CANC CAN

Sovereign People or Sovereign Governments

edited by
H. V. Kroeker

Proceedings of a Conference
Sponsored by
The Institute for Research on Public Policy
and the Government Studies Program,
Dalhousie University
Halifax, April 1979

The Institute for Research on Public Policy
L'Institut de recherches politiques

Montreal

© The Institute for Research on Public Policy 1981

Printed in Canada
ISBN 0 920380 34 4

Legal Deposit First Quarter
Bibliothèque nationale du Québec

The Institute for Research on Public Policy/L'Institut de recherches politiques
2149 Mackay Street
Montreal, Quebec
H3G 2J2

Typesetting and Printing by Tri-Graphic Printing (Ottawa) Ltd.

Founded in 1972, THE INSTITUTE FOR RESEARCH ON PUBLIC POLICY is a national organization whose independence and autonomy are ensured by the revenues of an endowment fund, which is supported by the federal and provincial governments and by the private sector. In addition, the Institute receives grants and contracts from governments, corporations, and foundations to carry out specific research projects.

The *raison d'être* of the Institute is threefold:

— To act as a catalyst within the national community by helping to facilitate informed public debate on issues of major public interest

— To stimulate participation by all segments of the national community in the process that leads to public policy making

— To find practical solutions to important public policy problems, thus aiding in the development of sound public policies

The Institute is governed by a Board of Directors, which is the decision-making body, and a Council of Trustees, which advises the board on matters related to the research direction of the Institute. Day-to-day administration of the Institute's policies, programmes, and staff is the responsibility of the president.

The Institute operates in a decentralized way, employing researchers located across Canada. This ensures that research undertaken will include contributions from all regions of the country.

Wherever possible, the Institute will try to promote public understanding of, and discussion on, issues of national importance, whether they be controversial or not. It will publish its research findings with clarity and impartiality. Conclusions or recommendations in the Institute's publications are solely those of the author, and should not be attributed to the Board of Directors, Council of Trustees, or contributors to the Institute.

The president bears final responsibility for the decision to publish a manuscript under the Institute's imprint. In reaching this decision, he is advised on the accuracy and objectivity of a manuscript by both Institute staff and outside reviewers. Publication of a manuscript signifies that it is deemed to be a competent treatment of a subject worthy of public consideration.

Publications of the Institute are published in the language of the author, along with an executive summary in both of Canada's official languages.

iv

v

Institute Management

Gordon Robertson   President
Louis Vagianos   Executive Director

David MacDonald, P.C.   Fellow in Residence

Raymond Breton   Director, Ethnic and Cultural Diversity Program
John M. Curtis   Director, International Economics Program
Rowland J. Harrison   Director, Natural Resources Program
Ian McAllister   Director, Regional Employment Opportunities Program
William T. Stanbury   Director, Regulation and Government Intervention Program
Zavis P. Zeman   Director, Technology and Society Program

Donald Wilson   Director, Conference and Seminars Program

Dana Phillip Doiron   Director, Communications Services
Ann C. McCoomb   Director, Publishing Services

Tom Kent   Editor, *Policy Options Politiques*

Foreword

Our society has grown more complex and our governments less accessible in the century since the founding of Canada's parliamentary system. The context within which our governors govern has changed, and one side-effect is the increasing "distance," real or perceived, between government decision makers and the general public. The response has been a demand for greater citizen participation in the governing process.

Reforming our parliamentary system to provide more opportunities for public input is no easy task. First, what degree of participation is optimum, from the extreme of direct participatory democracy to representative democracy? Second, what procedures could be established to allow public input without bogging down government's legislative function? Finally, who in government would listen?

The question of citizen participation is essentially a question of the role and purpose of government. These essays on the subject were presented at a conference designed to assess how government can be made more sensitive and responsive to the will of the governed. It is our hope that this publication contributes to that goal.

Gordon Robertson
President
January 1981

Avant-propos

Au cours du siècle qui s'est écoulé depuis l'établissement d'un régime parlementaire au Canada, notre société est devenue plus complexe et nos gouvernements moins accessibles. Le contexte au sein duquel nos gouvernants gouvernent s'est modifié et s'en est suivi, entre autres, un accroissement de l'« écart », réel ou perçu, entre les décisionnaires du gouvernement et le public. On y a réagi en exigeant une plus grande participation des citoyens au processus de gouvernement.

Il n'est pas facile de réformer notre régime parlementaire de façon à permettre au public d'y contribuer davantage. Il faut savoir tout d'abord quel est le degré optimal de participation à privilégier entre les deux extrêmes que sont la démocratie de participation directe et de la démocratie de représentation. En deuxième lieu, il s'agit de déterminer quelles méthodes permettraient la contribution du public sans enliser les travaux législatifs du gouvernement. Enfin, qui, au gouvernement, écouterait?

La question de la participation équivaut en somme à celle du rôle et de la raison d'être du gouvernement. Ces essais ont été présentés lors d'une conférence visant à évaluer comment rendre le gouvernement plus sensible à la volonté des gouvernés. Nous souhaitons que cette publication contribue à l'attente de cet objectif.

Le président,
Gordon Robertson
Janvier 1981

Acknowledgements

A successful conference often owes as much to the people responsible for administrative arrangements as to the participants. Debbie Wiles did a magnificent job in making the conference a success and was very supportive and helpful in completing the editing of the conference proceedings. I would also like to thank Ms. Marilyn Slater of the School of Public Administration, Dalhousie University, Halifax, and Ms. Suzanne Cobb of the Ministry of State for Economic Development, Ottawa, for their help in transcribing the conference proceedings and preparing the final papers for printing. I would like as well to acknowledge the energy, inspiration, and support of Mike Kirby in the planning and running of the conference. Finally, the students of the Dalhousie School of Public Administration require a special acknowledgement for their work and dedication throughout the conference.

Table of Contents

Notes on Contributors*

Jalynn BENNETT
Ms. Bennett is a member of the Ontario Economic Council, Chairman of the Council's Committee on Regulation, and is an assistant vice-president with Manufacturers Life Insurance.

Robert B. BRYCE
Mr. Bryce is a member of the board of directors of the Economic Council of Canada, was chairman of the Royal Commission on Corporate Concentration, and has held senior deputy head positions in the Government of Canada, such as Clerk of the Privy Council Office and Secretary to the Cabinet; Deputy Minister of Finance; and Economic Adviser to the Prime Minister on the Constitution.

Dalton CAMP
Mr. Camp is an author and journalist and former president of the Progressive Conservative Party of Canada. His most recent book is *Points of Departure*.

J. Alex CORRY
Dr. Corry is chairman of the Council of Trustees of The Institute for Research on Public Policy, former principal of Queen's University, the author of many books on political institutions and structures, and has held many positions with public organizations, such as member of the board of governors of the Canadian Broadcasting Corporation and member of the Canada Council.

J. Stefan DUPRÉ
Dr. Dupré is a professor of political science at the University of Toronto, and a member of the Council of Trustees of The Institute for Research on Public Policy. He has served many public organizations, has been chairman of the Ontario Council on University Affairs and president of the Social Sciences and Humanities Research Council of Canada.

Douglas M. FISHER
Mr. Fisher is a political journalist and commentator in the Parliamentary Press Gallery. He is a former Member of Parliament and has served as chairman of the board of Hockey Canada, and was a member of the Ontario Committee on the Legislature.

J. King GORDON
Professor Gordon is currently an adviser to the president of the International Development Research Centre. He has taught at a number of Canadian

universities, was the United Nations Development Plan representative in Egypt, and is one of the authors of *Social Planning for Canada*.

John F. GRAHAM

Dr. Graham is a professor of economics at Dalhousie University, former chairman of the Nova Scotia Royal Commission on Education, Public Services and Provincial-Municipal Relations, former chairman of the Public Accounts Board of the Province of Nova Scotia, and the author of books and articles.

Marjorie HARTLING

Ms. Hartling is executive director of the National Anti-Poverty Organization.

Tom KENT

Mr. Kent was president and chief executive officer of the Sydney Steel Corporation and has held deputy head positions in the Government of Canada, such as Deputy Minister of the Department of Regional Economic Expansion and Deputy Minister of the Department of Manpower and Immigration. He is a former editor of the *Winnipeg Free Press* and assistant editor of the *Economist*.

Harold V. KROEKER

Mr. Kroeker is visiting professor at the School of Public Administration at Dalhousie University. He has held positions with the Government of Canada, such as Assistant Secretary to the Cabinet Committee on Priorities and Planning. He is the author of books and articles on government.

André LAROCQUE

Mr. Larocque is Associate Secretary General of the Executive Council of the Government of Quebec and a former professor at the University of Montreal.

Gérard V. LaFOREST

Dr. LaForest is a commissioner with the Law Reform Commission of Canada. He was Assistant Deputy Attorney General in the federal Department of Justice, Dean of Law at the University of Alberta, has served on a number of Royal Commissions, and is the author of numerous books and articles.

Bayless MANNING

Dr. Manning is with the law firm of Paul, Weiss, Riskind, Wharton and Garrison. He is former Dean of Law at Stanford University and has served American presidents in a number of positions, such as president of the Council of Foreign Relations.

Jim McNIVEN
Dr. McNiven is executive vice-president of the Atlantic Provinces Economic Council and has taught in a number of Canadian universities.

William A.W. NEILSON
Mr. Neilson is a professor of law at the University of Victoria, and was Deputy Minister of the British Columbia Department of Consumer and Corporate Affairs.

P.M. PITFIELD
Mr. Pitfield is the Clerk of the Privy Council Office and Secretary to the Cabinet. He was former Deputy Minister of the Department of Consumer and Corporate Affairs and Deputy Secretary (Plans) in the Privy Council Office.

Victor RABINOVITCH
Dr. Rabinovitch is with the education branch of the Canadian Labour Congress and was director of health and safety standards in the Manitoba Department of Labour.

Gordon S. SMITH
Dr. Smith is Deputy Secretary (Plans) in the Privy Council Office and has served as adviser to the minister of National Defence and as a member of the Department of External Affairs.

Peter STUDER
Mr. Peter Studer is editor of *Tages-Anzeiger*, Zurich, Switzerland.

Kitson VINCENT
Mr. Vincent was the founding executive director of the Canadian Arctic Resources Committee.

Blair WILLIAMS
Dr. Williams is a professor of political science at Concordia University and former executive director of the Liberal Party of Canada.

---

* At the time of the conference, April 1979.

Introduction

Citizen Involvement in Government: The Art of the Possible

The papers and commentaries in this book leave little doubt that the participatory eggs laid in the political activism in the 1960s came home to roost in the late 1970s as very tough and angry chickens. Without major reforms to improve citizen participation in government policy making, the early 1980s could have all the bitterness and blood of a cock fight. The third in the series of national conferences on governmental processes organized by The Institute for Research on Public Policy provided an opportunity to examine more closely the basic institutions of democratic government and search for modifications or new arrangements that would ensure individuals greater access to, and involvement in, the process of government. For some of the participants, holding such a conference in 1979 appeared to be more of an opportunity to indulge in the nostalgic optimism of the 1960s with its emphasis on participatory democracy. For others, it was an opportunity to push for a revitalization of more direct democratic principles intended to enable citizens to control the expansionist and ubiquitous influence of government in the spirit of California's "Proposition 13" and other current popular views associated with the need to reduce the role and pervasiveness of government.

From the point of view of the organizers, the conference was a further development of the theme underlying the group of national conferences examining various aspects of the processes of government. These conferences have the explicit purpose of assessing how government can be made more sensitive and responsive to the collective and individual expectations of the governed. In dealing with citizen participation, the conference also provided a further dimension to some of the points raised at the first conference on the legislative process, held at the University of Victoria in March 1978.

In the closing address of that conference, the late Dr. John P. Mackintosh, who was a Member of Parliament in Britain, set the framework for many of the specific issues raised in this book in his discussion of the future of representative parliamentary democracy. In his usual brilliant, eloquent, and incisive manner, Dr. Mackintosh explored the tensions between representative and direct democracy, especially in relation to participation and consensus seeking. Dr. Mackintosh was a man who believed in holding opinions, and he came down firmly in favour of representative democracy and the need to revitalize the institutions associated with it. Specifically he asked:

> If it were possible for us to consult everybody, to have real direct democracy—would that be preferable to representative democracy through an elected assembly? Do not think that this is such a crazy idea because [one minister thought that m . . . there will come a day when . . . before the 9:00 news, there will be your fifteen minutes for legislating the nation's affairs. The screen will feature Mr. ''X'' who will explain why certain amendments to the current bill being enacted ought to be rejected, to be followed by Mr. ''Y'' who will explain why these amendments should be carried. Then the public will have a few minutes to think before pressing the red button on your set for the ayes or the blue button for the nays. The big computer will whirl and the figures will be tabulated in Whitehall to show the national will.
>
> . . .
>
> The problem about politics is that the system must put choices before people and these are usually complex choices. The answer to each choice situation involves a whole series of policies and programmes that are interrelated and must come out of a limited fund of resources. It is impossible to boil them all down to a set off between red buttons and blue buttons. That is nonsensical. Instead, we need to have party leaders come before the electorate with a coherent programme, with an attitude and an approach to these matters and a readiness to take responsibility for their overall judgements. Then the voters know whom to sack or reward at the next election.
>
> I think we have failed to make the case for representative government, not as a poor alternative to direct democracy, but as the proper way of conducting democracy in any modern society. If we could do that, I think we would be in a much stronger position to try to get the sort of atmosphere into our political life which would allow our parties and our backbenchers in Parliament to make use of the techniques that are already available in order to get adequate control over the executive.[1]

The objective of the third national conference on governmental processes was intended, of course, to deal both with a wider range and in a more substantive manner with the general concerns of citizen participation and involvement in government decision making, especially regarding how and what improvements might be possible. This concern is neither new nor novel; it undoutedly began with the idea of politics itself. While the notion of citizen participation and involvement can be traced back to the Greek writers of the fifth and fourth centuries B.C., there has been an interesting renaissance in the 1960s and 1970s in this concept. Surprisingly, this renaissance, which first found its articulation in the ''left'' of the 1960s, appears to have become the crusade of the ''right'' in the late 1970s and into the 1980s.

Whatever the underlying motivations or philosophic underpinnings, this renewed interest has had a dramatic impact on the political life of Western industrial democracies and in North America in particular. It is hard to imagine, for example, a city council in a major Canadian city today planning a significant neighbourhood redevelopment without actively seeking citizen participation. At the senior levels of government, ''consultation'' has been adopted as a guiding "spiritual" if not practical policy-making tool. In the electoral process itself, candidates have become very aware, sensitive, and often fearful of the political power and potency of citizens who have organized themselves around single issues.

This renewed interest in citizen participation, even in those instances where governments actively promote it, is often flawed and still more frequently inadequate. Some observers look at these "new" innovations with cynicism, since attempts by governments to involve citizens appear to involve little more than pouring old water into new jugs. That is, that while the political process appears to be responding to citizens, it is in reality designed primarily to co-opt or mute political dissent. Many others are more optimistic or at least believe the challenge to find new structures is fundamental to the continued survival of some reasonably coherent form of democratic government. Part of the spirit of Dr. Mackintosh's address at Victoria was based on that optimism and a belief that without a deliberate programme of reform, existing democratic institutions will be paralysed by the anarchy of factions and interests or open to more totalitarian and demagogic leadership. The convergence of "left" and "right" political interests, to the extent such labels are ever relevant, underscores how important and urgent this concern has become in contemporary democratic societies.

The major impediment to change, however, is that reform rests on a dilemma. This is in finding the right balance between vesting enough power in the governors to govern, while still enabling the governed to exercise final control and engage in effective involvement in the process of governing. In the sweep of time, this indeed has been the essential critical, philosophical, and practical dilemma facing all societies. As Bertrand Russell noted:

> Social cohesion is a necessity, and mankind has never yet succeeded in enforcing cohesion by merely rational arguments. Every community is exposed to two opposite dangers; ossification through too much discipline and reverence for tradition, on the one hand; on the other hand, dissolution, or subjection to foreign conquest, through the growth of an individualism and personal independence that makes co-operation impossible. In general, important civilizations start with a rigid and superstitious system, gradually relaxed, and leading, at a certain stage, to a period of brilliant genius, while the good of the old tradition remains and the evil inherent in its dissolution has not yet developed. But as the evil unfolds, it leads to anarchy, thence, inevitably, to a new tyranny, producing a new synthesis secured by a new system of dogma. The doctrine of liberalism is an attempt to escape from this endless oscillation. The essence of liberalism is an attempt to secure a social order not based on irrational dogma, and insuring stability without involving more restraints than are necessary for the preservation of the community. Whether this attempt can succeed only the future can determine.[2]

A FRAMEWORK FOR ADDRESSING THE ISSUES OF CITIZEN INVOLVEMENT AND PARTICIPATION

In reviewing the conference proceedings, there is a sense of urgency that emerges from the participants' papers and discussions regarding the need to reform the manner in which citizens participate in the process of governing. At the same time, speakers and commentators were equally clearly aware that defining what such involvement should mean or how it might be implemented is a very illusive and difficult task.

The simplest definition of democracy, rule by the people, implies participation and involvement. However, the nature of such participation or how involvement is to be exercised by individual citizens is a function of which of the many theories of democratic politics one chooses to follow. In an effort to provide greater precision to the notions of participation and involvement, some scholars have focused exclusively on examining the possible meanings of these and related words such as consent and consensus.[3] Such exercises in lexography, while important, can lead to even greater confusion or alternately to the development of arbitrary statements or definitions built on the logical momentum of scholarly deduction. There has also been extensive interest in the historical and traditional concepts of participation and involvement. These range from studies of Plato and Aristotle to the seminal philosophers of the eighteenth and nineteenth centuries who have shaped our current democratic institutions.[4]

While a considerable amount of scholarly material exists on this subject, the conference was not primarily academic in focus. Rather it was intended as an opportunity to seek out practical reforms in addressing the problems of participation especially in the context of Canadian parliamentary government. There was no deliberate attempt, therefore, to analyse the range of possible definitions associated with the notions of citizen involvement, participation, consensus seeking, or consent. Within the context of the conference, however, a broad framework did emerge within which the practical problems of citizen involvement were addressed. This framework can be briefly described as follows.

• *First*, the manner in which citizen participation or involvement takes place provides an important indication about how effectively a political process works. This point was a particular concern of J. Alex Corry and Bayless Manning.

• *Second*, involvement between the members of society and their government is not a simple direct relationship as might exist between, say, the members of an association and those who are elected from within the association to exercise authority over a couple of dozen members. The papers by Robert Bryce, Gérard LaForest, and Peter Studer provided excellent illustrations about the complexity of these relationships.

• *Third*, the members of modern democratic societies seek to participate and attempt to influence government decisions through a multitude of associations, groups, and structures. That is, democracy is no longer viewed as a "one-dimensional process" if indeed it ever was, rather, as commentators and speakers such as Victor Rabinovitch, Jalynn Bennett, and J. King Gordon noted, it is a process through which a person may seek to affect political events simultaneously through his labour union or business association, his neighbourhood or community group, through a special interest or issue group (say, an environmental organization), as well as through his elected political representative.

• *Fourth*, along with this acceptance that the political process of modern states flows through a pluralistic complex of associations, institutions, and organizations, there now exists a strongly held belief that the "actors" in the political process who influence and shape decisions are not only elected politicians. In the view of many, such as Tom Kent and Doug Fisher, it is the bureaucrats who are as important or who play an even more important role. Effective citizen involvement means, therefore, having access to this level of decision makers.

THE PROBLEMS OF CITIZEN INVOLVEMENT AND PARTICIPATION

There were two distinct views expressed at the conference regarding the problems of citizen involvement in the decision-making process of government. The first related to how various forms of participation might be expanded, and the second was concerned with reinforcing the processes of government to take decisions and provide leadership. Both of these concerns lead to institutional changes, but reforms intended to address one objective may often conflict with reforms intended to meet the other.

For the most part, the conference examined the first problem, that is, how to expand and make citizen involvement more effective. A theme that emerged very strongly from the conference discussion sessions was that the existing institutions and structures of government are not only inadequate for effective citizen involvement and participation, but in many instances they actively discriminate against ensuring effective citizen involvement. The majority of the sessions therefore attempted to seek out what changes could be adopted to improve this situation. As a result, papers such as those by Robert Bryce, Gérard LaForest, and William Neilson examined existing institutions and structures and assessed possible improvements or adaptations. In assessing past attempts at citizen involvement, Michael Pitfield's paper also considered how much participation citizens could realistically cope with, while Dalton Camp's amusing and reflective paper examined the extent to which traditional mechanisms such as political parties could be used to channel citizen interest and involvement. The range of these reforms was very successfully brought together in Tom Kent's conference summary, where he concentrated on reforms that would reinforce Canada's parliamentary form of government.

The second point of view regarding the need to reinforce government's ability to govern was admirably articulated by both J. Alex Corry and Bayless Manning. Dr. Corry, in his elegant key note address to the conference, and Dr. Manning, in his provocative presentation, highlighted how the push for greater participation has significantly reduced the ability of elected politicians to govern. Both speakers concluded rather pessimistically that without careful attention to the effects of expanded citizen participation and the "rights" that are attached to it, the ability of elected politicians to govern could seriously be impaired and eventually lead to government paralysis and inaction.

This notion was not dealt with as a major theme of the conference, but because of its association with current ideas about the need to reduce the overall role of government (this theme is a significant part of the fourth national conference[5]), it is worth examining more closely in this introduction. This view has been articulated in particular by the so-called "neo-conservative" school, which generally argues for less government, greater decentralization of decision making, and a return to "market principles" in determining the allocation of social and economic capital as well as the success or failure of individual enterprises. It would be a disservice, however, both to the proponents of this "school" as well as to those more generally concerned about the effective functioning of government, to reduce this issue to a particular point of view. Obviously, even the most ardent "interventionist" or socialist is or needs to be concerned about how well government is able to deliver policies and programmes. The tendency to associate this concern with more "conservative" views (that is, views calling for less government activity) reflects one obvious solution to the problem by arguing that government will be more effective in its role when it has less to do and can concentrate its resources.

Put in the more general context, the concern about the ability of governments to govern is also a concern that the process of governing in democracies must more clearly and visibly vest power and responsibility with elected governments. The dissipation and confusion in the exercising of political powers, it is argued, has greatly weakened effective government, and the broadening of political participation has reduced the elected politician's ability to forge the consensus necessary for action. While this concern has been described in a variety of ways, a very succinct statement of these problems, especially as it relates to citizen involvement and participation, has been provided in the Trilateral Commission's report entitled *The Crisis of Democracy*, which states:

> Quite apart from the substantive policy issues confronting democratic government, many specific problems have arisen which seem to be an intrinsic part of the functioning of democracy itself. The successful operation of democratic government has given rise to tendencies which impede that functioning.
> (1) The pursuit of the democratic virtues of equality and individualism has led to the delegitimation of authority generally and the loss of trust in leadership.

(2) The democratic expansion of political participation and involvement has created an ''overload'' on government and the imbalanced expansion of governmental activities, exacerbating inflationary tendencies in the economy.

(3) The political competition essential to democracy has intensified, leading to a disaggregation of interests and the decline and fragmentation of political parties.

(4) The responsiveness of democratic government to the electorate and to societal pressures encourages nationalistic parochialism in the way in which democratic societies conduct their foreign relations.[6]

In essence, the argument is that the stress on the rights of individual participation has been at the expense of the rights, interests, and needs of the community. Without the central focus of community, the ability to achieve consensus has been lost and this has seriously damaged the democratic process. In the words of the Trilateral Commission authors, ''consensus-building is at the heart of democratic politics.''[7] By extension, the inability to bring about a consensus, to focus political attention, and to reduce individual objectives and pluralistic interest-group ambitions risks destroying the very democratic institutions and structures in which citizens seek to participate.

There is clearly a paradox inherent in this view since the desire to ensure that governments are able to govern is usually equally matched by the desire to bring government more directly under the control of citizens. While this paradox is not easily reconciled or dismissed, the proponents of these seemingly conflicting views would perhaps argue that greater direct democracy is required to ensure that politicians and the bureaucracies of governments remain continually conscious of and sensitive to the ''public good'' but that this requires a reduced span of government activities.

There are no obvious answers to this set of concerns, and to the extent that it was raised in conference discussion, speakers such as Bayless Manning did so as a warning regarding the consequences of over-enthusiastically adopting totally participatory approaches in the making and implementation of government policies and programmes. Certainly those individuals or groups who wish to pursue special and sometimes parochial interests are rarely the ones who must accept the direct responsibility for or be subject to accountability for their actions to society.

As in most discussions involving politics, we are in the end brought face to face with the principle and values we hold regarding democracy. We are also confronted, once again, by the dilemma touched on earlier in this introduction: namely, that tensions exist between actions required to achieve the coherence and dedication to a common purpose essential for economic and social stability, and those needed for securing the maximum in individual freedom to enable a person to pursue his own interests and aspirations.

Clearly, effective citizen involvement and participation in the decision-making process of government do present problems. Briefly these might be summarized as follows:

- First, there is disagreement about what represents an adequate level of citizen participation necessary to achieve the objectives of social cohesion and those aimed at individual and minority-group political freedom.
- Second, all government is, by its very nature, coercive in terms of individual interests; democratic government involves a means of enabling the majorty to set the framework within which such coercion will take place.
- Third, the paradox of democratic government is that the linkage between private and public interest rests on developing individual responsibility for social and political action. That is, there is an almost inherent and timeless conflict in the objective of developing an individuals' social and political sense of responsibility in a democratic liberal society, because these are precisely the conditions that make it potentially difficult to gain cohesion or consensus at the community or ''public'' level.
- Fourth, responsibility is a function of knowledge, which in turn must be built on an involvement and understanding of the processes of governing; this is basic to fostering commitment while simultaneously encouraging a dialectical dialogue.
- Fifth, any process attempting to expand or intensify citizen involvement must ensure that final responsibility clearly rests with elected political leaders who are seen to be accountable for their actions.

This is a formidable and virtually irreconcilable set of problems. In pursuing the various aspects and nuances found in these problems, the conference participants were simultaneously exhilarated and depressed.

CONCLUSIONS

The principal focus of the conference was on how citizen involvement and participation in the decision making of government could be improved. In examining this concern, the conference participants concentrated on how existing institutions or organizations might be reformed. There was also a limited but very useful discussion of the relevance and adaptation of major structural changes such as the Swiss experience with direct democracy. On the whole, however, the participants favoured reform that was built on the principle of parliamentary democracy.

Within this context, a number of provocative questions were raised concerning whether reform should be sought solely or largely in terms of the democratic representative institutions themselves (that is, Parliament, the Members of Parliament, and political parties), or whether the major area of concentration should be on those institutions and organizations that enable greater access to and have a more direct impact on the bureaucracy (such as commissions, task forces, regulatory or public policy agencies—in all cases, the intention would be to expand the roles of such groups). The conference was an important step in the much larger exercise required to help resolve these questions. As such, it has provided a significant basis on which a more analytical and studied approach in both areas could be undertaken.

For purposes of this book, the conference proceedings have been organized into two parts. Part One contains the major theme papers presented at the conference. These four papers were provided by eminent practitioners and scholars, three of whom have individually had a significant impact on Canada's political history and institutions—J. Alex Corry, J. King Gordon, and Tom Kent. Bayless Manning, through his extensive involvement in American politics and academic life, provided a critical sounding-board based on American experience and against which possible reforms of Canadian institutions can be very usefully assessed.

Part Two contains the seven other papers presented at the conference, each of which dealt with a specific institutional or structural concern. The quality of these papers was equal to the theme papers. Michael Pitfield and Robert Bryce, for example, have had considerable experience within the Canadian federal public service. Others, such as Doug Fisher and Dalton Camp, have had an equally considerable experience on the public or political side of Canadian politics both through direct involvement in the process and recently as journalists. Gérard LaForest and William Nielson brought a combination of practical involvement as well as thoughtful insight regarding the use of the law or legal institutions and regulatory agencies as vehicles for advancing citizen participation. A major benefit to the conference and an important counterpoint to the largely or exclusively Canadian focus of participants was the enlightening and helpful presentation of the Swiss experience with direct democracy provided by Peter Studer, editor of the *Tages-Anzeiger* of Zurich, Switzerland.

A particularly fortunate aspect of the conference was the quality of commentary on each of these papers. All commentaries have been included. Each commentator brought a special contribution and provided the conference with a significantly greater degree of depth and experience.

NOTES

[1] John P. Mackintosh, "The Future of Representative Parliamentary Democracy," in *The Legislative Process in Canada: The Need for Reform*, edited by W.A.W. Neilson and J.C. MacPherson (Montreal: The Insitute for Research on Public Policy, 1978), pp. 315-16.

[2] Bertrand Russell, *The History of Western Philosophy* (London: George Allen and Unwin, 1961), p. 22.

[3] Such an examination can be found in the writings of J.P. Plamenatz, *Consent, Freedom and Political Obligation*, 2d ed. (Oxford: Oxford University Press, 1968), or P.H. Partridge, *Consent & Consensus* (London: Macmillan, 1971).

xxvi / *Sovereign People or Sovereign Governments*

⁴ There is almost an inexhaustible supply of these kinds of studies but the ones the author found most useful in preparing for the conference were by Lawrence A. Scaff, *Participation in Western Political Tradition: A Study of Theory & Practice* (Tuscon: University of Arizona Press, 1979); Carole Pateman, *Participation & Democratic Theory* (London: Cambridge University Press, 1970); Bertrand Russell, *The History of Western Philosophy* (London: George Allen and Unwin, 1961); and C.B. Macpherson, *The Life and Times of Liberal Democracy* (Oxford: Oxford University Press, 1977).

⁵ The fourth national conference on governmental processes dealt with the problems of reducing government expenditure in times of economic restraint. The underlying or basic theme was also, however, how to reduce the role and activities of government. The conference was held in Toronto, 19-20 September 1979. See Peter Aucoin, ed., *The Politics and Management of Restraint in Government* (Montreal: The Institute for Research on Public Policy, 1981).

⁶ Michel J. Crozier, Samuel P. Huntington, and Joji Watanuki, *The Crisis of Democracy*, a report on the governability of democracies to the Trilateral Commission (New York: New York University Press, 1975), p. 161.

⁷ *Ibid.*

La participation des citoyens aux affaires gouvernementales : l'art du possible

Les études et les commentaires publiés ici mettent en évidence le fait que les germes de participation implantés au cours des années 1960 ont donné, dans les années 1970, des sujets virulents. Si l'on ne procède pas à d'importantes réformes en vue d'accroître la participation des citoyens à l'élaboration de la politique d'État, on pourrait, au début des années 1980, être témoin d'une lutte âpre et sans merci. La troisième de la série de conférences nationales sur les procédés gouvernementaux organisée par l'Institut de recherches politiques constituait une occasion propice pour examiner de plus près les institutions de base du gouvernement démocratique et essayer de les modifier ou de mettre au point de nouveaux mécanismes de façon à donner aux particuliers une plus grande possibilité d'accès et de participation aux procédés gouvernementaux. Le fait de tenir une telle conférence en 1979 a semblé fournir à certains des participants une occasion de se replonger avec nostalgie dans l'optimisme des années 1960, où l'on mettait avant tout l'accent sur la démocratie de participation. D'autres ont profité de la conférence pour promouvoir la revitalisation de procédés démocratiques plus directs susceptibles de permettre aux citoyens de restreindre l'influence expansionniste et omniprésente du gouvernement dans l'esprit de la « proposition treize » en Californie, et d'autres théories à la mode relatives à la nécessité de réduire le rôle du gouvernement et son infiltration dans tous les aspects de la vie des citoyens.

De l'avis des organisateurs, cependant, le sujet de la conférence constituait uniquement une extension naturelle du thème de l'ensemble des conférences nationales qui portent toutes sur les divers aspects des procédés gouvernementaux. Ces conférences visent explicitement à évaluer les moyens de rendre le gouvernement plus sensible et plus ouvert aux aspirations collectives et individuelles de ceux qu'il gouverne. Vu qu'elle portait sur la participation des citoyens, la conférence a aussi permis d'élaborer certains des points établis lors de la première conférence, qui portait sur le processus législatif, qui s'est déroulée à l'université de Victoria en mars 1978.

Dans le discours qu'il avait prononcé au moment de la clôture de cette conférence, le regretté M. John P. Mackintosh, député au Parlement britannique, avait soulevé plusieurs des questions traitées dans le présent ouvrage quand il s'était penché sur l'avenir de la démocratie parlementaire représentative. Avec son intelligence, son éloquence et son ton incisif habituels, M. Mackintosh avait examiné les tensions qui existent entre la démocratie représentative et la démocratie directe, surtout relativement à la participation et à l'obtention d'un consensus. M. Mackintosh croyait dans la nécessité d'avoir une opinion sur toutes les questions importantes et avait appuyé énergiquement dans son discours le principe de la démocratie représentative tout en insistant sur l'importance de revitaliser ses institutions. Il avait demandé notamment :

> Si nous pouvions consulter tout le monde et instaurer une véritable démocratie directe, est-ce que ce serait préférable à la démocratie représentative appliquée par une assemblée élue? N'allez pas croire que cette notion soit tellement farfelue, puisque [un ministre pensait que] (...) le jour viendra òù (...) avant les nouvelles de 9 heures, quinze minutes seront réservées pour légiférer les affaires de l'État. On pourra voir à l'écran M. *X*, qui expliquera pourquoi certains amendements au bill qu'on en est en train d'adopter devraient être rejetés, et il sera suivi de M. *Y*, qui expliquera pourquoi ces mêmes amendements devraient être adoptés. On laissera ensuite quelques minutes de réflexion au public avant de lui demander d'appuyer sur le bouton rouge incorporé au téléviseur pour indiquer « oui » ou sur le bouton bleu pour dire « non ». Un gros ordinateur additionnera les résultats et communiquera les chiffres à Whitehall pour indiquer quelle est la volonté du peuple (...)
>
> Le problème en politique provient du fait que le système doit permettre au public de faire certains choix et que ces choix portent ordinairement sur des questions complexes. La décision dans chaque cas doit tenir compte de toute une série de politiques et de programmes interreliés et met toujours en cause des ressources limitées. C'est impossible de réduire le tout à un choix entre un bouton rouge et un bouton bleu. Ce serait insensé. Il faut au contraire que les chefs de parti présentent un programme cohérent aux électeurs, qu'ils expliquent leur façon d'envisager et d'aborder toutes ces questions et qu'ils montrent qu'ils sont prêts à assumer la responsabilité de leurs décisions. Cela permet aux électeurs de savoir qui il convient de rejeter ou de récompenser lors des élections suivantes.
>
> Selon moi, nous n'avons jamais essayé d'établir de façon satisfaisante que le gouvernement représentatif, loin d'être un pis-aller dont nous devons nous contenter faute d'instaurer un régime de démocratie directe, constitue le système démocratique le plus approprié à toute société moderne. Si nous y parvenions, nous serions, à mon avis, beaucoup plus en mesure d'instiller dans notre vie politique une atmosphère susceptible de permettre à nos partis et aux députés de l'arrière-ban d'avoir recours aux moyens qui sont déjà à leur portée pour exercer une mainmise adéquate sur l'exécutif[1].

Bien entendu, la troisième conférence nationale sur les procédés gouvernementaux devait en principe porter sur des sujets plus variés et traiter de façon plus approfondie les questions générales de la participation et de l'apport des citoyens à la prise des décisions par le gouvernement et plus particulièrement des améliorations à apporter et de la façon de s'y prendre. Cette notion est loin d'être neuve; elle a sans doute vu le jour en même temps que l'idée de la politique elle-même. Le principe de la participation et de l'apport des simples citoyens aux affaires publiques peut bien sûr être retracé jusqu'aux auteurs grecs du Ve et du IVe siècle avant notre ère, mais il est intéressant de noter qu'il a connu une certaine renaissance au cours des années 1960 et 1970. Fait étonnant, cette renaissance, qui était à l'origine l'apanage de la gauche des années 1960, semble être devenue le cheval de bataille de la droite à la fin des années 1970 et au début des années 1980.

Quels que soient ses motifs et ses fondements philosophiques sous-jacents, ce renouveau d'intérêt a eu des répercussions considérables sur la vie politique des démocraties industrielles du monde occidental, surtout en Amérique du Nord. On peut difficilement imaginer, par exemple, que le conseil municipal d'une grande ville du Canada songe à élaborer un projet important de rénovation d'un quartier sans essayer activement d'obtenir l'avis des citoyens. Pour leur part, les échelons supérieurs du gouvernement ont adopté la « consultation » comme outil d'orientation « spirituelle » sinon pratique pour l'établissement de leur politique. Pour ce qui est du processus électoral lui-même, les candidats aux élections se rendent maintenant très bien compte et ont même souvent peur du pouvoir politique et de l'influence que peuvent exercer les citoyens qui se sont regroupés autour d'une même question.

Ce renouveau d'intérêt pour la participation des citoyens, même dans les cas où le gouvernement l'encourage activement, est souvent seulement partiel et encore plus souvent insuffisant. Certains observateurs considèrent ces supposées innovations avec cynisme parce que les efforts du gouvernement en vue de faire participer les citoyens à la vie politique ne semblent viser qu'à maintenir le *statu quo* sous une forme différente. En effet, même si les institutions politiques semblent subir l'influence des citoyens, elles visent surtout en réalité à attirer les dissidents politiques dans leurs rangs ou à les faire taire. Bien d'autres observateurs sont plus optimistes ou croient du moins qu'il est essentiel de chercher de nouvelles structures pour assurer la survie d'une forme raisonnablement cohérente de gouvernement démocratique. Le discours de M. Mackintosh à Victoria s'inspirait en partie de cet optimisme et de la conviction que, si l'on n'adopte pas un programme de réforme positif, les institutions politiques actuelles seront paralysées par l'anarchie des diverses factions politiques et des divers groupes de citoyens, ou prépareront la voie à une forme de gouvernement plus totalitaire et démagogique qu'à l'heure actuelle. La convergence des groupements politiques de gauche et de droite, dans la mesure où ces qualificatifs peuvent vraiment vouloir dire quelque chose, souligne la nécessité pour nos sociétés démocratiques contemporaines de se pencher de toute urgence sur cette question.

Le principal obstacle au changement provient du dilemme que pose toute tentative de réforme. Pour maintenir l'équilibre, il faut en effet accorder aux gouvernants suffisamment de pouvoirs pour gouverner tout en permettant aux gouvernés de contrôler en définitive les affaires publiques et de participer réellement à la direction du pays. Cela a toujours constitué le principal dilemme philosophique et pratique des sociétés à travers les âges. Comme le dit Bertrand Russell :

> La cohésion sociale est une nécessité et l'humanité, jusqu'à présent, n'a jamais réussi à forcer la cohésion par de simples arguments rationnels. Chaque communauté est exposée à deux dangers opposés : la sclérose, par trop de discipline et de respect pour la tradition, d'une part; d'autre part, la dissolution ou la soumission à des conquêtes étrangères dues à la croissance d'un individualisme et d'une indépendance personnelle qui rend la coopération impossible. D'une manière générale, les civilisations importantes débutent avec un système rigide et superstitieux qui se relâche graduellement et conduit, à un certain moment, à une période de génie brillant, lorsque le bien de la vieille tradition demeure et que le mal, inhérent à sa dissolution, ne s'est pas encore développé. Mais, à mesure que le mal se déploie, il conduit à l'anarchie, puis, de là, inévitablement, à une nouvelle tyrannie qui produit une nouvelle synthèse soutenue par un nouveau système de dogmes. La doctrine du libéralisme est une tentative pour échapper à cette oscillation finale. L'essence du libéralisme est une tentative pour garantir un ordre social qui ne soit pas basé sur un dogme irrationnel et pour assurer la stabilité sans impliquer plus de contraintes qu'il n'est nécessaire pour préserver la communauté. Une telle tentative peut-elle réussir? Seul l'avenir en décidera[2].

L'ÉTABLISSEMENT D'UN CADRE POUR LA DISCUSSION SUR LA PARTICIPATION ET L'APPORT DES CITOYENS

Les mémoires présentés lors de la conférence et les discussions qui s'y sont déroulées témoignent de l'importance qu'accordent les participants à la nécessité de modifier au plus vite la façon dont les citoyens participent aux processus gouvernementaux. Par ailleurs, il est bien évident que les orateurs et les commentateurs qui se sont exprimés au cours de la conférence se rendent tous compte que la définition de cette participation et des moyens de l'obtenir constitue une tâche hautement abstraite et complexe.

La définition la plus simple de la démocratie, c'est-à-dire le gouvernement par le peuple, laisse entendre une certaine participation et un certain apport. Par ailleurs, la nature de cette participation et de l'apport individuel des citoyens dépend de celle des nombreuses théories de la politique démocratique que l'on choisit de suivre. Certains experts se sont efforcés de préciser davantage les notions de participation et d'apport en se penchant uniquement sur les significations possibles de ces notions et d'autres mots dans le même ordre d'idées, comme consentement et consensus[3]. Même si de telles études de lexicographie sont importantes, elles peuvent créer encore plus de confusion ou encore donner lieu à des déclarations ou à des définitions arbitraires qui ne seraient que la conclusion logique de certaines déductions savantes. Bien des auteurs se sont aussi penchés sur les notions historiques et traditionnelles de la participation et de l'apport des citoyens. Ceux-ci vont de Platon et d'Aristote jusqu'aux philosophes du XVIIIe et du

XIXe siècle qui nous ont donné les premiers fondements de nos institutions démocratiques actuelles[4].

Il existe évidemment une quantité considérable d'ouvrages savants sur cette question, mais la conférence ne s'attachait pas surtout aux aspects purement théoriques du sujet. Elle visait plutôt à permettre aux participants de trouver le moyen d'apporter des réformes pratiques afin de résoudre le problème que pose la participation, spécialement en ce qui concerne le gouvernement parlementaire canadien. Les participants n'ont donc pas essayé délibérément d'analyser l'éventail des définitions possibles de notions comme l'apport des citoyens, la participation, l'obtention d'un consensus et le consentement. Par ailleurs, la conférence a fourni un cadre qui a permis de faire un examen général des problèmes pratiques reliés à l'apport des citoyens. Voici, dans les grandes lignes, ce qui en est ressorti :

• Premièrement, la façon dont les citoyens participent à la vie politique ou influent sur le gouvernement constitue un indice important de l'efficacité des processus politiques. MM. J. Alex Corry et Bayless Manning ont insisté particulièrement sur ce point.

a Deuxièmement, les rapports entre les membres de la société et leur gouvernement ne sont pas de simples rapports directs comme il peut en exister, par exemple, entre les membres d'une association et ceux qui sont élus pour diriger quelques douzaines de membres. Les documents présentés par MM. Robert Bryce, Gérard LaForest et Peter Studer contiennent d'excellents exemples de la complexité de ces rapports.

• Troisièmement, les membres des sociétés démocratiques modernes veulent participer aux affaires publiques et tentent d'influer sur les décisions du gouvernement par l'entremise d'une multitude d'associations, de groupes et d'organismes. La démocratie n'est donc plus considérée comme un « processus en une seule dimension », si toutefois cela a déjà été le cas, mais plutôt, ainsi que l'ont signalé des commentateurs et des orateurs comme MM. Victor Rabinovitch, Jalynn Bennett et J. King Gordon, comme un procédé qui peut permettre à un particulier d'influer sur les affaires politiques par l'entremise à la fois de son syndicat ou de son association professionnelle, de son association de quartier ou de localité, d'un groupe qui s'intéresse à une question spéciale (un organisme de protection de l'environnement, par exemple) et de son représentant élu.

• Quatrièmement, en plus d'accepter la notion que les processus politiques des États modernes mettent en cause un ensemble pluraliste d'associations, d'institutions et d'organismes, bien des gens sont convaincus que ce ne sont pas seulement les hommes politiques élus qui participent activement aux procédés politiques qui influent sur les décisions gouverne-mentales. Selon bien des observateurs comme MM. Tom Kent et Doug Fisher, ce sont les bureaucrates qui ont la prépondérance et ils jouent un rôle encore plus important que les hommes politiques. Pour que l'apport des citoyens soit efficace, il faut donc que ceux-ci aient accès à cette catégorie de décisionnaires.

LES PROBLÈMES DE L'APPORT ET DE LA PARTICIPATION DES CITOYENS

Les participants à la conférence ont exprimé deux préoccupations distinctes relatives aux problèmes de la participation et de l'apport des citoyens à la prise de décisions. La première a trait à la façon de promouvoir diverses formes de participation, et la deuxième concerne le renforcement des mécanismes qui permettent au gouvernement de prendre des décisions et de diriger le pays. Ces deux préoccupations visent à entraîner des changements institutionnels, mais les réformes conçues pour atteindre un objectif peuvent souvent entrer en contradiction avec les réformes visant à atteindre l'autre.

Pendant la conférence, les participants se sont surtout penchés sur le premier problème, c'est-à-dire sur la façon de promouvoir la participation des citoyens et de la rendre plus efficace. Les diverses séances de discussion ont fait clairement ressortir un point important, soit que les institutions et les structures actuelles du gouvernement sont non seulement peu susceptibles d'assurer un apport et une participation efficaces de la part des citoyens, mais aussi qu'elles empêchent dans bien des cas les citoyens de participer efficacement aux affaires publiques. Pendant la plus grande partie des séances, les participants se sont donc efforcés de déterminer quels changements on pourrait apporter pour améliorer la situation. Plusieurs mémoires, notamment ceux de MM. Robert Bryce, Gérard LaForest et William Neilson, faisaient donc l'analyse des institutions et des structures actuelles, et examinaient les améliorations et les modifications qu'on pourrait leur apporter. Le mémoire présenté par M. Michael Pitfield examinait les tentatives du passé en vue de faire participer les citoyens aux affaires publiques et visait aussi à déterminer jusqu'à quel point on peut vraiment s'attendre à ce que les citoyens influent sur le gouvernement, tandis que l'exposé amusant et avisé de M. Dalton Camp examinait la mesure dans laquelle les mécanismes traditionnels comme les partis politiques peuvent servir à orienter l'intérêt et la participation des citoyens. Dans son résumé de la conférence, M. Tom Kent a réussi de façon brillante à faire le rapport entre toutes ces réformes tout en insistant davantage sur celles qui seraient susceptibles de renforcer le régime parlementaire canadien.

M. J. Alex Corry et M. Bayless Manning ont tous deux exprimé de façon admirable la deuxième préoccupation relative à la nécessité de renforcer le pouvoir de gouverner du gouvernement. M. Corry, dans son élégant exposé du thème dominant de la conférence, et M. Manning, dans un discours qui a su enflammer l'imagination des participants, ont expliqué comment le mouvement en vue d'accroître la participation des citoyens a réduit considérablement le pouvoir de gouverner des dirigeants élus. Les deux orateurs ont conclu de façon pessimiste que si l'on n'analysait pas soigneusement les conséquences d'une participation accrue des citoyens et les « droits » qui y sont rattachés, la capacité de gouverner des hommes politiques élus pourrait s'en trouver diminuée de beaucoup et mener éventuellement à la paralysie et à l'inaction du gouvernement. Cette notion n'était pas l'un des thèmes principaux de la conférence. Cependant, vu qu'elle se rapproche du sentiment populaire selon lequel il faudrait réduire le rôle général du gouvernement (ce thème a fait l'objet d'un examen poussé lors de la quatrième conférence nationale[5]), cela vaut la peine de l'examiner plus à fond dans le cadre de la présente introduction. Cette idée a été adoptée notamment par le groupe désigné sous le nom de « néo-conservateurs », qui préconise une réduction du rôle du gouvernement, une plus grande décentralisation de la prise de décisions et un retour aux « principes du marché » pour déterminer la répartition des ressources sociales et économiques, de même que le succès ou l'échec des entreprises individuelles. Il serait cependant injuste envers les partisans de cette école de pensée et ceux qui se préoccupent de façon plus générale du bon fonctionnement du gouvernement de réduire toute cette question à un seul point de vue. Il est bien évident que même les « interventionnistes » et les socialistes les plus ardents doivent ou devraient se préoccuper de savoir si le gouvernement est tout de même en mesure d'instaurer des politiques et des programmes. Ceux qui ont tendance à rapprocher cette notion des idées plus « conservatrices » (c'est-à-dire celles qui préconisent une réduction des activités gouvernementales) notent qu'il existe une solution bien évidente au problème puisque le gouvernement sera certainement plus efficace s'il a moins à faire et peut concentrer ses ressources.

Dans une optique plus générale, la préoccupation concernant la capacité de gouverner des gouvernements se traduit par le sentiment que les processus gouvernementaux d'une démocratie devraient confier de façon plus évidente et plus visible les pouvoirs et les responsabilités du gouvernement aux dirigeants élus. Les partisans de cette théorie affirment que la dissipation des pouvoirs politiques et la confusion qui entoure l'exercice de ces pouvoirs ont sensiblement affaibli le processus gouvernemental, et que l'insistance accrue sur la participation politique a réduit la capacité des hommes politiques élus à obtenir le consensus nécessaire pour prendre les mesures qui s'imposent. Cette notion a été décrite de bien des façons, mais on peut trouver un exposé très succinct de ces problèmes, surtout en ce qui concerne l'apport et la participation des citoyens, dans le rapport de la Commission trilatérale intitulé *The Crisis of Democracy* (la crise de la démocratie), où l'on peut lire ce qui suit :

> Mises à part les importantes questions de politique auxquelles les gouvernements démocratiques doivent faire face, il existe maintenant de nombreux problèmes précis qui semblent intrinsèquement liés au fonctionnement de la démocratie elle-même. Le bon fonctionnement du gouvernement démocratique a engendré certaines tendances qui font obstacle à ce bon fonctionnement.

1) La poursuite des vertus démocratiques de l'égalité et de l'individualisme a entraîné la délégitimation de l'autorité en général et la perte de confiance dans les dirigeants politiques.
2) L'accroissement démocratique de la participation et de l'apport politiques des citoyens a surchargé le gouvernement et causé une expansion mal équilibrée des activités gouvernementales, ce qui a exacerbé les tendances inflationnistes de l'économie.
3) La rivalité politique essentiellle à la démocratie s'est intensifiée et a entraîné une séparation des intérêts ainsi que le déclin et le morcellement des partis politiques.
4) La tendance que témoigne le gouvernement démocratique à se plier devant les désirs des électeurs et à céder aux pressions exercées par la société encourage les sociétés démocratiques à adopter un esprit de clocher nationaliste dans la conduite de leurs relations étrangères[6].

Cela revient essentiellement à dire que l'on a insisté sur les droits à la participation individuelle au détriment des droits, des intérêts et des besoins de la collectivité. Puisque l'on néglige le point de vue essentiel de la collectivité, il est devenu impossible d'obtenir un consensus, et cela a gravement affaibli le processus démocratique. Comme le signalent les auteurs du rapport de la Commission trilatérale, « l'obtention d'un consensus est le noyau de la politique du système démocratique »[7]. Par extension, l'incapacité d'obtenir un consensus, de concentrer l'attention politique sur une seule question et de réduire l'importance des objectifs individuels et les ambitions d'une multitude de groupes à intérêts distincts risque de détruire les institutions et les structures démocratiques mêmes auxquelles les citoyens veulent participer.

Cette notion est clairement paradoxale puisque le désir d'assurer que les gouvernements soient capables de gouverner est ordinairement accompagné par le désir de soumettre plus directement le gouvernement à la mainmise des citoyens. Même s'il n'est pas facile de concilier ces deux idées ou de nier l'existence de ce paradoxe, les partisans de ces deux principes apparemment contradictoires pourraient prétendre qu'il faut instaurer un processus démocratique plus direct si l'on veut permettre aux hommes politiques et aux bureaucraties gouvernementales de rester plus ouverts et plus sensibles au « bien public », mais que cela exige une réduction de l'étendue des activités gouvernementales.

Il n'existe aucune solution évidente à ces problèmes et, si la question a été soulevée au cours de la conférence, les orateurs comme M. Bayless Manning ne l'ont abordée que pour mettre les participants en garde contre les conséquences que peut avoir une acceptation trop enthousiaste des mécanismes de participation totale lorsqu'il s'agit d'élaborer et d'appliquer les politiques et les programmes gouvernementaux. Certes, les particuliers ou les groupes qui veulent promouvoir leurs intérêts spéciaux et parfois restreints sont rarement ceux qui doivent assumer directement la responsabilité de leurs gestes ou en répondre devant la société.

Comme dans toutes les discussions concernant la politique, nous devons inévitablement revenir à nos propres principes et à nos valeurs vis-à-vis la démocratie. En outre, nous devons encore une fois faire face au dilemme mentionné plus tôt dans la présente introduction, c'est-à-dire qu'il existe certaines contradictions entre les mesures requises pour assurer la cohésion et le dévouement à une cause commune qui sont essentiels à la stabilité économique et sociale, et les mesures nécessaires pour donner aux particuliers le maximum de liberté pour poursuivre leurs propres intérêts et aspirations.

Il est donc bien évident qu'une participation et un apport efficaces des citoyens aux affaires publiques posent certains problèmes. On peut les résumer brièvement de la façon suivante :

- Premièrement, les experts ne s'entendent pas sur la question de savoir ce qui constitue le niveau de participation des citoyens nécessaire pour atteindre les objectifs de cohésion sociale et les objectifs reliés à la liberté politique des particuliers et des groupes minoritaires.
- Deuxièmement, de par sa nature même, tout gouvernement doit restreindre les intérêts des particuliers; le gouvernement démocratique vise à permettre à la majorité d'établir les limites à l'intérieur desquelles ces restrictions doivent s'appliquer.
- Troisièmement, le paradoxe du gouvernement démocratique provient du fait que, pour former un lien entre l'intérêt des particuliers et celui de la collectivité, il faut inciter les particuliers à assumer la responsabilité des affaires sociales et politiques. Autrement dit, il existe une contradiction presque inhérente et constante dans l'objectif qui consiste à inculquer aux particuliers un sens de leurs responsabilités sociales et politiques dans une société démocratique libérale parce que c'est justement ce facteur qui pose des problèmes lorsqu'on veut obtenir un consensus ou une certaine cohésion à l'échelle collective ou publique.
- Quatrièmement, la capacité d'assumer ses responsabilités dépend de ses connaissances, et ces connaissances ne peuvent être acquises qu'en participant aux processus gouvernementaux et en les comprenant; cela constitue un facteur essentiel à tout engagement politique et favorise en même temps le dialogue dialectique.
- Cinquièmement, tout mécanisme en vue d'étendre ou d'accroître la participation des citoyens doit garantir que la responsabilité finale appartient clairement aux dirigeants politiques élus qui doivent être visiblement comptables de leurs gestes.

Cela représente un ensemble de problèmes gigantesques et presque impossibles à concilier. Il est facile de comprendre pourquoi l'analyse des divers aspects et des éléments de ces problèmes a tour à tour enthousiasmé et déprimé les participants à la conférence.

CONCLUSIONS

Le thème principal de la conférence consistait à déterminer comment améliorer l'apport et la participation des citoyens à la prise de décisions du gouvernement. Dans leur étude de cette question, les participants se sont concentrés sur les moyens d'apporter certaines réformes aux institutions et aux organismes actuels. Ils ont aussi abordé de façon restreinte mais fort utile l'application possible et l'adaptation de certains changements structuraux importants telle l'expérience de la Suisse en matière de démocratie directe. Dans l'ensemble, cependant, les participants penchaient plutôt en faveur de réformes fondées sur les principes de la démocratie parlementaire.

Dans cette optique, les participants ont soulevé plusieurs questions probantes portant sur la nécessité de déterminer si la réforme doit viser uniquement ou principalement les institutions de la démocratie représentative elles-mêmes (c'est-à-dire le Parlement, les députés et les partis politiques), ou si elle doit se concentrer surtout sur les institutions et les organismes susceptibles d'offrir un accès plus direct à la bureaucratie et d'influer davantage sur celle-ci (par exemple, les commissions, les équipes spéciales, les organismes de réglementation ou de politique publique—dans tous les cas, il s'agirait d'accroître le rôle de ces organismes). La conférence a donc constitué un élément important de l'entreprise beaucoup plus vaste qui consistera à essayer de résoudre tous ces problèmes. Elle a permis d'établir une base à partir de laquelle on pourra entreprendre une étude plus analytique et plus approfondie dans les deux domaines.

Aux fins du présent volume, les délibérations de la conférence ont été regroupées en deux parties. La première partie contient les principaux exposés thématiques présentés lors de la conférence. Ces quatre mémoires sont l'oeuvre d'experts et d'observateurs reconnus, dont trois, MM. J. Alex Corry, J. King Gordon et Tom Kent, ont influé énormément sur l'histoire politique et les institutions du Canada. M. Bayless Manning, grâce à sa grande expérience de la vie politique et universitaire des États-Unis, a permis aux participants de faire une évaluation très utile des réformes possibles des institutions canadiennes en s'appuyant sur l'expérience américaine.

La seconde partie contient les sept autres mémoires présentés à la conférence et qui portent chacun sur un aspect bien précis de la réforme institutionnelle ou structurale. La qualité de ces mémoires rivalise avec celle des exposés thématiques. Notons, par exemple, que MM. Michael Pitfield et Robert Bryce ont une expérience considérable dans le domaine de la fonction publique fédérale du Canada. D'autres, comme MM. Doug Fisher et Dalton Camp, ont acquis une grande expérience de l'aspect public ou politique de la scène politique du Canada, d'abord grâce à leur participation directe à cette activité et, plus récemment, à titre de journalistes. MM. Gérard LaForest et William Neilson ont fait profiter les participants de leur expérience pratique en la matière, et ont donné un aperçu perspicace de l'utilisation de la loi ou des institutions juridiques et des organismes de réglementation pour promouvoir la participation des citoyens. Enfin, l'excellent exposé de l'expérience suisse en matière de démocratie directe présenté par M. Peter Studer, rédacteur du *Tages-Anzeiger* de Zurich, a été très utile aux participants et a fourni un contrepoint important à l'orientation principalement ou exclusivement canadienne donnée à la conférence. Un aspect particulièrement utile de la conférence a été l'excellence des commentaires qui ont été faits sur chacun de ces exposés. Tous les commentaires ont été inclus dans le présent volume. Chaque commentateur a contribué un point de vue spécial à la discussion et a accru d'autant la portée et la signification de la conférence.

NOTES

[1] John P. Mackintosh, « The Future of Representative Parliamentary Democracy », dans *The Legislative Process in Canada: The Need for Reform*, W.A.W. Neilson et J.C. MacPherson (éd.), Montréal, l'Institut de recherches politiques, 1978, p. 315 et 316.

[2] Bertrand Russell, *Histoire de la philosophie occidentale*, traduit de l'anglais par Hélène Kern, Paris, Gallimard, 1952, p. 19 et 20.

[3] De telles analyses font partie des ouvrages de J.P. Plamenatz, *Consent, Freedom and Political Obligation*, 2ᵉ éd., Oxford, Oxford University Press, 1968; ou de P.H. Partridge, *Consent & Consensus*, Londres, Macmillan, 1971.

[4] Il existe une multitude d'études de ce genre, mais ceux qui ont le plus aidé l'auteur à se préparer pour la conférence sont les ouvrages de Lawrence A. Scaff, *Participation in Western Political Tradition: A Study of Theory & Practice*, Tucson, University of Arizona Press, 1979; de Carole Pateman, *Participation & Democratic Theory*, Londres, Cambridge University Press, 1970; de Bertrand Russell, *Histoire de la philosophie occidentale*, traduit de l'anglais par Hélène Kern, Paris, Gallimard, 1952; et de C.P. Macpherson, *The Life and Times of Liberal Democracy*, Oxford, Oxford University Press, 1977.

[5] La quatrième conférence nationale sur les procédés gouvernementaux portait sur les problèmes que comporte la réduction des dépenses gouvernementales pendant une période de restriction économique. Le thème sous-jacent de la conférence concernait cependant la façon de réduire le rôle et les activités du gouvernement. Cette conférence s'est déroulée à Toronto les 19 et 20 septembre 1979. Voir Peter Aucoin (éd.), *The Politics and Management of Restraint in Government*, Montréal, l'Institut de recherches politiques, 1981.

[6] Michel J. Crozier, Samuel P. Huntington et Joji Watanuki, *The Crisis of Democracy*, a report on the governability of democracies to the Trilateral Commission, New York, New York University Press, 1975, p. 161.

[7] *Ibid*.

Part One

A Survey of the Issues

Chapter One

Sovereign People or Sovereign Governments

by
J. Alex Corry

My severest trouble will be to avoid talking and thinking like a lawyer. Sovereignty in its most precise and sharply defined meaning is a legal conception, basic to the lawyer's search for the law, pure and undefiled. It is even subtler than sovereignty-association, which we struggle to get hold of now. We are not concerned here with legal sovereignty but with a much looser, flabbier notion—political sovereignty. The question here is whether the people are able any more to control their governments or whether they are reduced to waiting to be told by their governments what is going to be done to them, for them, or against them. Is government to be master or servant? In what sense can governments be said to be democratic any more?

Despite the treacherous bog that is political sovereignty, there are a few places around the edges with firm footing. Given the present-day range, complexity, and interlocked character of the policies and programmes of central governments, whether federal or provincial, the people cannot be telling these governments what to do in the manifold detail of their various activities. About all they can do is purr when they are pleased and howl when they are hurt. But that is an old truth, not a new one. Even in a much simpler world, they could never give detailed direction: they had to wait to praise or punish in the next general election. The main change is that they now have much more to howl about.

The fact is that wherever we get beyond the lower levels of community, the rural township, or the small town, the people lack the knowledge, the face-to-face relationships that rouse spontaneous debate and shape cells of dominant opinion on general issues. At the higher, more populous levels, how do they organize themselves in relation to the more complex issues? As far as I can judge, the interest and attention most people can muster for public matters tend to focus on the specifics of what governments are doing to them or for them in their immediate lives, and so draw them into launching or joining competing pressure groups. Out of these comes confusion of tongues rather than the rudiments of a public mind.

It was not always thus. It used to be easier to get a sense of the shifts in the drift of opinion. Did sharply partisan newspapers impart an excitement to public debate and sharpen issues even if they did not clarify them? When we were more ignorant did we come more easily to sturdy convictions? Was it that the arena of public contention was both smaller and more largely occupied by matters more easily relatable to the broad public interest? Or was it because there were fewer specific sore spots where the government shoe pinched to get hot and bothered about? At any rate, it is said that Abraham Lincoln, in the years before the Civil War, was avidly reading newspapers from every state in the Union. He concluded that the great bulk of the people would come out strongly for the Union, and he placed himself there to lead them. I do not know how Mackenzie King read Canadian opinion, but I think he had earthier sources than the spirits he communed with.

In sum, in the contexts I have just been dealing with, the people are not sovereign. They are ruled or led or both, showing faint red or green lights here and there. But this must not be taken to mean that they are powerless. In so far as Canada is in some sense a community, has some kind of organic unity, even though defective, and is not merely a carpentered construct, the people still possess some elements of political sovereignty. In so far as they, the people, are conscious of being a community, whether it be a local neighbourhood, the Quebec community, or the Canadian community, there is a core of common beliefs and attitudes that is the foundation and the cement of the community. It is expressed in widely shared opinions about right and wrong on a variety of subjects, including what governments should be doing or not doing. Within this range, once the community is aroused, opinion is king. The king's servants, the government, ignore it at their peril. The last time the Canadian community was massively aroused was in relation to World War Two.

Even then, we were not as close to being united all across the country as we were in the middle twenties on wanting to shake off the last vestiges of colonial trappings and to embrace Dominion status. The American people in the Watergate imbroglio came out decisively for constitutionalism and the rule of law. These several issues, when stripped of their obfuscations, revealed themselves as open to commonsense judgements in which the people come more easily to firm opinions and are, on occasion, wiser than governments. More than that, the initial decision in these instances was to be against something. Usually, it is easier to muster opinion against something than decisively for concrete action.

Valiant efforts have been made recently to rouse public opinion against environmental pollution and with considerable success. However, the specifics of actions needed to clean up the environment call for a wide range of measures that outrun commonsense considerations. They raise many abstruse scientific and technical questions and engage many diverse and conflicting interests. How is a clear and decisive public opinion to emerge from such a *mélange*?

Put briefly, complexity is making popular guiding and control of government an almost impossible task. At the same time, drastic changes in the character of most national communities are crippling their ability to face up to the task. The sense of what is right and fitting is strong, pervasive, and easily read in long-established traditional communities, at least until the cement of tradition moves towards an advanced stage of decay. Hints of what I mean will be enough. It is said that people died of shock when they learned that Charles I had been beheaded. It is true that sweet old ladies in Kingston wept when Edward VIII abdicated.

As we all know, the acids of modernity have been wearing down all traditional communities for varying lengths of time. To what extent the unity of this nation or that has become a flimsy facade is difficult to say. At the least, we understand better now the prophets who have long been warning us that Leviathan, the mortal god, is an unreliable object of worship.

In Canada, at any rate, identifiable surges of genuine national feeling are rare. (Much as we may decry feeling as a component in statecraft, it is nevertheless always an element in the precipitation of public opinion.) What emerges now with us is rather regional and group clashes over shares in the national pie or hot contention about capital punishment, abortion, seal hunts, and what not. Important as these issues are, discussion of them sheds more heat than light. The overall impression of the strident dialogue on these and other topics is best put in the words of Thomas Hobbes: "the windy blisters of a troubled water."

Governments, it appears, are not getting clear readings of public opinion from public debate, members of legislatures, or newspapers. Perhaps that is because there is little out there to read that is legible. Opinion polls flourish and are always telling us more than they really know. Presumably, governments scan these polls anxiously but are nevertheless tempted to resort to plebiscites. Whether it be polls or plebiscites, what they test is not considered opinion matured by discussion pro and con, but off-the-cuff impulses that may change next month, if not next morning.

Governments find it difficult to act resolutely in pursuit of coherent policies if faction, always present in a vigorous free polity, comes to dominate the field. Faction is rising dangerously near to dominance. This is inevitable, in my view, because we now live, in Canada and elsewhere, in what someone has aptly called the Special Interest State. In the time and space available here, it is not possible to chart the rise of the Special Interest State or to diagnose in detail the derangements that flow from it.

In the briefest terms, the flourishing diversification and enlarging bounty of economic life in the last century has brought into being hundreds and hundreds of diverse and contending economic interests and social groups, all wanting to safeguard and/or advance their special and particular concerns. Whether governments have helped or hindered in developing the increased productivity, they have been seen as closely associated with it. Incessant social and economic change threatens stability and the entangled interrelationships of various groups of interests. Governments have had to preside over the processes of social and economic change. In coping with these complexities and disturbed interrelationships, they have given special concessions and advantages to many groups while denying others or saddling them with special burdens not equally imposed on all.

The emissaries of special interests fill the antechambers of governments and get as much space and time in the media as they can. None of them wastes time in taking their troubles to the Lord in prayer; they seek at once solace and assuagement from governments. Even hearing their demands is a mounting burden and distraction as governments struggle for coherent policy. Such members of the public as are not lined up in support of one or other group interest—and they are many—are shocked and confused. The issues arising out of the clamour are always complex and almost always beyond the grasp of the ordinary citizen.

I am not concerned here to make judgements. As long as manoeuvring in the Special Interest State is kept within the bounds of the law, who is to deny the right to petition governments for protection or for redress of what are thought to be special grievances? But I do note several points of fact. First, this kind of activity is a main source of rising faction among us. Second, in so far as government responds with special concessions, it does encroach on what was once a central democratic principle. The early struggle for democratic control of government drew massive popular support by demanding equality before the law, the destruction of special privilege or status hitherto enjoying sanctification by law. The cry echoes down the years: "equal rights for all and special privilege for none." The extent to which this principle is honoured or ignored is still perhaps the best measure of the repute of governments with the uncommitted public.

Governments, of course, have to say that our affairs are now so complex that slavish adherence to equality before the law often would not meet the requirements of the public interest. If governments have to be intervening in so many corners of our lives as they now are, this is no doubt true. But the chains of reasoning that link special treatment of this or that group with the urgent public interest are often long and involved, based on recondite facts and statistical estimates, and not infrequently tortuous.

Difficult though it may be to make these links clear in simple language, a government that wants to maintain its legitimacy with the public should be making a desperate effort to do just that. Recent instances that come to mind are the decision of the federal government to upgrade the ice-rinks in four cities, and that of the government of Ontario to give large subsidies to the pulp and paper industry. I assume that both programmes are well linked to the public interest, but no sufficient demonstration has come to my attention. In fairness, I must add that I have not conducted a survey of the national press to find out.

Without such a demonstration, these and other special concessions are incomprehensible to citizens other than ice-athletes and those deeply and directly concerned with the pulp and paper industry in Ontario, and they are likely to be seen as forms of indefensible privilege. If it were to be said that giving all the lengthy explanations required in scores of similar decisions is too heavy a burden for governments to handle, then I would be driven to conclude that the circuits that carry the decision making of governments are indeed overloaded. The proof that there is a serious problem of communication here is the ready credence given in many quarters to charges of conspiracy between special interests and governments, and the willingness to believe in sinister collusion between powerful but incorrigibly diverse interests.

Such charges and suspicions are mostly nonsense. Our governments have not fallen to this level. Occasional accommodations of convenience may take place between interests basically distrustful of each other, but the notion of systematic collusion between disparate, self-centred, and conflicting interests strains the imagination. However, what is believed is often more important in politics than is the truth. Dark suspicions of conspiracy can be put down as a main cause of the precipitous decline of public confidence in governments to a point well below the level of a healthy scepticism.

What is the portent of all this for the subject, sovereign people or sovereign governments? The people cannot rule what is so massive, complex, and interlocked and not to be unlocked by common sense alone. Members of Parliament and of legislatures can—and do—get a grip on sectors of government activity that are of special interest to themselves, their constituencies or regions, but rarely ever extend to the volatile and shifting scheme of things entire: one may question whether even prime ministers, premiers, and cabinets are really in sure command of the whole. In so far as they approach that command, it is only because they have at their beck and call cohorts of knowledgeable public servants whose whole time can be given to mastering the intricacies. And indeed they are indispensable for the present tasks of government: one need not concede that government is sovereign or even invoke Parkinson's Law to account for the rapid rise of the mandarins.

As the burgeoning special interests infect the electorate, their influence spreads to the elected Members of Parliament and legislatures. They, the members, become less sure of having a solid base of support in the constituencies. Their hesitations appear in party caucuses and weaken the united fronts contrived there. What members of the majority party will put brutally to the Cabinet in caucus narrows considerably on the floor of the legislature. The opposition becomes much surer of the utter general incompetence of the government than of the specific defects of particular policy proposals. As a result, the government gets from the legislature a smudged reading of what majorities of electors in the several constituencies are likely to support, tolerate, or reject. Beyond that, again, where there are more than two parties in the field, it is not clear whether the electorate in the next general election will return an overall majority for any one party. Minority or coalition government brings instability and uncertainty. A policy cobbled up today may be inconsistent with one cobbled up yesterday. The representative legislature on which a sovereign people has to rely for its effective control of government falls short of serving its purpose. The link between government and people weakens.

However, governments must govern somehow. As the legislature's contribution to policy weakens, its control becomes more tenuous, a gap opens up that must be filled. In large measure, it is filled by the knowledgeable expert members of the public service. They contribute to policy initiatives and suggest alternative lines of action for the Cabinet to ponder and compare. They assemble the data and make the analyses needed for assessing alternatives. They explore such existing programmes as are thought to be defective and study the compatibilities of new proposals with established programmes. They share largely with the Cabinet in the shaping of policy. We do not know where and how much, if at all, the Cabinet yields assent to the superior knowledge and grasp of their advisers. At the least, the Cabinet and the higher civil servants are much closer to sovereign power than are the people. In substance as distinct from form, we are closer to understanding how it can be said that the real rulers of a society are undiscoverable.

Everyone knows that I have not been privy to the inner workings and dominant anxieties of cabinets and prime ministers. I should think, however, that they must be concerned with the weakening of their links with the general public, particularly when their actions reach into so many corners of the lives of the citizens. Their most extensive, if not the most intimate, connections with citizens now are restricted to general elections, the hunting season when every politician is fair game, and they are more likely to be showered with buckshot than favoured with temperate and considered use of the franchise.

The experience of cabinets with professors as consultants has taught them that political wisdom is not always associated with erudition. They may well have had similar stirrings of doubts about some of their higher civil servants. In any case, political wisdom that goes beyond common sense to cover our entangled complexities is one of the rarer commodities. Cabinets must want to use such gems wherever possible as measures of the fineness of their own acumen. How widely to throw the net is the question.

The general public is restless too. So much is remote and dark to the citizens that they have run out of words to explain what is going on. They would like to be closer to the centres of power and decision to find out more about what is going on, and to say what they think. This is particularly true of such members of the public as are worried about the fate of democracy—for example, the members of this institute, as witness this conference and its agenda.

We are faced with finding ways and means of enlarging citizen involvement and perhaps control. I shall not trespass on ground that later speakers and commentators are likely to be covering. But I shall ask some questions that I hope speakers will address, and all of us will think about.

First, is what government would want from easier accessibility and wider involvement with citizens close to what the general public would want or could contribute? One thing I think government sorely needs, and perhaps wants, is ways to break more gently the burden of its measures on to the backs of the public, to explain simply why it is doing this or that, to say in five-letter words, or four, how concessions to special interests are related to the public interest. Many people do not know because these arcane matters have never been put in language that conveys meaning to the man in the street. But would the devices to be explored here help government with this exercise?

Of course, the general public wants to know more about why and how. This is vital if the public is to enforce responsible government. But what are the risks that the citizens who actually participate will want much less of what government now provides or imposes, will have less concern for more understanding, and put more weight into pressing new wants that hitherto have not managed to rock the boat? Will more would-be clients of the Special Interest State turn up, adding to the babel of voices now heard? If so, will government conclude that it would prefer more apathy than less?

Let us say firmly that we want less apathy. Will the devices that students a decade ago called participatory democracy and joint decision making be defeated, as students said they found, by the oligarchic tendency of all large organizations, including governments? Which of the devices under consideration can be counted on to put an enduring dent in the widespread apathy?

The universities learned two lessons from the student revolt, which are relevant here. Often the spokesmen who lectured us sternly about the right of everyone to share in decisions in a democracy came down off their high horse in response to an innocent assertion: wider sharing would be easier to face if we could always count on having perceptive fellows like you! Then there is the analogue from an earlier time: the professor who campaigned stoutly for more openness and more sharing in decisions relating to the faculty. Later, he himself became the dean of the faculty and set new high standards of secretiveness and unilateral decision.

In these instances, the underlying urge, of which I think the protagonists themselves were unaware, was a strong desire to join the élite. Is citizen involvement likely to be diverted into a competition for places in the élite? If so, and if we need to recruit élites from a wider field, this would be useful. But is this what we want to get from citizen involvement?

There is something else universities learned from the push for participatory democracy. When, in due course, student representation was provided for on various governing bodies and active committees, the interest of students in these bodies declined sharply and quickly: within a few short years, it was difficult to get the students to elect or appoint their representatives, and still more difficult to ensure their attendance. Why? When first given membership, they turned up keen as mustard, sure that now they would find out all the sinister or stupid things that were going on. To their surprise, they could not find any skulduggery and not nearly as much stupidity as they had expected.

They also found that most items on the agenda were not simple, that great application to detail would be required to make them knowledgeable. On top of that, much of the detail was boring, if not stupefying. At the least, the siren calls of other extracurricular excitements stirred them more. They found, in many instances (not all), that they did not want to be in this or that particular élite.

This outcome recalls Oscar Wilde's judgement on the case that was being made for guild socialism in Britain in the early years of this century. None of you will be old enough to remember that the running of the economy and many other social activities were to be in the control of numerous guilds composed of the workers by hand and brain across the country. They would all be up to the neck in the many decisions of the several guilds of which they were members. Wilde said the trouble with guild socialism was that there would not be any more free evenings.

Another critic on the economic side said it simply was not true that every worker had a director's cigar in his vest pocket. What proportion of our fellow-citizens want, or would feel equal to, involvement with matters of comparable weight and movement? May it be that most people would prefer to leave such matters to knowledgeable élites they could trust, if only—and it is a big ''if''—their stewardship could be tested in commonsense judgements of its fairness and effectiveness?

I ask these questions because I think they bear on the topics to be discussed here and because I do not know the answers. I conclude with a comment on student involvement in university government that came late in the sixties, which I am sure about. In one respect, it has been a marked success. Having got access to the inner councils, they found there senior officers and members of teaching staff making decisions with thought and care. They learned that there were reasons for doing this and not doing that which had never occurred to them. They found almost nothing of the skulduggery suspected. Interest in heavy participation fell off rapidly without being utterly extinguished. They made the commonsense judgement that as long as these senior officers and members of academic staff continued worthy of trust, they themselves had other and better things to do.

If persistent dark rumours circulate or if a sequence of decisions or actions puzzle the students, they can quickly make fuller use of the representation guaranteed them and turn up regularly at meetings. If their concern is not abated, they have a forum in which to express it vigorously. This is a main reason why the campuses have been more peaceful in the seventies. Although citizen involvement with governments is a much more lumpy and knotty matter, some of its forms to be examined here might have similar beneficial results.

I hope so, because I continue to believe that the best, if not the only, guarantee of an ultimately sovereign people is a large renewal of trust in representative and responsible government. I suspect that much of the clamour for citizen involvement will not be stilled merely by involvement and participation in multifarious detail, because it arises for other, and not immediately apparent, reasons: first, because of the lengthening reach of central governments into the daily lives of the people, or at least into matters that affect their daily lives; second, a suspicion that decisions that impinge sorely on them are actually being made, not by their representatives in the legislatures or by ministers directly responsible to their representatives. The suspicion is that many decisions are being made on high by persons nameless and faceless to them. Add to that the fact that the reasons for the decisions are often dark to those affected and tainted with mystery. Even God Himself has suffered a loss of confidence in many quarters for very similar reasons.

If there is anything in this conjecture, then one of the benefits of more citizens getting closer to, and more involved in, what is going on may be that they will see what a tangled web their representatives in the legislatures are dealing with. One would hope that even if they do not see governments checked on as tight a rein as in the past, they might decide that the loose rein is more appropriate to our circumstances and still adequate to hold governments accountable. In short, they might decide that their representatives are worthy of renewed trust.

Chapter Two

Past Is Prologue

by
J. King Gordon

Your chairman, a student of Canadian political history, discovered me on the page of a book describing certain events that took place in Regina some forty-six years ago.* He has produced me for this distinguished gathering, if not as a living artifact, at least as an archeological relic. And in this capacity I have chosen to speak, not on the topic listed in your programme, but on a much more modest theme: Past is Prologue.

The difficult times to plot policy makers and policy making are times of historical discontinuity. Then the pressure points shift; the power factors rise and wane; and new forces suddenly make their appearance and reveal surprising strength.

Such a time was the Great Depression. Such a time is today.

In 1932, a little publication appearing in Montreal carried this story:

> Premier Bennett, speaking in Toronto said: The acquisition of property comes to a man of ability in this world if he has done his job properly. And it lies between him and his God what he does with it.

Four years later, in 1932, I was travelling in the Atlantic provinces and wrote to a friend from Fredericton.

> Sunday afternoon I went for a drive into the beautiful surrounding country. We visited Marysville, one of the Canada Cottons towns. In sheer industrial ugliness I have seldom seen its equal. The better houses are red brick boxes of uniform size and proportions. The worst are unpainted clapboard, no plumbing, outhouses behind each house, central tap from which apparently all get their water. At the last election, a company official stood at the polling booth and told the men that if Bennett were not elected the town would close down. There is a club building for the "help." It is called Dawson Hall. Also tennis courts. Last year the officials got very worried about the morals of the employees because the girls were wearing shorts to play tennis.

After all these years, the two stories hold some interest. The first, setting forth the philosophy of the man of property in a way John Galsworthy could not improve upon, fairly expressed the attitude that was generally acceptable to policy makers in business and government. The second story had a more personal interest—although its insight into industrial relations of the day is very revealing: at the time it was written, of course, Bennett had been defeated and the mill was still running. The Dawson after whom the millhouse hands' clubhouse was named was president of Canada Cottons and also chairman of the board of governors of United Theological College in Montreal. Every Sunday morning he taught a large Bible class of women in St. James United Church.

I had been a professor of Christian ethics at United Theological College. Along with Eugene Forsey and another McGill professor, we put out a little research bulletin on social and political developments that might be of interest to the church. In one issue, we reported that in a textile mill in Quebec, the girls were being paid $9.50 a week although the provincial minimum wage was $15.00: through a special arrangement, the law had been waived because the textile plant was an infant industry.

The times were difficult and the college was hard pressed for funds. After I had been teaching for two years, it was found necessary to discontinue the chair of Christian Ethics as an austerity measure. At the time I wrote the letter, I was travelling secretary of the Fellowship for a Christian Social Order, a socially aware group made up for the most part of young United Church ministers and members.

During that trip, I had touched base with Father Coady and the rector of St. Francis Xavier at Antigonish, borrowed the rector's car to drive out to Harbour Bushey to see the co-operative lobster factory, caught a glimpse of the misery of unemployed families in Newcastle, addressed a meeting in a United Church basement in Dalhousie, New Brunswick, and gone on from there to speak to a meeting of the Pulp and Paper Workers Union in the union hall.

Now what has all this got to do with policy making?

In the summer and autumn of 1931, two groups, mainly of university professors, gathered around Frank Underhill, a Canadian historian in Toronto, and Frank Scott, a McGill law professor, in Montreal, to discuss forming the equivalent of the British Fabian Society. A number of the group had been exposed to Lasky, Hobson, G.D.H. Cole, and the Webbs during their academic sojourn in England. In January 1932 in Toronto, with the group now enlarged by devotees from Queen's, Victoria, and Trinity, the League for Social Reconstruction (LSR) was launched.

The manifesto of the LSR began as follows:

The League for Social Reconstruction is an association of men and women who are working for the establishment in Canada of a social order in which the basic principles regulating production, distribution and service will be the common good rather than profit.

Then, within these general guide-lines, followed specific prescriptions for social planning in Canada, not only to meet the widespread suffering produced by the Depression but to lay the groundwork for a reconstructed social and economic order in which social justice rather than profit making would be an accepted principle of organization and action.

The LSR prospered and extended its membership beyond academic circles. It held meetings. It issued pamphlets. It sponsored conferences. Its leading members were under constant call to speak at public meetings, student seminars, church gatherings, union meetings. In 1935, after much labour, it produced an impressive book, *Social Planning for Canada*. The chief public relations man for the CPR contributed an anonymous pamphlet attacking the book and its authors. Sales shot up and we had to go into a second printing.

It would be a mistake to give the impression that the LSR became a potent propaganda or political force in the country. It was the timing that was important. At a time of economic breakdown, general uncertainty, and widespread distress for which no adequate relief was available, the LSR provided an articulate analysis of the situation and proposed certain lines of government policy to meet it.

It was a time of political ferment, political searching. On university campuses, the Student Christian Movement became a radical force. In presbytery and conference and general council, the United Church condemned the iniquities of the economic system. The new industrial trade unions became politicized. Here in the Atlantic provinces, the Extension Department of St. Francis Xavier University, under the dynamic leadership of Father Tompkins, Father Coady, and A.B. MacDonald, carried out a quiet revolution through study groups and co-operatives. And into all these manifestations of discontent and protest, the LSR made its contribution—through the personal participation of its members, through radio, through the printed word.

The political expression was inevitable. After a preliminary conference at Calgary in 1932 of a parliamentary group of farmer and labour members, the Co-operative Commonwealth Federation was launched at Regina in July 1933. Its manifesto bore a strong resemblance to the manifesto of the LSR—which was not surprising since Frank Underhill was the original author of both.

If we read those manifestos now and view them against the ongoing tradition of democracy and the increasing recognition of human rights free from discrimination, it is difficult to believe that when they appeared, they were considered to be radical documents. In fact, much of what was advocated is now incorporated into legislation and public policy. It is not merely that we have seen that three provincial governments of the CCF or its successor have had an exemplary influence elsewhere. It is rather that the major parties, partly as the result of challenge of the philosophy of the new party, partly as a result of the pressure of their own membership, were forced to embody principles of social planning and broad social security into their political programmes and legislative practice. An inveterate CCFer likes to think that eventually social, moral, and political realities assert themselves.

I turn now to the present. I said at the beginning that the difficult times to plot policy makers and policy making were times of historical discontinuity—the pressure points shift, the power factors rise and fall, and new forces suddenly make their appearances and reveal surprising strength.

The period in which we have been involved during the mid-thirties seems light years removed from today's world. But I suggest that its similarity is based on the fact that now, as then, we are probably in the midst of one of the great discontinuities of history. I shall even suggest that the great economic, social, and moral issues are not dissimilar.

As I recall it, on that trip to Halifax in 1936, I left Montreal at about ten o'clock in the morning and arrived in Halifax the next day, twenty-five hours later, at twelve noon. A couple of months ago, I left Montreal at eleven o'clock one night, spent ten hours in Paris the next day, and arrived at Douala, Cameroun, just after midnight their time—about twenty hours after leaving Montreal. It was a conference on the law of the sea. People had come from London, Geneva, Washington, New York, Sri Lanka, Tokyo, Halifax, and all parts of Africa—all with travel time under a day. The *world* today is much smaller than Canada was in the 1930s.

And the shrinkage is due not only to the substitution of subsonic and supersonic jets for the old iron horse and steamship. Modern technology has placed mankind on a communications network that leaves out no one. An event in Harrisburg, Pennsylvania, has instant reaction in Japan and West Germany. Modern technology, with its enormous potential for resources development as well as for communication has for the first time in human history opened up common goals and aspirations for all of mankind.

Had the political order of the world been left unchanged by the war, the implications of the new framework of human expectations would have been less significant. Cameroun was a former German colony, then a League of Nations mandate—or rather two mandates under French and British jurisdiction. Now it is an independent state as are almost all former colonies in Africa and Asia. Our new world—and we have not begun to realize all its significance—is made up of independent nations: the established industrial nations of the north and the newly independent nations of the south. They are now part of one world community.

Recently, at a conference of the vice-chancellors of Commonwealth universities held in Kingston, Jamaica, Shridath Ramphal, Commonwealth Secretary General and former foreign minister of Guyana, made the following statement in referring to the ending of colonialism:

> But political independence was not an end in itself—it was a mechanism in a much wider process of democratising the international community and applying to it the norms of equity and social justice, which the war had been fought to secure as a basis of human existence. In some ways, decolonisation was the counterpart at the global

level of the dismantling of feudal and elitist structures within Western societies more than a century earlier. But just as in Europe, for example, the political reforms of the 18th and early 19th century were not enough in themselves to install social and economic justice there, so decolonisation after 1945 was not enough to install social and economic justice in our wider global community.

The process of decolonization left the pattern of economic power and control unchanged. The rich nations, comprising about a third of the human race, controlled over 80 per cent of the world's wealth, 93 per cent of its industry, and close to 100 per cent of its institutions of research and higher learning. Some 800 million persons lived—and live today—on ''a margin of existence totally dominated by malnutrition, disease, high infant mortality, low life expectancy, and illiteracy.''

With stark realism, the author of *Proverbs* wrote:

> The rich man's wealth is his strong castle: the destruction of the poor is their poverty. (10:15)

At first, in the years after the war, the governments and peoples of the developed world tended to regard the situation as analogous to that of the poor and underprivileged and handicapped in their cities. What was needed was a global united appeal. Bilateral and international aid programmes were inaugurated. A goal of .7 per cent of GNP was set but reached by only a few of the rich contributing countries. Canada rose to .56 per cent but slid back to .46. After two so-called ''development decades,'' the plight of the poor in the Third World remains unchanged.

Then, during the late sixties and early seventies, a new unity emerged among the nations of the Third World, a ''trade union of the poor,'' as it was called—not just more aid but a fundamental restructuring of trade commodity controls, and prices; international monetary mechanisms with greater consideration for the needs of developing countries; as well as increased access for Third World countries to scientific and technological resources. The insistence of this demand was underscored by the formation of OPEC, the oil embargo of 1973, and the demonstrations of solidarity between the rich and the poor developing nations. A special session of the United Nations General Assembly in 1975 called for a ''new international economic order.'' Canada identified itself with these objectives in a speech by the prime minister at the Mansion House in London:

> The human community is a complete organism, linked again and again within itself as well as with the biosphere upon which it is totally dependent for life. This interdependency demands of us two functions: first, the maintenance of an equilibrium among our activities, whatever their nature; second, an equitable distribution world-wide of resources and opportunities.

And then, with greater precision, he went on to say:

> The proper discharge of these functions calls for more than tinkering with the present system. The processes required must be global in scope and universal in application.

In their imagination, if not in their conception, they must be new. Of their need no one can doubt.

The sentiments were repeated at a conference of the Commonwealth heads of state in Jamaica in the summer of 1975, and through a special committee, a consensus was worked out for Commonwealth countries, for the affluent north and the disadvantaged south, for the upcoming special session of the United Nations General Assembly. In Ottawa, to give reality to this decision and co-ordinate policies, an interdepartmental committee relating to developing countries was set up.

Meanwhile, a series of developments had reinforced the concept of interdependency—perhaps even calling into question the adequacy of the nation-state as a satisfactory base for policy making. The seriousness of the threat to the environment by man's technological progress was emphasized at Stockholm in 1972. The critical world food problem, accented by serious droughts in India and the Sahel in Africa, was examined at a world food conference in Rome. The findings of the Club of Rome, later dramatized by the oil crisis of 1973, gave top priority to a global concern for the continuing availability of the energy and mineral resources needed to sustain the industrial societies of the north and meet the legitimate aspirations of the south for the means to a decent life. And the world economic recession, with high inflation and high unemployment in the developed countries, raised the suspicion that the poverty of the Third World and the economic disarray of the developed world had to be considered as mutually related.

As one might have predicted, there have been a number of expert studies made at the international level to provide guidance for policy makers in this new and dangerous global situation. They cannot be seen out of the context of the ongoing north-south dialogue. They reflect the historical discontinuity that finds expression in the contemporary situation. In some cases, based on a radical analysis of post-war economic and political developments, they attempt to lay the groundwork for the new international order that is called for. For some, who regard recent events in the developed world as aberrations that will soon be overcome with the restoration of the market economy, they represent at best idealistic fantasies, at worst dangerous and subversive ideology. Increasingly, they are being regarded as intellectually respectable and morally responsible efforts by scholars and statesmen in developing as well as developed countries to design global strategies to control the process of change in which we are caught up, and to guide it towards a more just and stable international order.

One of the first of such studies was carried out by the Pearson commission at the request of the World Bank. It took into account some of the developments in the late sixties, to which we have referred, and may be regarded as a link between the international assistance approach and the more radical approach called for in the goal of the new international economic order.

In the last few years, there have been a whole series of studies among which the following might be noted:

- The Leontieff study[1] commissioned by the United Nations
- A study by the Dag Hammarskjöld Foundation in Uppsala produced under the title *What Now?*[2]
- The study co-ordinated by Jan Tinbergen and prepared by a distinguished group of scholars from developed and developing countries: *Reshaping the International Order*[3]
- A study on *Basic Human Needs* by John and Magda McHale[4]
- A series of studies carried out by Marc Nerfin on *An Alternative Development*[5]
- The North-South Roundtable sponsored by the Society for International Development in Rome in May 1978[6]
- The study of the Willy Brandt commission, established by the World Bank, which is now awaited.

Alongside of this research and study being carried out with greater or less degrees of urgency, we see the slow but inevitable accommodation of international institutions, international practice, even international law, in order to carry out the world's business and, in some measure, meet human needs. Oscar Schacter's *Sharing the World's Resources*[7] describes the contemporary process of international law in the making.

By and large, however, the nations of the developed world, having recovered from some of their shock of the early seventies and their ethical and political commitment to a new international economic order, have regained their complacency and await the return to normality. One is forced to the conclusion that it is not lack of knowledge or indeed failure of moral realization that inhibits positive steps towards international co-operation for development within a new international order. It is the persistence of old power patterns, of old concepts of national sovereignty that fail to recognize the new, emergent global realities. A very disturbing report by Peyton Lyon of Carleton University and two colleagues in a recent issue of *International Perspectives*[8] indicated that concern for the Third World registered a low priority among a representative group of senior Canadian policy makers.

It would almost appear as if the global issues, given high priority by the prime minister and other Cabinet spokesmen, are somehow beyond the parameters of the practical policy makers, who act in terms of traditional patterns and more immediate political pressures.

In the thirties, it appeared to be the highest possible goal when it was insisted that social justice should be available to all the Canadian people. And it was assumed with confidence that this goal could be achieved through social planning by the Canadian government.

We are part of a different world. The goals of social justice, the sharing of the world's resources, now belong to all members of the human community. And the achievement of that goal is attainable, in this interdependent world, only through co-operative and concerted action. Our own well-being, our own security, are beyond the powers of our government, acting alone.

Shridath Ramphal, Commonwealth Secretary General, put the issue dramatically:

> Perhaps it is this insight of the world as a community of people needing each other for survival and having a common interest in the quality of the human condition world-wide that will, more than any other single factor, determine the fate of the dialogue between North and South, between rich and poor, in the remaining years of this century. But it will determine much more than that: for international co-operation and development, or as I prefer to see them more conjoined, international co-operation for development, is not a thing apart. It could be human destiny entire. It is not, as we once conceived it, a little bit of goodness measured in aid, like alms on Sunday; it has to do with the structure of human relationships in all its facets.

In poetic language, reminiscent of John Donne's ''No man is an island, entire of itself,'' the Canadian government expressed almost the identical argument in *Foreign Policy for Canadians* in 1970:

> A society able to ignore poverty abroad will find it much easier to ignore it at home; a society concerned about poverty and development abroad will be concerned about poverty and development at home. We could not create a truly just society within Canada if we were not prepared to play our part in the creation of a more just world society.[9]

So the policy line is laid down. Now it is just a matter of implementation.

NOTES

* *Editor's note*: Dr. Gordon was one of the authors and signators of *Social Planning for Canada*. This book has come to represent the classic thought of Canadian socialism in the 1930s and was recently reprinted. See F.R. Scott, Leonard Marsh, Graham Spry, J. King Gordon, Eugene Forsey, and J.S. Parkinson, *Social Planning for Canada* (Toronto: University of Toronto Press, 1975).

[1] Wassily Leontieff, Anne P. Carter, and Peter A. Petri, *The Future of the World Economy*, a United Nations study (New York: Oxford University Press, 1977).

[2] ''What Now: Another Development,'' *Development Dialogue* (July 1975).

[3] Jan Tinbergen, *Reshaping the International Order*, a report prepared for the Club of Rome (New York: Dutton, 1976).

[4] John McHale and Magda C. McHale, *Basic Human Needs* (New Brunswick, N.J.: Transaction Books, 1977).

[5] Marc Nerfin, ed., *Another Development: Approaches and Strategies* (Uppsala: Dag Hammarskjöld Foundation, 1977).

[6] See *International Development Review* 20, No. 2 (1978): 3-42.

[7] Oscar Schacter, *Sharing the World's Resources* (New York: Columbia University Press, 1977).

[8] P.V. Lyon, R.B. Byers, and D. Leyton-Brown, "How 'Official' Ottawa Views the Third World," *International Perspectives* (January-February 1979): 11-16.

[9] Canada, Department of External Affairs, *Foreign Policy for Canadians: International Development* (Ottawa: Information Canada, 1970), p. 9.

Chapter Three

The Limits of Law as a Substitute for Community Responsibility

by
Bayless Manning

It is a common failing of people from my country, the United States, to presuppose that the circumstances in our country and yours are, if not exactly the same, very similar. As a result of my work with the Council of Foreign Relations, I have arrived at a point where I recognize that this assumption is often wrong. I am therefore reticent to address the general thesis I am going to talk about today in any context other than that of my own country. I hope you will receive these remarks with that in mind.

The topic I would like to address is a little different from the formal title. It is a thesis that has only recently begun to develop a certain degree of attention within the United States. It is very interesting that in the past four years in the United States, attention has focused on the limits—the inherent limits—of the regulatory process and of the legal process. It is a topic that never existed before and an issue that was never identified until quite recently. Today, it is a significant part of the political environment within the United States, particularly within those segments of the population who are informed about and concerned about governmental processes.

Let me begin by giving you a couple of facts. We have something called the *Federal Register* in the United States. The *Federal Register* contains all of the regulations of the federal government and its agencies. In 1970, the *Federal Register* had 20,000 pages in it. By 1977, it had grown to 65,000 pages! In the first 181 years as a republic, we had by 1970 accumulated 20,000 pages of regulations; in the next seven years, we accumulated 45,000 more pages.

Since 1961, the United States government has created 236 departments, agencies and bureaux; it has eliminated only 21. A little while ago, a few people finally began to wonder about the costs of our regulatory system. Not only the direct cost of our regulatory system—direct in the sense of the money for the staff and the paper and the pencils and all that—but about the indirect costs and problems. The most serious study was done by a federal commission, wonderfully named "The Commission on Federal Paperwork." That study concluded that today we spend $93 billion a year filling out governmental forms in the United States. That works out to be $500 per citizen. That is the indirect cost of regulations; it is the distribution and the hidden cost of all those people, all those companies, all those individuals filing things and filling out things.

To offer another example, we estimate that a public trial costs $250 per hour. This is just the cost of the judges, bailiff, the infrastructure, the clerks, and so on, who make the judicial process operate as a going machine, and is apart from the plant, the facilities, the equipment, and the lawyers. One more instance: General Motors estimates that today it employs a total of 25,000 employees who do nothing but fill out governmental forms. They may be exaggerating, so let us cut their figure in half and say that they hire only 10,000 employees for this purpose.

We are afflicted with a serious social disease, which I have called "hyperlexis"—too much law. It is a pathological condition that is basically caused by an overactive law-making gland.

Hyperlexis is a very serious disease and not simply an annoyance. In the first place, it is terribly costly, as I have already indicated. For example, apart from the military, we have approximately fifteen million government employees in the United States today who are directly paid for by taxes. Our regulatory overload is also terribly expensive in terms of the hidden costs that I spoke of before.

Second, cost aside, the legal system is clogging and choking into paralysis. We all know that the enforcement of the law within the United States has sunk to a new low. Judicial and administrative backlogs make it impossible to dispose of matters expeditiously. Our criminal process particularly can only be described as being in a state of epilepsy. Some efforts are being made to do something about this condition, for example, the effort to create no-fault insurance arrangements that eliminate tort proceedings in automobile accident cases. This reflects the problem that our court system, particularly in our major cities, is unable to operate because of the backlog of automobile litigation.

There is an additional interesting aspect of the problem of judicial backlog that is seldom recognized. We are now able to document this problem very specifically from a major study that was done through the Association of the Bar of the City of New York. This study showed that when the legal process jams, when the judicial process and the administrative process clog so that it is impossible to put material through it and enforce a legislative mandate, the consequence is to deprive the legislature of the opportunity to make policy decisions.

The study I refer to examined the experience under the so-called "get-tough drug laws" that were adopted in the State of New York in 1973. The study attempted to find out for the first time whether the imposition of really stiff criminal sanctions in the drug field would or would not have a measurable impact on the street and on drug use. The question is important, since many people feel very strongly on each side of the proposition, but no one had any data one way or the other as to the truth. What did the study conclude? It found that it could not give an answer. Why? Because the statute was never enforced. Why? Because the statute could not be enforced. There was no conceivable way in which the court system, indictment system, and public defender system that were in place could handle the arrest levels and the trial levels that would have been required to enforce it vigorously. Further, plea bargaining was outlawed under the 1973 statute; therefore, every defendant had to confess to a major offence with very severe penalties or plead innocent and insist on a full trial. The result was to totally jam the system. It therefore did not make a particle of difference whether the legislature wanted permissive drug laws or tough drug laws. Nothing was going to happen anyway.

The point is an obvious one. The legal system is ultimately and fundamentally dependant upon voluntary compliance. Unless you presuppose something very like an occupation army, and even then it is very hard to do, no legal system functions because it is enforced. It functions because there is some effective enforcement here and there and almost everybody else complies voluntarily.

As we keep piling on the regulatory process, the amount of law, and the number of injunctions, we are witnessing an increasing disregard for and decline in voluntary compliance. This has happened for a number of reasons, some of which are psychological, some of which simply emerge out of ignorance on the part of regulatees who do not know the rules and find it too difficult and expensive to find out. Non-compliance in turn brings a kind of disrespect, which in the long term can be very dangerous indeed. Furthermore, it is dangerous in another respect to have more law than can be enforced. If the statute and regulatory books are overloaded with mandates and injunctions, then of necessity some rationing process must go to work. That typically means that somebody, usually at the prosecutorial level, begins to hold the key that turns enforcement on or off. This is to say nothing of the almost inevitable likelihood that some segments of the community will be disfavoured in that discretionary process, and will find that the law is enforced against them but not enforced against others. No democracy, I think, can tolerate that kind of discrimination or tolerate that kind of local petty despotism. And yet, no system can avoid it if one attempts to get more out of the system by regulation and legislation than in fact the system can handle.

The purpose of most of our regulation is uniformly laudable. Most of it is aimed at attempting to achieve the elimination of discrimination or unfairness, or trying to arrive at varying kinds of elevated purposes for eliminating social disparities of one kind or another. It is aimed at trying to protect people against themselves or against others and designed primarily to help the disadvantaged, in some sense of that term disadvantaged. The operational reality is, however, that overload of the system operates primarily to the disadvantage of people in the middle and at the bottom of the society. This is because in a highly regulated environment, only people at the top of the economic ladder can afford to hire law firms and other professional experts. They can afford to hire people who have the formal education to pick their way through the maze and can spend the time to figure out how to do it. We have created or we are creating a new class of form-filling consultants. Most people do not have the resources and are correspondingly disadvantaged by the process.

Before I close this sad list, let me mention one more thing. Most of the noise that one hears about this problem, to the extent that one hears about it at all, comes from the private sector. It comes from the business community who feel, quite properly, that these regulatory processes are making it harder and harder to make decisions or to achieve decisions. It is seldom further observed, however, that increasingly heavy regulation of economic activities and governmental activities is also making it impossible for the goverment itself to make decisions. The goverment is tying its own hands in the process, often for the most laudable purposes.

For example, the City of New York is in the middle of a fight that has been going on for four years. It is about whether to build a highway along the Hudson River to replace the one that has physically collapsed. A monumental war is going on among one department of the federal government, another department of the federal government, a major agency of the State of New York, and the City of New York administration. They cannot work out an agreement and so they sue each other back and forth. Each of them is able to invoke on its side a set of regulatory mandates. Each agency is headed by a kind of hero, a civil servant who is thoroughly honest and who is doing his best to discharge the particular mandate of his agency.

Despite the usual presentations of the public media, there are almost no worthwhile contests between bad guys and good guys. Most contests, indeed, are not even between bad guys and bad guys. They are usually between good guys and good guys. A dramatic example of this may be seen in the energy area, where major efforts are being made to preserve our forests while other efforts are being made to feed, clothe, and supply an industrial society. There is no way to avoid such conflict. But if regulatory structures and decision mechanisms cannot operate, then at some point the society has wholly incapacitated itself from decision making.

Today, in the United States, our hearing system and our decisional system have come to a point where every man believes he not only has the right to a day in court, but that he is entitled to a hundred days in court. The principle of one man, one vote has become one man, one veto. I do not think that society can operate on this basis.

I am a lawyer and I am talking as a lawyer with you today. I am not talking ideology and I am not talking economics. I am saying that the legal circuitry in the United States today is so overloaded that it cannot function. It cannot function because we have arrived at some kind of an interior limitation on the use of law itself as an instrument for regulating society. This is true regardless of one's preferences as to what regulation is to be used for.

This statement is not a standard one, and it is easy to misintrepret and vulgarize it, as routing conservative *laissez-faire* argumentation. That is not what it is. I am only pointing out a built-in operational reality about the legal system itself and its own limits.

If the situation is so serious in the United States, why do we not take steps to remedy it? One reason we do not fix it is that we only recently began to discover our disease. The second reason is far more important. The truth of the matter is, in Pogo's immortal words, "We have met the enemy and he is us." Here are some of the factors.

In part the problem is a function of our multi-layered federal system. Hundreds of governmental units are daily grinding out new laws quite regardless of what anybody else is doing. We have no machinery for integrating this output.

At least four different ideological elements are at work among us. One of them is that in an earlier day, a general notion existed about the appropriate scope and limit for governmental action. Over the course of the last three generations, that ideological barrier has virtually eroded. Most people no longer really say, "Well, of course, the government cannot do X because that would not be a proper governmental function." An important constraint on law making has thus vanished.

Second, a major ideological drive of our era is the movement toward a minimum equality of opportunity for every ethnic group, every age group regardless of gender or location. It manifests itself in extensive regulation.

Another major ideological drive is the effort, if not to create a riskless life, to create a life in which all risk is equally distributed. Instead of leaving risk to rest where it initially falls, our law has for decades been moving toward distributing the losers widely. Protection is extended to pension holders, to security buyers, to bank depositors, to people who are hit by automobiles, to people who are less than efficiently operated on by their doctors, to persons of low income, and so on. We achieve those "risk distributions" by massive injections of law of one kind or another: regulatory, judicial, or through tribunals.

The fourth ideological point, and one for which the United States is particularly renowned, is our deep and historical concern with procedure. We are horrified by the unequal confrontation of the powerful state against the individual, and continuously strive to create procedural safeguards for the latter. It is a marvellous part of our tradition. It is all wrapped up with the first ten amendments, freedom of speech, and the Peter Zeeger case, and a lot of things we feel very strongly about. Of late, we have translated and transported into our general regulatory environment the elaborate structural arrangements for hearings, procedural niceties, witnesses, and for lawyers that heretofore had been thought appropriate only for the most heinous of crimes and the most severe sanctions. We have even arrived at a point where it appears that a whole trial procedure, with an appeal and everything else, can be triggered by a student who does not like the grade that he got in a course. I do not believe that a society can successfully operate that way.

There are other factors at work behind our flood of law making. The way we do our legislating is one of them. Basically, our political system for decision making at the congressional level is built on a series of coalitions and trade-offs among elected representatives of interest groups, some geographic, some industrial, some ethnic, and so on. While we may say that we wish we had less law and less regulation, the fact of the matter is that every economic, ethnic, geographic, religious, or ideological group wants something supported, regulated, or banned by the government. Each group does everything it can to pressure, capture, or harness the machinery of the state—that is, the legislatures, the judiciary, and the administrative system—in pursuit of its particular ideas of the good and the true and the profitable. The U.S. government is today the oldest governmental system in the world because it contains within itself the trade-off mechanisms to make it possible to function. But these coalition voting patterns shift from year to year, and new regulation and legislation are an inevitable, continuing product of that process.

Changes in technology have triggered social dislocations, which in turn lead to a variety of different kinds of governmental intervention. Surely, too, the bureaucracy itself is self-perpetuating. Spiders produce spiders, spiders issue cobwebs: bureaucracies produce bureaucracies and they issue regulations. That is of their nature. And they are not biodegradable and do not go away.

One last point: all of these forces and factors, and some I have omitted, are pressing in the direction of continued expansion of regulation. But there are no significant forces inside the system that tend in the opposite direction. The system has no brakes, no governor, no countervailing force. As a result, the law-making engines operate like the fairy story of the salt mill in the bottom of the sea. It just grinds out salt endlessly.

Is there no hope for improvement? By far our most important need is for a change of attitude and for public education about the hyperlexis problem. I would like to offer you half a decalog—a pentalog—of propositions. These are five true statements that should be, but never have been, focused upon and absorbed by the public, by government officials, and by the public media.

- **Proposition I.** To declare a law is very cheap: to administer or enforce a law is very expensive.

- **Proposition II.** However great the direct, visible costs of a law may be, the secondary indirect costs are always far greater.
- **Proposition III.** The capacity of the law and law enforcement to change human behaviour is very limited.

Even when the public as a whole supports a law (as in the case of laws against violent crime), the effects of the law are marginal. Where public opinion is negative or voluntary, compliance is spotty, then the effects of the law will be minimal, regardless of the investment in its enforcement.

- **Proposition IV.** Even when a law works to achieve its primary purposes, it will generate negative side-effects that often will be too great to warrant retention of the law.

A tariff generates smugglers; harsh criminal penalties create plea bargaining; all-out enforcement campaigns precipitate civil rights problems; procedural safeguards clog the judicial process; consumer protections costs increase to consumers; minimum wage legislation contributes to unemployment; and so forth. Inevitably, any law or regulation will produce by-products that are undesirable.

- **Proposition V.** Many problems are not amenable to law at all.

A law cannot create resources, repeal economics, or supplant psychological causes of human behaviour. Law is a useful tool but not an all-purpose tool.

We Americans act as though regulatory law was costless, an all-purpose tool and free of negative side-effects. We treat law as what economists call a ''free good.'' The truth is that regulatory law is in fact expensive, of limited utility, and frequently accompanied by significant harmful side-effects.

I shall skip over some thoughts about what we might do in the United States in addition to public education, because I think they may not be applicable to Canada. I do want to emphasize in closing, however, what it is I am saying and what I am not saying. As I mentioned at the beginning, it is very easy to misunderstand and mischaracterize what I have said here today as oratory decrying governmental programmes and opposing social reform. That is not my view and it is not my general political stance either. As I see it, government will and must often intervene directly in the social process through regulation and other law. I think many government programmes in effect today are essential to a decent society, and I think we have imperatives, particularly in our cities, that will require still more intervention. That is not in debate here. The thesis I am arguing here is a clinical one—a matter of cost-benefit analysis. As new programmes are proposed, we must recognize that the cost of regulation and law making is very great, and the costs rise geometrically as we load on more. At the same time, as the nation's legal institutional circuitry becomes increasingly overloaded, the pay-offs of regulation decline correspondingly.

Law is not a free good. Perhaps if we poured enough economic resources into our judicial system and our administrative enforcement system, we could, right now, enforce everything we have on the books. But I doubt it. It is also only a hypothetical point, because we do not allocate these resources and we will not do so because the costs would be so astronomical. If we continue to generate new laws at the rate we are going, however, then tomorrow no amount of resources would be sufficient to administer the regulations efficiently.

It happens that today, for the first time, we have a political environment within the United States that is beginning to be sensitized to this problem. I think we have an opportunity now to try to get at the hyperlexis problem. If we let it go by—and I fear we will—hyperlexis will slowly and steadily drag our whole system to the ground. We will have lost one of the most valuable and priceless national treasures we have. We will have destroyed the confidence of the people in—and their voluntary compliance with—the law.

Chapter Four

Parliamentary Government and Citizen Involvement: A Conference Summation*

by
Tom Kent

I had hoped to get away with a simple summary, but early yesterday I realized that that would not be very helpful. To summarize the papers and commentaries, even with as much brevity and wit as possible, would result in a sort of dog's breakfast. The topics, presentations, and commentaries have been too diverse; any attempt at a summary would consist of too many bits and pieces.

I have decided to take a different approach. This reflects my view that a characteristic common to the papers is that while they disagree in little, that is because they are, on the whole, long on diagnosis but pretty short on prescription. I decided that what I should try to do would be to summarize on the basis of accepting the sort of diagnosis that has been given and considering the implications as to the kinds of things we should be doing, or the possible policy conclusions we might draw. Essentially, my approach is to recognize that the demands for more individual involvement in decision making have increased greatly, to examine how they have come about, and to make some suggestions about how they might be dealt with.

That was my plan yesterday. The necessity of rearranging today's programmes means that I am summing up in advance of some of the speeches and discussion. I therefore begin by apologizing to today's speakers and to Mr. Camp, most particularly, for the fact that what I am going to say will not take account of his paper. As a result, I am sure that however great might have been the inadequacies of the summation, they will certainly be very much greater now.

I would like to begin by giving you my impression of the basic problem with which we are dealing. There has not been, as far as I know, any challenge to the conference starting point that the citizen does not have enough involvement in decision making. Since this might be said about many societies at many times, one might begin by asking whether there is any special reason why this unmet need is so much a theme today. I think there is.

The reason lies in the paradox that arises from the particular nature and the uniquely rapid speed of recent technological change. We are experiencing, to use a rather inadequate summary word, an "information revolution." Our communications by comparison with the past have eliminated distance. Our ability to utilize data has been transformed. We are experiencing the effects of all the extra resources that our grandfathers and fathers devoted to universalizing and prolonging education. The result is that we now very quickly generalize the effects of much more massive information and its immediate communication. This makes us very different indeed from past societies. If one tries to sum up the distinct and significant feature of contemporary social change, it really is that vastly more people have enormously more information.

The crux of this change is that the power that technology gives, power to exploit many new resources, is dispersed among many more people, either as individuals or in small groups. This is the positive side. It means that most individuals have wider options, they have more capability to live how they choose. But there is also the negative side, or different side. It is that with a more complex technology, people are more interdependent; if the technology changes quickly, the interdependence increases at a rate to which people have difficulty adjusting their ideas and values.

Rapid technological changes, in the information area above all, mean that more and more things that the individual used to do, or in which he shared as a member of a family or a small community, are replaced by activities that are necessarily those of large-scale organizations acting on behalf of large numbers of people. A society that lives that way is necessarily a more governed society. It is also a society in which the increased number and complexity of the decisions that government must make are sure to result in government being a process from which the individual feels more remote.

The result is that we have this paradox of the individual with diminished independence but greater power. He knows more, he can do more, yet within the structure he is less and less his own master. He is more and more dictated to by large and largely anonymous forces over which he has no sense of control or even, for the most part, influence. To put it another way: our society is at one and the same time becoming both more collectivist and more individualistic. The individual is far more capable to "do his own thing," but there are many more things than in the past that now can, in fact, get done only by large-scale organization for large numbers of people.

This paradox is at the root of a lot of the tensions of our society: the enormously increased difficulties of the management process in industry; the strength and separatist tendencies of racial, regional, and other groups; the contemporary phenomenon of terrorism, demonstrating the enormous power in the hands of an individual or small group. The contemporary power of the individual in his setting was not envisaged in the classical theory of the freedom of the individual. J.S. Mill never contemplated what it means to have an armed individual in the fragile environment of a jumbo jet.

Fundamentally similar factors result in the increased power of many trade unions to behave in the manner of old guilds or modern medical associations. These are groups that in contrast to the original purpose of defending the underprivileged, can now impose what are really highwayman terms on a society which, by becoming so complex, has become more dependent on each of its specialist groups.

So much for the obvious diagnosis, but I think we have to remind ourselves of it. What it means for the relationship between goverment and individuals is, I think, very clear. The individual is more capable but he is more subject to stronger external forces; and the only tolerable response is that he should be more effectively involved in the governmental decision making that attempts to cope collectively with those external forces.

How do we do that? No one, as far as I have heard, has suggested any departure from the basic nature of representative government. In that case, the fundamental participation of the individual in government continues to be that we elect people to govern. But obviously that process as it now operates is an involvement of somewhat rapidly diminishing adequacy. The questions that seem to me to fly out of the sort of discussion we have had are what changes can we make in the electoral process that would make it a more effective involvement, and what additional involvement processes can we institute or improve?

Without lessening the importance of the answers to these questions, I would want to emphasize, however, that they are only half of the decision-making problem. The other half is that in the face of the increased complexity of government, decision making has slowed down. That has also happened in the private sector, but to a great extent this reflects the influence of government. Much of our contemporary discontent, in my opinion, is due not only to the way decisions are made but also the failure to make any decisions when the time is right for them.

Mr. Fisher talked yesterday about his discovery, I would say forty years late, that much of the power of government lies with major bureaucrats or quasi-bureaucrats. Of course, there is a large element of truth in that. But there was much more truth than there is now. An earlier generation of bureaucrats did largely run things in Ottawa. But Mr. Clarke died a long time ago and even Mr. Bryce has retired. Their successors do not have the same power. Indeed, the greater truth about Ottawa today is that no one runs things in the way in which they used to be run. The overburdened system has broken down. So while our subject today is involvement in decision making, I would plead that it must be involvement that avoids the danger of yet further slowing down the process. Indeed, on the contrary, there has got to be faster decision making, which I believe can be consistent with and indeed helpful to better citizen involvement.

On the basis of the above generalization, what I would like to do is to try to state ten conclusions that in my mind emerge.

My diagnosis started with the information revolution. I really do not see how there can be any other view than that we have to respond to that with more open government. There really is not any choice. Indeed, the necessity of increasing openness is guaranteed by the way bureaucratic government itself now works, by the tools it has adopted. Practically every piece of paper, however supposedly internal and secret, gets photocopied in its scores and hundreds. At the moment it is still an affectation of the system, but it is no more than that. You pretend to treat certain kinds of policy papers with the secrecy that probably was appropriate in the days when they were written with a quill pen. Attitudes that were perhaps reasonable in the days of the quill pen are theoretically still maintained in the internal business of government policy consideration, but they are bound to break down and in fact are visibly doing so.

I am not for one moment suggesting that government or any other decision-making process can operate without there being confidential expressions of opinion. Such discussions have to take place within any honest decision-making process, and some of that confidential expression of opinion has to be written. This is the equivalent of continuing quill pen, if you like. But the volume of such paper is really quite limited. Within the total volume of public paper, it is very small indeed. The work of government now could be organized so that most of its paper is freely available. Clearly, a fundamental change of attitude in that respect would in itself do a great deal to contribute to more effective, broader involvement in decision making.

However, while that is significant and I think it is important to start with it, it is certainly not by any means as important as changes related to the political structure. If we are right to assume, as we all seem to, that we are sticking with representative government, that means sticking with political parties; and they, of course, are the central failures of our system. When we hold a seminar about citizen involvement, what we are saying, fundamentally, is that the political parties are not what, in the theory of representative government, they should be. Our parties have succeeded in bridging the country after a fashion but only by being non-ideological machines. The last thing they want of their membership is policy involvement. Perhaps that is a slight overstatement. More precisely, they do not like it and they bother only occasionally even to pretend seriously to want it, in certain special circumstances, but never for very long and certainly not when in office. Those facts have a very large part in present popular frustration. They are the reason why so many people are looking for substitutes for political parties, for more specific mechanisms for participation on particular issues.

That is a natural response but it is not very satisfactory. Any fundamental improvement must mean going back to the basics. If we are going to keep representative government, the most important improvement in participation is to find ways to force the parties as such to be more concerned internally with policy. How do we do that? There are all kinds of tinkering that can help a little and indeed some of it has been done. However, I can see only one way of getting adequate change. This is to change the electoral system.

I was brought up on the classical political theory as to the merits of the two-party system and therefore the desirability of election by simple plurality of non-transferable votes in single-member constituencies. I still recognize that there are very considerable merits in this system, and in our Canadian situation I would not move away from single-member constituencies. I would, however, introduce the simple alternative or transferable vote. That is to say, the voter can express first, second, and third preferences among candidates; if no one has a majority of the first preference votes, those for the bottom candidate are redistributed according to second preferences; and so on until one candidate has a majority.

Such an electoral system has its problems, but I cannot see any other way in which we can shake the party structures and provide a chance to restore real policy concerns to the party process. The politicians will not want that; indeed, they will hate it and they will be completely against it. But in all seriousness, I would say that if a group such as is here today is really concerned about participation, then by far the most significant thing that could be done would be to mount a major campaign to force this issue. In the absence of such a campaign, I have a horrible fear that involvement in government decision making is going to continue to be groups like this talking among themselves in nice little seminars.

There is another, in my view, necessary electoral reform. If we have the alternative vote, the chances are that elections will become more frequent. That is not a bad thing, provided we abandon the ritual of the two-month campaign. Obviously, with television and jets it is completely unnecessary. It continues, I think, because it is so convenient for the party machine. If you have a long election campaign, then between elections the parties can have very small organizations and not be bothered too much about people. There is time to summon up the troops after the election has been called. If we had a three-week campaign, or something reasonably similar, it would be far more important to the parties that they start with people already in place, with people already interested and concerned. Parties would need continuing organization, they would have to keep people more actively involved, and that could be done only by having a more active, continuing concern with discussion and debate about policy. This would put pressure on the party in office to provide better access to government, to sustain a steady concern with policy decisions. It would also change a party out of office; the party would have to have a continuing, more lively concern for policy rather than adopting the simple oppositionism that is more traditional and that causes the participation-seeking citizen to feel that the political process is not his instrument.

Those are my two prescriptions for electoral reform. To step back, my first three conclusions are more open government; the transferable vote; and the three-week election. The obvious fourth point is parliamentary procedure. I am not going to use time to make detailed proposals on that. There has lately been some improvement in Parliament's performance and role. Its fundamental role in our system is to provide the focus of public debate about policy. That has been greatly helped by the televising of Parliament. There have also been some beneficial procedural changes and important steps to provide some policy-related assistance to members. These changes have improved the effectiveness of Parliament appreciably, but there is no doubt that procedural changes could do a lot more to improve its effectiveness as a focal point for general debate; part of the need in that respect is to improve committee effectiveness.

I would like to treat that aspect of parliamentary procedure as part of my next point. We need, obviously, better inquiry and advisory committees. Working openly, they are an attractive way of increasing involvement. Equally obviously, though, they are effective only if they are not greatly multiplied. If they are greatly multiplied, then, like everything else, their value is depreciated; you get duplication and delay. I wonder, therefore, whether we should not experiment with mixed committees that are partly parliamentary made up of M.P.'s and partly lay members—gifted amateurs, if you like. This might be seen as the equivalent to the existing type of joint committees of the House and the Senate except that the non-M.P. members would not have to be senators; they would not have to pay that price. In my view, this kind of committee would be for many purposes more effective than the royal commission, the ministerial advisory committee, or the task force. It would improve participation both directly and by relating to the basic participation focus of the parliamentary system. That is suggestion five.

Number six is more controversial because it relates to the fundamental style of government. The Lambert report[1] has just been published and I have not read it, but from press reports I am happy to acknowledge that on one point it seems, at least partially, to endorse what I have urged in a number of places over a considerable period. This is that for effective participation as well as to escape from the bind of non-decision making that distinguishes Ottawa, we really have to insist that government programmes should be presented in the context of a statement of expectations and provisional plans for five years ahead.

I emphasize that I do not mean five-year plans in the sense of plans that succeed each other at five-year intervals. I mean that each year the government sticks its neck out and looks ahead, as best it can, for the next five years. It says what it thinks may happen, can happen, should happen. To take a controversial example, it talks about what it thinks the exchange rate is going to be. Pray heavens what it says today is that the rational exchange rate for Canada for a long time to come is about 80 cents compared to the U.S.

dollar. The main point is that whatever the government's view, it takes it and states it publicly. Thereby it provides a better basis for decision making in the private sector; and it provides a far better base for public interest, concern, and debate about public policy. People can participate on a rational basis if they know what government is thinking, not only about today and this year, but about the next five years, at least. What I am suggesting is a fundamental change in the style of government. Many people would say that I am asking politicians to be heroes. I do not think so, once the first plunge into the water was taken. In any event, the change of style is, in my view, absolutely essential for effective democratic government in the circumstances in which we now live.

My seventh point concerns government structure. I have become increasingly sceptical that structural changes in themselves do any good. But there are some structural changes that will help if we make them in support of other changes. If we retain representative government, then ministers and senior officials are going to continue to be people who have responsibilities for both the formation and the implementation of policy. That is the nature of the basic system. In both functions, the top group is supported by advisers, and the bureaucracy otherwise consists of people who are essentially administrators. They are the people with whom the public generally has to deal on specific matters. They are busy people; and as busy people, bureaucrats are not, generally speaking, good listeners.

The administrative structure nowadays is headed by hundreds of directors general and the like. I would suggest—and I emphasize that this is perfectly compatible in my view with reducing the total size of the bureaucracy—that we need to develop, in addition to directors general, some counsellors general. I do not mean more policy advisers, permanent or temporary, economists or management consultants or merchants of mumbo-jumbo non-decision. We have more than enough of those. I mean generalists who can listen. They would be required to listen. It would be on that basis that counsellors general would make an input into policy making. This could be very important in the system of government; certainly it would be a specific improvement in the way in which the public is interested, concerned, listened to. It could be a distinct improvement in the way public involvement is brought into the decision-making process.

My eighth suggestion is about devolution. As you have gathered, I am no great admirer of the present state of the federal government. But I am an entirely unregenerate believer that this country cannot work as ten countries. Large responsibilities have to stay firmly and effectively with Ottawa, with the federal government. The doubt about this must be resolved, and I would underline the essentiality of that. The challenge is to make it clear that we are going to continue to have a federal government carrying the major responsibilities for the governing of this country. Unless and until that issue is resolved, everything else is academic. But if that issue is resolved, if we can be confident of a continuing central government, which provides reality for a Canadian national economy, then there is enormous scope for effective devolution of the management of public responsibilities to smaller units, by areas and by functions. Under these conditions, government operations could be managed with more flexibility, and smaller areas would make possible much more effective public citizen involvement. But I emphasize that these merits of devolution depend on it being genuinely devolution, not a disguise for the attrition of basic federal jurisdiction.

My ninth point, since I do not want to make this entirely governmental, is about the media. We can only envy the media standards that are possible in older and more densely populated countries. In our thinly populated land, and perhaps for other reasons too, we are not going to be able to equal the great European newspapers and opinion periodicals in the foreseeable future. But I do not think we have to be resigned to the degree of sloppiness that now characterizes most of both the print and electronic media in this country. Since our regional markets are too small for a competitive media environment to provide adequate standards, they can be secured, to some degree, only through the appointment of an ombudsman for the press. If it is the appointment of a genuine ombudsman, with assurance of a careful appointment by the Supreme Court or some similarly objective process, I am not afraid of hollow cries about the freedom of the press. An ombudsman system could shame the media into approaching a little closer to the standards that competition produces in larger societies. It would be useful if it resulted in even modest improvement in the media quality we have today. I think it could be a considerable help to citizens to be more effectively involved in public policy, which does require that they have quality media assistance available to them.

My tenth and last conclusion is my favourite one. This is a sophisticated group of people and what I plead with you above all is to be all the time on the side of ''plain words.'' I say this especially to the researchers and teachers but also to the bureaucrats and managers. Obscurity is never anything but a cover for uncertainty or cowardice or both. There is nothing that is relevant to participation in public policy, nothing that is useful or significant to say, ''that cannot be said simply in plain words.'' Simplicity is hard work, much harder often than talking and writing in more specialized words, at greater length, and with less precision. But if we are not prepared to do that work, then there is not much reality to any claim to concern about citizen involvement. If such involvement is to be effective, there has to be a common communication. Involvement most certainly does not call for the arrogant sin of lowering standards in thought or content. It does require the true intelligence of directness in communication by plain language.

Mr. Chairman, I have talked long enough and I certainly have talked on false pretenses, in the sense that this clearly has not been a summation in the ordinary sense of the word. I can only hope that as a subjective set of conclusions, it at least has some provocative contribution towards making our deliberations more meaningful for each of us.

Let me therefore end by restating quite starkly my ten examples of the things we should be trying to bring about if we are serious in our diagnosis of the need for more citizen involvement:

1. Government information and the government decision-making process to be much more open
2. Electoral reform by the alternative vote
3. Three-week election campaigns
4. Reformed parliamentary procedure
5. Joint Parliament-public inquiry and advisory committees
6. Open five-year forecasts and plans by government
7. Counsellors general as government listeners
8. Functional and area devolution to small units of sustained federal responsibilities
9. An ombudsman for the media
10. Plain words.

NOTES

* *Editor's note:* because of problems of flight arrangements for some of the speakers, Mr. Kent was generous enough to reschedule his summary remarks and give them at lunch of the second day of the conference, prior to Mr. Manning's and Mr. Camp's presentations.

[1] Royal Commission on Financial Management and Accountability, *Final Report* (Ottawa: Minister of Supply and Services Canada, 1979).

Part Two

An Assessment of Existing Institutions and Structures and Possible Reforms

Chapter Five

The Citizen and Government: Co-operative Forms of Policy Making

by
*P.M. Pitfield**

I have been asked to discuss "The Citizen and Government: Co-operative Forms of Policy Making." There is a certain nostalgia to this topic. I am sure you will recall that ten years ago this summer, "participatory democracy" was officially declared a "great cliché" by the Task Force on Government Information.[1]

Even while so declaring, however, the task force reflected the flavour of that time. Ten years later, older and wiser, we can still admire the elegant simplicity of the task force's prescription for dealing with its "depressing discovery" that millions of Canadians know little, if anything, about their federal or provincial governments.

"Someone," the task force suggested, "should tell those people something."

With the accumulated wisdom of a decade, however, it is clear that the question of how that "someone" tells those people "something" is more difficult than we had thought. Equally important, it is possible that we have not questioned nearly enough the idea that everyone *should* be informed, that everyone *should* participate. The idea that everyone *should* contains, when it is examined closely, a certain authoritarian strain—"We have ways of making you participate."

And I am not sure that the consequences of this strand of thought have not contributed to the assumption inherent in the topic I have been asked to discuss today. At the very least, the assumption is that "good" policy making requires the participation of the citizen with government. What "citizen"? The interested? The disinterested? Both? What do we mean by "government"? The bureaucrats? The politicians? Both?

The assumption can easily be taken further to imply that—in decision making—the citizen and government share power; that they are in an almost adversarial situation, one against the other, requiring new instruments to allow them to reconcile their differences, new mechanisms to represent the citizen *against* government.

Government, however, is not *against* the citizen. It cannot be, or it cannot be for long. It is there to represent the citizen, to exercise power that the citizen has delegated to be exercised on his behalf and in his interest by the government. Yet, the main interest of many citizens most of the time is to be left alone to deal with their own lives.

In view of that, perhaps we should ask whether pursuing increased participation in myriad ways has not set government against these citizens by setting government against their interest in non-participation in most issues most of the time.

This may have contributed to that modern paradox, the fact that those who wish to be left alone by government—all government—have become a significant political force. Certainly the existence of such a political force set against government is implicit in the topic I have been given.

Because some citizens do not wish to participate does not mean that government has no responsibility to them, nor does it mean that they are indifferent to the result of government action. In fact, if anything, government's responsibility is greater, but it is not the responsibility to develop new means of entangling them in what they do not want to do. Rather, it is to exercise the authority they have delegated to government in a way that allows them to deal with their own lives.

What, then, are the parameters of today's topic? It seems to me that in general, we are not talking about taking from government the responsibility to decide. Nor are we talking about forcing participation on those who do not wish to participate.

Rather, we are talking about those who wish to be involved in public affairs, about providing them with access to the information on what and how government is deciding that they require in order to participate. We are talking, not about the means to share power, but about the means by which citizens delegate to government the responsibility to exercise power on their behalf and by which citizens hold government accountable for the results.

Let me approach the topic from the perspective of what we have been through. The last decade has seen great activity in the reform of the Canadian policy-making processes built on the experience of the 1960s. What marked the 1960s was the degree of willingness to experiment with new forms of policy making and citizen involvement.

Why the 1960s? Was it more education? Mass communications? Increased wealth? A sense that the lessons of the Depression and the Second World War having been learned, anything could be solved? The resulting sense of greater economic and political security? Or a sense that government, as it was put, was too important to be left to politicians in an age of nuclear war and Silent Spring? Whatever the reason or combinations of reasons, there was a growth in the willingness to become involved and to change, and an acceleration in the pace of change.

The Quiet Revolution in Quebec, the Royal Commission on Bilingualism and Biculturalism, the elaboration of federal-provincial relations through conferences and shared-cost programmes—all of these either responded to or were aimed at producing greater participation in the governmental processes of the nation.

In the context of government, there was also a willingness to experiment with devices that were outside the traditions of Parliament. One of the first such non-parliamentary or—if you like—executive devices, was the task force, imported from the United States, initially by Mr. Walter Gordon. This device came into considerable favour in Canada because after his election in November 1960, President Kennedy commissioned twenty-nine task forces in order to acquire "boldly innovative" ideas from outside his administration. There were other extra-parliamentary innovations as well. The establishment of the Economic Council of Canada and of the Science Council were among them.

Finally, there was dissatisfaction with the conduct of parliamentary business. A poll in 1964 showed that 45 per cent of those interviewed felt Parliament was doing a "poor" job, while some 16 per cent felt it was doing a "good" job.

There was, in brief, frustration with the conduct of public affairs. And one could find support in that frustration for either of the two main reformist impulses that had been marinating in the ferment of the 1960s—for the modernization and streamlining of Parliament in keeping with our traditions; or for the devices of more direct citizen participation and involvement that were not necessarily in keeping with our parliamentary traditions.

As participatory democracy was being decreed a "great cliché," the number of changes in place or in process, parliamentary and non-parliamentary, was large, growing, and acquiring tremendous new momentum.

On the parliamentary side, there were a number of significant reforms. The development of an active system of specialized committees flowed from the recommendations of the Special Committee on Procedures in 1968. There was a major streamlining of House rules in 1969. Funding of opposition research staff was provided for the first time in a parliamentary system. The white and green paper device was brought to a central position as a means of bringing Parliament and the public into the policy-making process at a much earlier stage of consideration. Bills were introduced for discussion rather than passage. Committees of the House travelled more extensively. The Library of Parliament was provided with the funding needed to establish a research capability within Parliament.

But the far more visible side of participation was on the non-parliamentary side. It was probably inevitable that it be more visible. Participation, by definition, involved direct and swift communication between government and public. The traditional, slow-moving processes of

Parliament necessarily paled beside the newer means of involving the public in policy making, newer means that were not barred by tradition and convention from the latest in communications technology, from television to survey research and computer analysis.

By 1969, the device Walter Gordon had imported into the Canadian governmental context only six years before, the task force, was in full flower. Some forty-five task forces were operating in and around the Canadian government, the majority using some form of survey research or "polling."

There were questions raised, of course. Fred Schindeler and Michael Lanphier raised one of the pertinent ones in a 1969 article. "Why after all, should it be necessary to 'bother' with representative institutions when, for a few thousand dollars, the premier can obtain a very accurate estimate of the 'general will' without reference to Parliament?"[2]

Such questions were not given great weight, however. Even Messrs. Schindeler and Lanphier did not take their own question seriously, arguing that Parliament as well could use polling techniques and inevitably was required to reconcile differences that would exist.

But, in addition, the interested public seemed to like being asked for its views. Participation was seen as desirable in its own right, regardless of how it came about.

The Task Force on Housing, one of the first of the last decade, crystalized many problems. The most public of the task forces, it evoked considerable response. One reason for the response was the fact that it was headed by a Cabinet minister, Paul Hellyer, who was perceived, as he conducted public hearings across the country, as having the authority to achieve results. With the release of the report[3] over Mr. Hellyer's signature, the minister was personally committed to the recommendations—before those recommendations had been studied by his Cabinet colleagues.

How could the minister's clear and public assumption of what he saw as his individual responsibility be reconciled with the imperatives of collective responsibility?

The answer was that this could be very difficult to do in a parliamentary system. As with the Gordon task force so with the Hellyer task force, the ultimate experience was that simply grafting a good idea on to the existing system did not necessarily make a better system. In fact, it could result in a considerably less effective system or, at least, a very disappointing one from the point of view of participation and sensitivity.

I use the example of the experience with task forces not because it was unique but because it reflects the effect of the frustrations and reformist impulses of the 1960s in dulling general awareness of the fundamental complexities inherent in involving the public directly, without the mediation of Parliament, in the processes of government.

Aside from task forces, there were other devices for encouraging direct public participation in the policy processes. Indeed some, like Information Canada and The Institute for Research on Public Policy, were the product of task force recommendations.

But, in addition, virtually every department of government established advisory committees. Departments or offices were established to deal with specific areas of new concern—environment, science, the status of women, and so forth. Decision making was decentralized in some areas—for example, in the processing of unemployment insurance claims.

There were new approaches to funding through Opportunities for Youth, New Horizons, and the procedures established by Justice Berger for the Mackenzie Valley Pipeline Inquiry. And, most important, there was an enormous growth in funding to voluntary organizations and individuals, to groups, and to groups of groups. By the 1975-76 fiscal year, this funding had been pushed to a very high and unprecedented level.

What about the results of these efforts at greater participation in policy making? The results are many.

One is that there has been demonstrated a clear willingness, indeed eagerness, on the part of the interested public to participate where they have been able to do so. From the *White Paper on Taxation*,[4] through the Mackenzie Valley Pipeline Inquiry and the National Unity Task Force, that has been clearly demonstrated and commented upon with some emphasis by those involved.

A second is that there are far more people who are far more knowledgeable about how to get government grants, and—more generally—how to work the system to advantage. The question, in many cases, is to whose advantage?

In short, while certainly not suggesting that this is always, or even usually, the case, one cannot reflect upon our experience in promoting consultation and participation without asking to what extent so-called ''spokesmen'' are not sometimes either entrepreneurs to whom the whole thing is just another money-making business, or self-appointed and single-minded élites totally concerned with their cause and not worrying beyond that about the representation of their supposed followers.

Not far removed from these is the growth of the single-issue phenomenon, that is, the attempt of one group to impose its undiluted view of its issue on society. Single-issue interest groups concerned about such issues as abortion, capital punishment, and nuclear power are becoming increasingly powerful. They are worrisome because they are by definition polarizing and destabilizing. It is not the issue they support that is troublesome but that they support it to the exclusion of all other questions. This militates against the compromise and consensus essential to ongoing government.

The single-issue phenomenon may not be a consequence of the participation effort of the last decade, but it has certainly not been discouraged—and may have received a considerable push—from that effort. Why? Because the basic signals of the participation effort sent to groups and individuals were that they could end-run the traditional processes of Parliament by bringing their views to bear in a forceful and focused manner elsewhere in the governmental system.

So, at least three major signals have come out of the participation effort of the last decade:

- First, and the basic one, public money is available for projects promoting citizens' participation.
- Second is the importance of publicity and information in determining the causes to which that money would flow.
- Third is the implication in the word "participation" itself—like the words "co-operative forms of policy making"—that there was power to be shared directly by the citizen with his government.

But as I said earlier, the system we have inherited and developed is based, not on the sharing of power, but on the delegation of power and the public assumption of responsibility for its use by those to whom it has been delegated.

However information might be gathered and communicated, ultimate responsibility for deciding is placed in the Cabinet. Whatever Cabinet might decide, it must ultimately answer for in Parliament. And whatever parliamentarians might decide, they must ultimately answer for to those who have delegated to government the responsibility to decide.

I think it can be argued that the participation effort may have created the impression it could be otherwise. That impression, I think it can also be argued, had the unintended effect of diminishing Parliament's role and status.

The decision to introduce television into Parliament has done something to restore the legitimacy of Parliament as the focus of public attention. Television has also had the effect, I would judge, of drawing the attention of parliamentarians to the shortcomings of the institution in which they serve and on the way that the constituents they represent view Parliament. How they overcome Parliament's shortcomings is clearly their decision.

But the improvement of Parliament's operations must surely be at the heart of concern among those seeking to improve the processes by which citizens delegate power to government, for Parliament is at the heart of the process of delegation. This inevitably leads to the working of political parties, on which Parliament is based.

The idea of party influence does not rest on a wide base of popular approval. Most opinion polls place parties and politicians quite low in public esteem.

Yet both are vital to our system of government. They are the principal instruments through which the public can participate in the process of delegating to government through Parliament the responsibility for decision and holding government accountable for its decisions.

Neither party nor Parliament was ignored in the decade just past. Funding for opposition research, for the parliamentary library, for political parties themselves through campaign contribution legislation—all of these recognized the importance of party in Parliament. Yet, it is fair to say that in terms of perception, despite the continuing and central role of Parliament and political parties in our system of government, other, more publicized efforts obscured the efforts to improve Parliament's capacity to fulfil its role.

How can the capacity of Parliament and political parties to fulfil their essential roles be further enhanced and be seen to have been enhanced? These, most assuredly, are not questions for bureaucrats. But they are among the most important questions our system of government faces and they were recognized to be so, for example, by the Lambert commission, whose report[5] has made an important contribution in the thinking on how to enhance Parliament's ability to hold office-holders accountable.

And they are complex questions requiring extensive, rigorous, and—above all—practical analysis, sensitive to the other delicately balanced elements of the system under which we live—to the principles of individual and collective responsibility of ministers, to the neutrality of the public service, to our legal traditions and federalism, to the needs of citizens who wish to participate in government, and to the needs of those who do not.

Such analysis needs to be based on the lessons of the 1960s and 1970s, on an understanding of why a number of devices that were grafted on to our system in an effort to allow citizens to play a greater role in government did not work or did not work well. It needs to be based, too, on an understanding of the critical role of political parties and parliamentary processes in delegating to government the responsibility to govern and holding it to account for how it does so.

This is the sort of analysis that this Institute is supremely capable of having done. It is a matter of first importance that it be done.

NOTES

* Due to illness, Mr. Pitfield's paper was presented by Gordon S. Smith, Deputy Secretary to the Cabinet (Plans), Government of Canada.

[1] Canada, Task Force on Government Information, *To Know and Be Known* (Ottawa: Queen's Printer, 1969).

[2] Fred Schindeler and C. Michael Lanphier, ''Social Science Research and Participatory Democracy in Canada,'' *Canadian Public Administration* 12 (Winter 1969), pp. 497-98.

3 Canada, Task Force on Housing and Urban Development, *Report* (Ottawa: Queen's Printer, 1969).

4 Canada, Department of Finance, *Proposals for Tax Reform* (Ottawa: Queen's Printer, 1969).

5 Canada, Royal Commission on Financial Management and Accountability, *Final Report* (Ottawa: Minister of Supply and Services Canada, 1979).

Commentary

by
Stefan Dupré

> In framing a government which is to be administered by men over men, the great
> difficulty lies in this: you must first enable the government to control the governed;
> and in the next place oblige it to control itself.
>
> James Madison
> *The Federalist*, No. 51[1]

"You must first enable the government to control the governed." It is in
search of this capacity that modern Canadian governments have sought to
encourage various forms of public participation in policy making. The
multiplicity and complexity of contemporary public policies invite the
assumption, in Mr. Pitfield's words, "that 'good' policy making requires the
participation of the citizen with government." There is much to support the
validity of this assumption. The direct participation of the interested citizen
in shaping policies that will influence his actions by regulation, taxation, or
expenditure is sought by government as a means of enhancing the legitimacy
of these policies and easing their implementation. The principal vehicles for
such participation are of relatively recent vintage in Canada, but an
expanding policy highway network is jammed with more and more organized
clientele groups travelling to increasingly diverse destinations in various
government departments, administrative boards, advisory councils, and task
forces.

But for all the emphasis on co-operative policy making, it rings true,
again to quote Mr. Pitfield, that "those who wish to be left alone by
government—all government—have become a significant political force."
Consider, for example, your friendly physician, studiously absorbed in the
development of health care policy by the Ontario Medical Association and
the Ministry of Health, yet full of sermons on the evils of government and a
dues-paying member of the Citizen's Coalition. What explains the paradox
that citizens increasingly wish to be left alone by governments in which they
have more avenues for participation than ever before? I submit that part of the
answer lies in the difficulty of achieving Madison's second directive: getting
government to control itself. Co-operative forms of policy making are part
and parcel of an unfolding tale about how governments, in the very process of
increasing participation to secure a supportive response from the governed,
have experienced mounting difficulties in achieving self-control, and in turn
rediscovered the problem of controlling the governed in the form of spreading
alienation.

When the story is couched in the context of Canadian Cabinet government, whether at the federal or provincial level, its basic outline is as follows. The initial and natural response to the need for positive government is to rely on a division of labour that leads to growing departmentalization in policy making and a greatly enhanced role for departmental experts. As government departments acquire more far-reaching influence, the portfolio responsibilities of individual Cabinet ministers become more and more consuming, and indeed ministers increasingly become spokesmen for their departments rather than spokesmen for their respective regions, constituencies, or party followers. To secure the consent of the governed to ever more complex governmental initiatives, co-operative forms of policy making multiply within departments, breeding in turn a multiplication of suggestions for yet more initiatives and for better (which often turn out to be more complex) ways of implementing them. At this juncture, the growing portfolio responsibilities of ministers take on the guise of outright portfolio loyalties, for to be other than a departmental spokesman is to risk incurring the wrath of increasingly involved clientele groups.

Within the Canadian executive, the classic mechanism for achieving co-ordination and control is of course the Cabinet. This mechanism begins to falter in a setting where its members are primarily the bearers of portfolio loyalties. The response is a series of adaptations that yield what I believe can most accurately be described as the institutionalized cabinet. Whether it is examined in Ottawa or in any one of the ten other laboratories for governmental experimentation in this country, the institutionalized cabinet almost invariably involves some combination of the following three things: standing committees of Cabinet designed and staffed to reduce clashes among related portfolios; expanded central agencies staffed by bureaucrats who serve Cabinet as a whole and the prime minister as master conciliator and arbitrator of Cabinet conflicts; and the promotion of other central agencies to departmental status under ministers whose sole portfolio responsibility is that of control (e.g., treasury boards and management boards).

There is thus no lack of evidence that contemporary Canadian governments have tried to achieve self-control. Their efforts amount to a transformation of Cabinet itself into an institutionalized body. Similar efforts in the United States have yielded what Richard Neustadt calls the "institutionalized Presidency." And in Canada, as Mr. Pitfield points out, the search for self-control has extended beyond Cabinet into Parliament itself, "reforming" many practices of the House of Commons.

Yet, for all this, governments are not perceived to be under control, horror stories about contradictory and ill-conceived programmes and policies multiply, and citizens who have acquired more opportunities for participation than ever before now wish governments to leave them alone. Individuals as intimately knowledgeable as Mr. Pitfield of what has already been at least a ten-year quest for greater governmental self-control urge yet further analysis in a quest for solutions.

I, for one, welcome Mr. Pitfield's invitation. The institutionalized cabinet is a relatively recent innovation and there surely remain means of improving its performance. Yet Cabinet alone should not be expected to do the job. Its members will inevitably remain influenced by their respective portfolio loyalties, and all the more so to the extent that it may at once be impractical and undesirable to depart from co-operative forms of policy making. The House of Commons remains a fertile field for innovations. Yet, I submit that no one can read John B. Stewart's masterful treatise, *The Canadian House of Commons: Procedure and Reform*,[2] without containing his expectations of what can be achieved there. Professor Stewart is himself a model of creativity in suggesting new remedies. But he also develops with great skill the sobering thought that there are limits on what can be expected from a legislative chamber which, given the fundamental principle of Cabinet responsibility, must operate according to an adversary process in which party teams rather than individuals are the fundamental actors.

At this point, I become mindful of my experience that nearly every conference features an idiot who tosses out a suggestion that is so simple-minded that there must be every reason for ignoring it. To assume the role of an idiot, I need only be myself and I shall now toss out the idea that, of all places, the Senate deserves focused and constructive attention. In his keynote address to this conference, Dr. J. Alex Corry spoke of the importance of subjecting the stewardship of government to commonsense tests if public trust is to be enhanced. Of what should commonsense tests consist when applied to modern government in all its complexity? I believe that they are a matter of posing questions like the following. Do programmes that purport to constitute a policy or a consistent expenditure menu hang together intrinsically? When does the existence of incompatible programmes reflect the pell-mell accumulations that can be a key symptom of a government that is not in control of itself? When and why may policies or programmes be sources of severe federal-provincial entanglement?

The setting of such examinations to me constitutes the essence of "the sober second thought" as it should be applied to the multiple and complex activities of modern-day government. The Senate beckons as the open forum, removed from the adversary process of the House, in which commonsense tests can be applied. Such tests must, of course, be applied publicly if government is to be seen to be in control of itself or prodded to achieve self-control. In all the search for answers to the riddle of modern government in Canada, far too little attention, in my view, has been paid to the Senate as the place *par excellence* for the application of Dr. Corry's commonsense tests. In particular, the recent operations of the Senate's Standing Committee on National Finance, focusing selectively as they do on significant areas of government spending, deserve far more scrutiny than they have received as indicating the potential of the upper house for supplying what the continuing quest for Cabinet and House reform has left missing.

Being an idiot, I am content for the moment to relegate to a matter of detail the question of whether or how the membership of the Senate might be altered. I cannot refrain from observing, however, that more than a few of our present Senators are precisely the kind of people who should be in charge of applying commonsense tests. My main point is to stress the importance, in the continuing analysis that Mr. Pitfield invites, of rediscovering the potential of the Senate, not as a substitute for the processes of federal-provincial relations, but as the place where commonsense tests will be applied to the stewardship of government and will help achieve Madison's objective, now more important than ever before, of obliging government to control itself.

NOTES

[1] Alexander Hamilton, James Madison, and John Jay, *The Federalist* (Cambridge, Mass.: Harvard University Press, 1961), p. 356.

[2] John B. Stewart, *The Canadian House of Commons: Procedure and Reform* (Montreal: McGill-Queen's University Press, 1977).

Commentary

by
Victor Rabinovitch

It seems appropriate for this conference on citizen involvement in policy making that so many individuals seem to have been involved in the presentation of Mr. Michael Pitfield's paper. Not only was the paper delivered by Mr. Gordon Smith on behalf of Mr. Pitfield, but there were also the considerable efforts of other nameless individuals who contributed selflessly to its preparation. Their collective paper expresses several important themes, deserving notice and critical response. The following brief comments will only highlight several of the more important themes and will offer some alternative viewpoints to those expressed by Smith-Pitfield.

The first theme that should be noted is particularly conservative in its thrust. Mr. Smith and Mr. Pitfield argue that "the main interest of many citizens, most of the time, is to be left alone to deal with their own lives." This sentence seems to sum up the philosophy of the entire paper. Citizens want to be left alone, we are told, and all this talk about "participation" is really an extension of "Big Government" into the private lives of ordinary people. But does this theme reflect a realistic assessment of the forces and powers that buffet the ordinary citizen in everyday life? Are citizens being "left alone" by the major business corporations, which dominate consumer markets, employment opportunities, and the quality of working life? Are citizens being "left alone" when their living environment is invaded by pollution from Reed Paper or by emissions from nuclear power plants?

At no time in history have citizens been genuinely "left alone." The endless rounds of wars, hunger, and natural disasters have meant that demands by one's rulers or one's neighbours have always been present. The argument that the main interest of a modern citizen is to be "left alone" is really based on a simplistic concept of what human society is, and a false notion of how most citizens perceive the pattern of social demands on their own lives.

A second theme that runs through the Smith-Pitfield paper concerns the alleged effects of participation upon citizens. There is a clear implication throughout the paper that increasing participation sets citizens up against their government. This is a complex and disturbing point. I suspect, however, that this theme is strongly coloured by the experiences of Mr. Pitfield and others in recent Ottawa politics.

"Civilization is at an end," Czar Nicholas reportedly said during the 1917 Russian revolution. What he meant, of course, was that the type of civilization enjoyed by himself and his family was coming to an end. Similarly, when an elected government senses itself to be under public attack and liable to lose an impending election, individuals closely identified with the party in power are liable to assert that the entire institution of democratic government is under attack. In other words, the theme of citizen versus government in the Smith-Pitfield paper should be taken as further evidence of a siege mentality prevailing in some parts of Ottawa during the spring of 1979.* The Smith-Pitfield paper does not provide any hard facts to defend the view that citizen participation promotes citizen antipathy to the institution of government.

A third theme concerns the apparent growth of single-issue interest groups in politics. A timely reference to this issue was made by Dr. Corry in his paper earlier. The Smith-Pitfield paper echoes a school of thought current in the United States, which holds that America is becoming ungovernable because of the rise of so many single-issue pressure groups. Such groups allegedly refuse to act within the confines of the traditional political parties, contributing in this way to political instability.

The current preoccupation with single-issue pressure groups should not hide from us the fact that single-issue politics is not a new phenomenon. Numerous examples of major single-issue campaigns can be found in the history of North American politics in this century. Some of those campaigns were successful; others were not. Democracy did not collapse under the onslaught.

Ironically, the most sophisticated form of single-issue activism is found in the government itself. Public service administrators (frequently and often unfairly termed bureaucrats) can be thought of as single-issue activists, for they are generally assigned the responsibility of developing unique expertise on very specific areas of public policy and administration. These public servants, and their opposite numbers within the specialized bureaucracies of business corporations, are the real single-issue activists of our day.

A final theme that deserves mention is particularly poignant. It concerns what might be termed our collective loss of innocence. Throughout the Smith-Pitfield paper, it is implied that we have outgrown the naïve sentiments and expectations of the 1960s' student radicalism. Those movements are dead, it is implied, and today we must all face a reality in which participatory democracy is merely a quaint slogan.

We should take good care to avoid swallowing the view that the movements of the 1960s are dead and gone. Many of the political urges first vocalized in that period—urges for greater public participation, improved information distribution, greater control by individuals over decisions affecting their lives—are alive and well and thriving in the late 1970s. Many of the individual activists who came to the fore in the 1960s are still to the fore in our own period. We need only look to the composition of the Cabinet of the Parti Québécois government in Quebec for a major example of familiar faces who began their careers in the militant student movement of fifteen years ago.

This leads us to some general observations to counter the themes expressed in the Smith-Pitfield paper. One point worth repeating is that many of the best democratic impulses identified with student radicalism and community politics of the 1960s are still with us.

Increasing attention to the issue of work-place democracy, expressed at times as the quality of working life or as the crisis in occupational health and safety, are now priority items within European and North American labour movements. The continuing wave of consumer activism, environmental protection awareness, co-operative community life-styles, and even minority challenges to the traditional professions are all expressions of the spirit of the 1960s activism. Even the convening of this conference on citizen involvement and control is a reflection of the issue of participatory democracy.

In a sense, these references to the 1960s are misleading because they imply that concern with the form and content of public participation in democratic institutions only began in the 1960s. This is far from true. Throughout the history of the nineteenth century reform movements in the British parliamentary system, there were active debates on the nature of democracy, the role of elected representatives, and the adequacy of the election process. There was a particularly vibrant public debate in the turn-of-the-century socialist and labour movement concerning the role of referenda for expanding public participation.

One of the tragedies brought on by the First World War, by the economic crisis of the 1930s, and the subsequent rise of Fascism was that the concern with increasing citizen participation that emerged in the early 1900s was diverted into the more pressing fight against the barbarity of Nazism and corporatist-Fascism. In a sense, the political movements of the 1960s marked a rebirth of democratic initiatives that first arose six decades earlier.

Of course, political debates in our own day take place under conditions that are vastly different from those faced by turn-of-the-century activists. Participation in public decision making is far more likely to occur with the spread of public education, the reduction in hours of normal employment, and the expansion of social protection associations such as trade unions. Many more individuals are now available to join special interest groups; many more citizens have the time, the money, and the education to participate. The luxury of participation has expanded considerably beyond the limited confines of a privileged economic élite.

In our examination of ways and means to expand citizen involvement, a number of key factors should be emphasized. One concerns public access to information. It is an obvious priority to evolve new laws defining the rights of citizens to gain access to information that is directly relevant to public policies. This means more than a freedom of information act with respect to government documents. It must also include rights of access to information generated within private bureaucracies, notably corporate business bureaucracy. Without fair and adequate access to these information sources, it is likely that the monopoly of information held within massive administrations will continue to thwart positive involvement in public policy making.

A second principle is based on the notion of good faith. In collective bargaining, there is a legal concept that binds both employers and labour organizations to bargain in good faith. Both parties are required to demonstrate a genuine will to arrive at a voluntary settlement of contentious issues. This notion of good faith should be fully applied to the issue of public participation.

Genuine participation in a democratic society is based on the premise that compromises can be achieved between different groups of citizens, as well as between citizens and their government. The sovereign power of the Crown cannot be used to justify the unilateral imposition of government decisions upon participating citizens. Yet, time and again, Canadian governments at all levels have invited participation from interested parties only to end the process with an abrupt announcement of a government decision. In effect, participation has not been invited in good faith. The spectacle of participation has been used only for public show.

Finally, it is important to deny the assertions of those who say that participation is not practical because apathy is rampant. My personal experience gained from frequent meetings and seminars with rank-and-file workers, shop stewards, and local union officials all across the country, particularly in many smaller communities, indicates repeatedly that there is much interest in government, in public decision making, and in democratic participation. There are so many ordinary working people prepared to give up entire weekends to argue about issues arising from their working life and their working conditions. Of course, this is only one area of public policy making, in which policy is generally of a local nature and has an immediate bearing on the conditions of one's life. But this policy area is directly linked to broader subject areas, notably those of economic investment and industrial development. Based on this experience of local participation, broader institutions for national participation can be built.

NOTE

* *Editor's note:* a federal general election was called in March 1979, and the conference was held in the early days of that election period.

Chapter Six

Citizen Involvement in Policy Formation Through Commissions, Councils, and Committees

by
Robert Bryce

I venture somewhat reluctantly to speak on this subject as one who has been involved over many years as a government official in making use of the reports of commissions, councils, and committees. I have also had two years of experience as Chairman of the Royal Commission on Corporate Concentration and some nine months as a part-time member of the Economic Council of Canada. What I say will be opinions based on my experience and observation plus a little hasty reading of articles and some parts of royal commission reports. This talk is not a research report, but the subject is worthy of more systematic study and detailed discussion.

First, about ''citizen involvement.'' I am taking it to mean some kind of action by people who are concerned about the public interest rather than the advancement of their own special interests, most often by what one of the titles refers to as ''gifted amateurs'' rather than professionals or executives acting as such. The category should include members of Parliament but not ministers, nor public servants, nor media people, no matter how inquisitive or brash they may be, but must include activists who have adopted a cause. While at times some such citizen involvement can be an awful nuisance, troubling to public servants and businessmen and members of other establishments, it is in my opinion generally a ''good thing.'' It has been growing rapidly in the past dozen years, forming what John Deutsch referred to as ''a new populism.'' However good it may be, it is difficult to deal with, and we should examine our governmental processes to see how we can best come to terms with it and use it productively.

The first of these processes I will speak about are commissions of inquiry. We have had a great many of these in the federal sphere, and many others in the provinces. I doubt if anyone has ever counted all of them, even those under the federal government. The Law Reform Commission of

Canada[1] says no source of information on the subject is complete, and indeed its report indicates the difficulty there is even in finding all the statutes that authorize the setting up of inquiries, in addition to the *Inquiries Act* itself.

Most of the official inquiries are not worth looking at for our purpose anyhow, as they are really specialized investigations of particular incidents, injustices, or allegations of wrongdoing. The Law Reform Commission makes a distinction between these "investigating" commissions, to which it feels special legal powers must be given and special legal contraints applied, and the other category, which it calls advisory commissions, whose subject matter is usually broader and whose legal powers and constraints need be less formidable. It is these advisory commissions that provide advice on public policy and in regard to which the question of citizen involvement arises.

It is worth taking note that the Law Reform Commission has recommended that the law require the granting by commissions of the opportunity for citizen involvement. It proposes the statute say: "An advisory commission *shall* accord to any person, group or organization satisfying the commission that he or it has a real interest in the subject matter of the commission's inquiry an opportunity to give evidence during the inquiry."[2] With this principle I think most people, and most ex-commissioners, would agree, though they might be uneasy about the implications of making it such a sweeping statutory obligation.

The Law Reform Commission goes further to deal with a matter that is much more controversial and difficult, and which arose in the inquiry on which I was engaged. They propose saying in the new act: "Where an advisory commission determines that it is appropriate in order to promote the full expression of relevant information and opinion it may pay all or any part of the legal, research and other costs of a person, group or organization giving evidence before it."[3] The words are simple, broad, and permissive. The principle would be clear. The application could in some circumstances be a nightmare when a government sets up a commission with this power, coupled with the duty to hear all persons and groups with a real interest in the subject. It must provide an appropriation for this purpose, just as appropriations have been granted for hearings and research.

I must say I am in favour of this principle but still puzzled as to what cases are to be judged as appropriate for granting costs, what sort of means test is to be applied, what scale of research and advocacy is to be supported, and how many and which of perhaps many contending and competing persons and groups are to be selected for support. This could become in itself a troublesome but important part of many inquiries.

In the case of the Royal Commission on Corporate Concentration, we did not accept any obligation to grant such support, nor ask any public funds to be used for the purpose as distinct from fees to be paid expert witnesses we selected. In only one case did a clearly qualified and needy witness ask for expenses to come and be heard, and in that case I was able to find a public-spirited individual who provided the money. Consequently, we really did not have a confrontation on the matter, although our subject seemed to favour the big rich corporations as witnesses compared to the concerned citizen. We met the problem also by arranging a whole series of evening hearings in small cities across Canada to which we invited all who were interested to come and speak to us, with or without a paper, whether or not they had any special knowledge or qualifications. We heard, in total, one hundred and twenty-seven witnesses at these informal hearings and engaged in active discussion with most of them. They were nearly all concerned citizens telling us what worried them about big business—at least big by their standards. This evidence did not assist us very much in forming an opinion about policies to recommend in regard to conglomerate mergers, which was the central problem we were to deal with, but it did help us to understand the complex and widespread social implications of corporate power.

When I look back at the dozen or more important royal commissions with whose reports I had to deal as a public official, I doubt if really any of them were much influenced by citizen involvement, or indeed if they made much effort to seek it out. They included many of the famous commissions—beginning with the Rowell-Sirois Commission on Federal-Provincial Relations[4] in the late thirties. That commission held eighty-five days of hearings in all provincial capitals and in Ottawa, and they must have heard a great deal of grief over the dreadful effects of the Depression and the parlous state of provincial and municipal finances, but most of their witnesses were there as representatives or speaking of their own particular interests. That commission inaugurated the practice of preparing voluminous expert research reports, and theirs were famous, as well as the commission's own account of the history of Canada's confederation and the troubles into which it fell in the great Depression, but these were the products of gifted professionals and I suppose are still used as texts in our universities.

Much of the same can be said of many of the other commissions whose works I remember—the Gordon Report on Canada's Economic Prospects,[5] though it got more individuals to appear with stars in their eyes; the Borden Report on Energy;[6] the Hall Report on Health Services;[7] the MacPherson Report on Transportation;[8] the Porter Report on Banking,[9] which used expert witnesses to good effect; the Glassco Report on Government Organization[10]—which, I believe, held no public hearings; and, of course, the monumental Carter Report on Taxation,[11] which involved 700 witnesses in its ninety-nine days of hearings, but most of them were representing specialized groups or industries. There were, I believe, more individuals on the staff of this huge inquiry than there were individuals who submitted their own briefs to the commission.

It was really later in the 1960s that the deliberate efforts to involve the typical citizens began with the "B and B" commission where, of course, the appraisal of public attitudes was vital. It continued—or reappeared—in the

Berger commission where it reached a high pitch of evangelical fervour, which later events must have frustrated.

In my opinion, the finest and most productive example we have seen of a royal commission, conscientiously, patiently, and skilfully involving the concerned citizens in its work has been the Porter Commission on Electric Power Planning in Ontario. I attended some of its hearings. I talked with the chairman early on about his approach, and I have read about its processes as well as studied its report on nuclear power in Ontario.[12] It had to deal with much that is detailed and technical but also important and troublesome. The commissioners had to consider one of the great public issues of our age, which has been the source of serious controversy and trouble both in Europe and the United States. The commissioners handled this task with scrupulous care, great patience, and thorough study. They held open, informal hearings on how they should proceed, then a round of lengthy hearings to provide public information on the issues involved, in which concerned individuals and groups were able to participate, and finally an extended series of debate stage hearings at which the issues identified and described by the commission were publicly debated with the commissioners by expert witnesses and those individuals and groups who wished to advance their views and question others. The commission financed research reports by consultants, individuals, and interest groups and paid expenses for them to attend meetings and take part in cross-examination of experts.

Out of all this effort has come a positive constructive report on the use of nuclear power and the measures that must be taken to safeguard both people and the environment at the various stages in its production. We can, I think, regard this report, together with the excellent report of the Cluff Lake Board of Inquiry[13] in Saskatchewan, and the earlier Ham Report[14] in Ontario on uranium mining, as largely settling for Canada one of the most important and difficult issues of our time by their careful attention to the views of concerned citizens and groups, and their balanced appraisal of where the public interest really lies. The government of Saskatchewan, I understand, has accepted the conclusions of the Cluff Lake inquiry, and I would expect Ontario to accept those of the Porter commission on this subject.

It is to be hoped that we can have more commissions of inquiry of this quality on issues that warrant the time and expense.

The second category I am to speak about is advisory councils. Around the federal government, there are perhaps a score or more of these, depending on where one draws the boundary, some of them far more active than others, and most of them with relatively narrow fields of interest advising a particular minister or department. Apart from the Economic Council on which I will comment, and the Science Council on which now I would not dare—although I was for some years an associate member—these advisory councils are usually made up of persons with special knowledge of and interest in particular industries or occupations, or specific government activities such as welfare, or special concerns such as those for consumers or the status of women. These councils can be and are, I believe, of real use to ministers and departments in the administration and the development of their programmes. The councils are normally composed of concerned citizens in a broad sense, but usually they are promoting their own interests as well as what they see as the public interest. Certainly that was quite evident in the one case I remember where I appeared before one of these advisory councils. Consequently, they are not really a field for the type of citizen involvement on which we are focusing today. Perhaps, however, this is a needlessly fine distinction, and we should regard specialized advisory councils as a field for useful public service for the concerned citizens, though perhaps not for gifted amateurs. The central government offices and departments in which I served were involved in such broad fields of controversial subjects that we had no standing advisory councils of this kind, though at the Finance Department we did have *ad hoc* outside committees that assisted us in our work. Sometimes it was very painful work for both sides, for example, when we had an outside committee of life insurance company presidents to help us to identify the problems involved in bringing such companies under the *Income Tax Act*, which was done in 1968.

The Economic Council of Canada is a larger and more general advisory council, which was established by the then new Liberal government in its multifaceted programme of 1963. I have had some familiarity with its reports as deputy minister of finance—when I endorsed some parts of its advice but not others—and of course, as a ''concerned economist'' since that time. During the past nine months, I have been one of the twenty-odd part-time, unpaid members who compose the council, along with the full-time chairman and two directors. The council was given in 1963 a long, statutory definition of its duties, which steer it toward the study of various economic questions, with the emphasis on medium- and long-term problems, and structural problems, but not really toward social problems. It was also to conduct studies in these various fields as it might be directed by the government to do, and to make recommendations on government policies in response to these references or on its own initiatives.

The council's mandate is very broad in the economic field and the council has been given the resources to follow it. The council has used its own staff of economists to do research and write reports, and has contracted research studies out to other professional economists, chiefly university professors. The scale of its activities recently is indicated by its total staff of about one hundred and thirty last year, roughly half of which were professionals, and by its expenditure of about $900,000 on outside professional services.

Under the statute, the part-time members of the council were to be appointed ''after consultation with appropriate representative organizations.'' The idea was that they were to be broadly representative of industry and commerce, organized labour, the professions, and consumers, as well as having the usual Canadian diversity of regional residence and the two official languages. This sort of representative diversity was achieved for a dozen years until the representatives of organized labour withdrew in 1976 at the time the government introduced wage and price controls. Moreover, the reports of the council itself, both its required annual review and its reports on particular issues, usually represented a consensus of views of the members without dissents in most cases and without minority reports. This consensus was achieved in many cases despite the fact that various members had conflicts of interest and probably some unwritten reservations.

Just how this council worked—how it managed to reach agreement—is hard to judge. Little has been published on it, as far as I know, though an analytical account of its own decision making would make a valuable study in itself because the council has managed to reconcile conflicting interests and produce useful consensus reports. Probably the chairman and two full-time directors, supported by their staff and buttressed by their outside professional researchers, have managed to dominate the council itself, by using discretion and skill in the knowledge of the personalities and the views represented around the table. The members serve as individuals and not as instructed delegates, though no doubt the trade-union members were subject to more constraints than others, and many others felt it was their duty to present the views of the sectors of society from which they were selected. However, there was no majority responsible to any outside organizations and the members must normally have been prepared to accept far more than they might advocate, and compromise or suppress their own opinions in order to produce an agreed report, just as boards of directors and public companies are believed to behave.

Is public service of this kind "citizen involvement" in the sense we are discussing it today? I would suppose it is, but in a rather specialized sense. It is not part of the new populism, and there is no role for the amateur activist and his various concerned groups, unless they have already become part of the "Establishment."

The council never has hearings, and it keeps even the economists in the public service distinctly at arm's length. It may on occasion seek to find what public opinion on a subject is, or the predominant view in academic circles, but it does not, so far as I can judge, pay much attention to dissident minorities.

It is worth noting that the future character and role of the Economic Council is under debate, and indeed changes are already under way. During the past year, under the new chairman, a dozen new members have been appointed. I have no idea what "representative organizations" were consulted (other than the Privy Council staff and ministers), but a large number of these new members are or have been professional economists; they come mainly from universities, but two are from business and one is a retired government executive. The representative character of the council is changing and it is becoming more expert. This trend will probably continue and will have some advantages, at least in the decisions on what research should be done and in the appraisal of the results and their economic implications. The presence of more economists on the council will probably lead to more controversy within it, and I would expect more dissent. Already the chairman is foreshadowing a rather looser concept of consensus and I think she is right. Eventually this trend may lead to fewer recommendations by the council on issues that are essentially social and political, and more emphasis on the purely economic analysis and options, which I think would probably be desirable. Economists generally—or I guess I would say the better ones—have been showing a more becoming humility in recent years as their very limited ability to find satisfactory answers to, or even analyses of, the world-wide problem of persistent inflation has been evident.

The third element in the title assigned to me today is "committees" and, manifestly, that word covers a multitude of activities and frustrations. There is no use my trying to comment on the possibilities of citizen involvement in the wide variety of government committees—internal, interdepartmental, intergovernmental—or even those formed to improve government relations with particular segments of our society.

However, I would like to say a few things about the most important committees—those made up by the most concerned and involved of all our citizens, the Members of Parliament. These committees used to be pretty ineffectual when I joined the public service over forty years ago, but they have improved greatly in the last dozen years particularly, and improved in ways that should permit a wider involvement in the policy process, not only for Members of Parliament themselves, but for other concerned citizens who appear before them or at least communicate with them. The advisory role of committees has been more visible in regard to the Senate—contrary to the usual situation—and has been carried out sufficiently far in advance of government decisions that it has had a useful preparatory value. We should give it more attention, and be more prepared to respond to general invitations to appear, as I ventured to do last year on the sensitive subject of the role of the Senate under a revised constitution.

However, it is the role of the committees of the House of Commons that has changed greatly since the changes in the rules of that House made during 1968 and 1969. As I understand it, these changes were primarily made in order to improve the working of the House itself, but they have had the valuable secondary effect of making the committees more useful. I guess I was one of the first deputy ministers to appear under the new rules in 1969, when our finance estimates got a good going over. What really impressed me, however, and for which I wish to express my gratitude, was the outstanding work of that House Committee on Finance, Trade and Economic Affairs in 1970 in its extensive hearings on and proposals concerning the government's

White Paper on Taxation. [15] Here there was intensive citizen involvement on a large scale. The committee received over five hundred briefs and over a thousand letters. The members of the committee decided to do a thorough job in reviewing the proposals, at considerable cost in their time. The committee held one hundred and forty six meetings on the subject and heard over two hundred briefs. It divided in two—in order to travel east and west to probe the views of concerned citizens—and there were very many concerned on that subject. Finally, it made scores of detailed recommendations as to how the government proposals should be modified. The government took the committee's comments very seriously and adopted many of its recommendations in the legislation introduced the following year. It was, I think, an outstanding example of what a parliamentary committee can do under our rules, given the support of the government. It is noteworthy that the committee was provided with staff and expert advisers to assist it in its inquiries and report.

It seems to me that experience in the past dozen years indicates that more can be done to use committees of the House constructively, not only in an advance role like the consideration of a white paper, but also in their regular duties in the consideration of estimates and government bills, and in the discussion of current policies for which these regular tasks provide an opportunity. To make the most constructive use of these opportunities, the committees, like the government, like the opposition now, like royal commissions and the Economic Council, need regularly the assistance of staff and "expert advisers." A lot of study needs to be given to how this staff should be organized, used, and controlled. We should not develop a great complex of rival bureaucracies. To avoid that may require care in organizing the control of the staff, and the normal use of term appointments and the means of selecting staff. The use in public hearings of testimony by, and cross-examination of, independent experts—even economists—should be developed. There will probably be resistance to this by some of the senior public servants, and by some ministers, but the government nowadays has so many thousands of experts in its own service that it should be able to defend its proposals and policies against expert criticism in Parliament, as well as in outside conferences where much of it has been going on in recent years.

To return to our concerned citizens, however, this public debate in parliamentary committees should also afford them—particularly the gifted amateur and not just the special pleader—a better opportunity to be involved in the policy-forming process in its broader and public aspects, and at the visible centre of our governmental process.

NOTES

[1] Canada, Law Reform Commission of Canada, *Administrative Law; Commissions of Inquiry: A New Act*, Working Paper No. 17 (Ottawa: Minister of Supply and Services Canada, 1977).

[2] *Ibid.*, p. 69, emphasis added.

[3] *Ibid.*

[4] Canada, Royal Commission on Dominion-Provincial Relations, *Report* (Ottawa: Queen's Printer, 1954).

[5] Canada, Royal Commission on Canada's Economic Prospects, *Report* (Ottawa: Queen's Printer, 1957).

[6] Canada, Royal Commission on Energy, *Report* (Ottawa: Queen's Printer, 1959).

[7] Canada, Royal Commission on Health Services in Canada, *Report* (Ottawa: Queen's Printer, 1964).

[8] Canada, Royal Commission on Transportation, *Report* (Ottawa: Queen's Printer, 1961).

[9] Canada, Royal Commission on Banking, *Report* (Ottawa: Queen's Printer, 1964).

[10] Canada, Royal Commission on Government Organization, *Report* (Ottawa: Queen's Printer, 1962-63).

[11] Canada, Royal Commission on Taxation, *Report* (Ottawa: Queen's Printer, 1966).

[12] Ontario, Royal Commission on Electric Power Planning, *Interim Report on Nuclear Power in Ontario* (Toronto: Queen's Printer, 1978).

[13] Saskatchewan, Cluff Lake Board of Inquiry, *Final Report* (Regina: Queen's Printer, 1978).

[14] Ontario, Royal Commission on the Health and Safety of Workers in Mines, *Report* (Toronto: Queen's Printer, 1976).

[15] Canada, Department of Finance, *Proposals for Tax Reform* (Ottawa: Queen's Printer, 1969).

Commentary

by
John F. Graham

No one is better placed than Dr. Bryce to assess the possibilities and limitations of citizen involvement and decision making through the kinds of bodies he has discussed. He had done a full enough job in distinguishing between the characteristics of commissions, advisory councils, and legislative committees that there is little need for much elaboration or comment.

However, I do take a rather different view than he does of what is meant by citizen involvement, or at least what we mean by the citizen who is involved. I do not believe we should see the citizen we speak of being involved in decision making or, better, perhaps "decision influencing," which is I think what we are really talking about, as being the "gifted amateur" who is concerned about advancing the public interest. This is a term that I do not like much anyhow. Rather, I believe we should be considering how private citizens or groups of citizens who do not represent a special professional or commercial interest can influence the legislation and regulation of the ubiquitous government that affects them in countless ways.

I have been very impressed by how clearly, and often eloquently, the ordinary citizen, whom you would hardly class as the gifted amateur, can express his concerns on particular issues that affect him. Frequently, his views are no doubt also the views of many fellow citizens. But it is usually a private interest, rather than some notion of a general public interest, that is being expressed. It is important to dispel any romantic notion of citizen participation or citizen involvement. Even with a bureaucracy dedicated to public service, with government and legislators dedicated to good government, and with media dedicated to informing the public about public issues—none of which we have to an adequate degree—it is likely that only a small part of the country's citizens would have much understanding of what is going on in the country, in the province, or even in the municipality, or would be interested in taking any initiative in expressing views or influencing decision, no matter how open the opportunities were.

Nevertheless, there is much value in providing citizens who do wish to do so with an opportunity to express their views. An independent commission, royal or otherwise, providing it is determined to do so, can offer one of the most effective opportunities for the views of citizens to influence recommendations as the policy, although actually influencing policy is another matter. I will come to that. The commission, of course, has to judge whether the arguments and points of view expressed by an always small number of citizens are representative of a general concern of the classes or types of people from which those citizens come, just as a teacher often has to judge whether a question raised by a student in a large class indicates a difficulty shared by many of his fellows in the class.

I do think it is possible for a commission to obtain a good understanding of citizens' concerns and to incorporate them in its analysis, findings, and recommendations. It is equally important for the commission, for its part, to add to citizens' understanding and information in the course of communication between citizen and commission. A commission can, even with respect to complex technical questions, represent citizens' concerns to government and often obtain a better understanding than politicians themselves, not only of what is socially desirable, but also of what is politically acceptable. Politicians preoccupied with the immediate, as they generally are, are often not the best judges even of their own political interests. But they are the ones who have to make the political decisions and live with them in the end, and that responsibility must be continually recognized and respected.

The citizen has to contend with a whole collection of experts, all of whom think they know more about any public matter, and about his interest, than he himself does, whether it relates to health services, education, nuclear reactors, zoning, or constitutional reform. He is beset by a host of governmental agencies that are supposed to be operating on his behalf and by the highly paid and often highly competent expertise that can be mustered by medical associations, teachers, unions, industrial lobbies, and so on.

A commission with the expertise and other resources at its disposal is in an ideal position to ensure that the citizens' interests are heeded and accorded their proper weight. The job of a commission is to define what it sees to be the public interest in the areas covered by its terms of reference and to determine how, in its judgement, the public interest can most effectively be upheld. In doing its job, the commission seeks to learn as well as it can what citizens perceive their interests to be and to combine this knowledge with its own independent analysis in order to arrive at its findings and recommendations. It is also faced, of course, with weighing and judging the usually more aggressive and well-financed submissions of special interest groups. Here it has an advantage over practically every other kind of advisory body, in that it has the independence, the resources, and usually the time to develop a coherent set of principles and recommendations that are not unduly influenced by special pleaders. Once a commission is established, it tends to have a life of its own and to assert its independence far beyond what the government expected of it. It is well placed, often better than the politicians, to assess the acceptability of its recommendations.

If a commission has done its job well, it becomes an effective advocate for the public interest, incorporating such views of the public interest expressed by the private citizens that have stood the test of argument. Often, it will also have contributed greatly to the understanding of citizens with whom it met and discussed the issues; for one virtue of commissions, if there is no other one, is their members become better informed than almost anyone else about the subject of their investigation.

The process has another effect: it gives rise to expectations of citizens that desirable changes will actually be made—that they will get better government as a result. Unfortunately, these expectations are not often fulfilled.

It is after the commission, assuming that it has done a good job of public consultation and independent analysis, has delivered its report that the endeavour, with few exceptions, goes awry.

Why? There are a number of reasons, and you can no doubt add to my list. The principal one, I believe, is the absence of any well-defined conception of justice—of principles of government for which our legislatures or governments stand. Our political system, preferable though it may still be, with all its faults, to most others, is composed principally of politicians who see every decision as being determined by political self-interest. There is ultimately no deep concern with providing good government. Politicians, including legislative committees, are sitting ducks for special pleaders on behalf of particular interest groups who know they can always bend politicians more easily than can independent commissions.

Another reason is a tendency for the bureaucracy of professional administrators and expert advisers to see themselves as knowing better what is good for citizens than do citizens themselves or commissions acting on the citizens' behalf. Often what seems to move them is what they see as best for themselves. And they are in a pre-emptive position to influence policy.

A further reason lies in our having media that are either unable or unwilling to inform those of the public interested in being informed, in a searching and continuous way, about the special interests of those involved and about the public consequences of administrative and legislative decisions.

The Carter report—*The Report of the Royal Commission on Taxation*[1]— to which Dr. Bryce refers, is a perfect example of a good report failing to prevail. This is a matter about which he probably knows more than anyone else. There are, of course, many exceptions to the mildly derogatory generalizations I made about senior members of the public service, a moment ago. Dr. Bryce is an outstanding exception, and probably more than anyone in public life at the time, he recognized the value of that report and did all he could to preserve its principles and support its implementation.

What happened there? Here was one of the most impressive and well-based and well-argued documents in this country's, or any other country's, history. It provided a comprehensive and coherent programme for the development of a rational system of taxation in Canada, rooted in a practically incontrovertible basis of equity—justice. It was and is considered internationally to be a landmark in the annals of taxation. I am not suggesting, for a moment, that even all economists agreed about everything in that report, but all were impressed by its sweep and its grasp and, I think, many, by its essential rightness with respect to the public interest.

It looked for a time as though this was one report the government was going to take seriously and in a way it did. Within a reasonable time, the government produced a *White Paper on Taxation*[2] that accepted the report's basic principles and was in some respects even an improvement on the original report. Dr. Bryce was one of those responsible for this white paper and deserves much credit for it.

As Dr. Bryce has described, committees of the House and the Senate were established to review the white paper and receive submissions on it. It is true that the submissions were numerous and that much of the original principles remained intact in the committees' reports. But it is also true that the reaction was dominated by the systematic onslaught against the reforms by powerful special interests. There were no corresponding advocacies of equal weight for the interests of the ordinary citizen, for what we might call the general public interest. Moreover there was the inevitable attrition that occurred over the prolonged period of discussion.

So what do we end up with? A so-called tax reform bill that is a pale shade, indeed a travesty, of the original proposals. I suppose we should consider it fortunate that we ended up with even the tax on 50 per cent of capital gains, the principal element of the reform bill that was eventually passed, although the Royal Commission on Corporate Concentration would like to reverse even much of that reform. However it was decided that the Carter report should not be implemented, the outcome can hardly be said to be the result of weighing the interests of Canadian citizenry in the common weal.

A few commissions have ended with a better fate—the Pottier *Report on Public School Finance*[3] in Nova Scotia and the Byrne *Report on Finance and Municipal Taxation*[4] in New Brunswick are examples. But generally, once a commission has done its job, the interests of the private citizen without a special lobby are likely to be thrown to the wolves.

It is easy enough to make these kinds of critical comments. Is there anything constructive that can be suggested about how all of the valuable efforts that are made by commissions can be made more effective?

The usual practice is that once a report has been completed and delivered to the government, the commission is discharged of its task. In a way, that procedure is correct and desirable. The commission has been asked to advise the government and it does as good a job as it thinks it can. It may not be desirable to have the commission enter the debate in the ensuing months or years ahead. The commission may jeopardize the outcome of its report if it engages in political controversy over it. Some commissioners of some commissions, as in the case of the Carter report, did engage in a lively defence of their document. And there is no doubt a period after the issuing of a complex report in which it is legitimate for the commissioners to help explain it to the public. But then it is reasonable that the government, which has to make the decision and be responsible for it, should be able to arrive at that decision without having the commission still involved in a very active way.

One thing that could readily be done that might make a difference is for a government, when it has come to a point where it is about to decide what it is going to do, to meet again with the commission and explain to it what it plans to do in its legislative programme with respect to the report and give the commission a chance to respond to its intentions. Often governments may think that they are implementing a report, when what they are doing is far from what the report recommended. It often appears that the members of government who are involved have not read the reports that they are ostensibly considering. Or, more kindly, there may not have been a sufficient opportunity for them to understand fully the arguments in support of recommendations.

Such a meeting would at least help to ensure that there was no misunderstanding about the report, would give the commission a further opportunity of influencing policy, and give the government the benefit of informed counsel at a crucial juncture.

This is one suggestion then to allow for at least this degree of continuity in the function of a commission.

I have said little about parliamentary committees or advisory councils. A problem with all party legislative committees is that they are often unwilling to arrive at any conclusions because none of the parties that are involved want to be committed to a common document. The hearings therefore tend to be perfunctory. This was not the case with respect to the parliamentary committees on the *White Paper on Tax Reform*; but that was exceptional. Citizens can be heard by such committees, but these considerations often make citizen consultation a very perfunctory exercise.

With respect to advisory councils, I do believe that these can be effective for particular matters, especially when they assume the function of the citizen advocate. I have had some experience with one kind of advisory council, an academic advisory committee to the Canada Council, when that council was still concerned with the social sciences and humanities. Given the constituency to which that body related, the committee was able effectively to represent the views of the members of that constituency and to arrive at policies and programmes that served it well.

The Economic Council of Canada, which Dr. Bryce cites as an example, has been a disappointment. I say this perhaps because I saw the functions of the council as being other than they have turned out to be. I saw it as a body publicly giving independent advice that might well run counter to current government policy. The Economic Council has done some valuable things. It has, for example, launched important independent studies, the findings of which are often not coincident with current or intended government policy. But the council itself has rarely come out with a series of proposals or policy recommendations that are very much at odds with government policy. When the council did that at one point, with respect to inflation and unemployment, it was roundly attacked by many in and associated with the government. It was argued that it was not the proper function of a body appointed by the government to oppose government policy. If the council is to be effective, it has to be prepared to do just that on occasion. The council has been in something of a bind itself in that it has not had the kind of guidance that it feels it has needed from government as to what the social goals followed by any particular government have been.

We find in reports of the Economic Council pleas for guidance as to what the social goals of government are. Lack of such guidance, however, does not absolve the council from saying "if it is to be a goal to eliminate poverty, or to provide this kind of environmental protection, or to provide that kind of programme with respect to housing, this is one way that this can be done and these are the social consequences, etc." What one would like to see is more speculative work of that sort coming from that kind of council.

Problems, of course, differ at different levels of government. In talking about these kinds of bodies, we have been talking mainly about the federal and provincial levels of government. When we come to the local level of government, there are even greater opportunities, perhaps not through these means but through more direct means, to permit citizens to have an opportunity to express their views on matters of public policy, matters relating to the physical and social development of their communities, before final decisions are taken about them. Because of the character and smaller scale of the local community, it is much easier to accomplish these things. Even there we find that the overriding interest is often in protecting the interests of developers, who, because they have acquired properties with values that have been created not by themselves, but through the social existence of those communities, are able to use the socially created but privately expropriated values in ways that are frequently in their own interests but not in the general public interest. There are thus certain elements that are inherent in the character and nature of our society that make it difficult for the public interests to be fully protected, or for citizens to have much effect ultimately over the decisions affecting their physical and social environment.

These comments have been mainly concerned with commissions. My principal conclusion is that commissions can have a special and valuable place for citizen involvement, but if there are not to be unrealized expectations, frustrations, and disappointments and wasted effort, there has to be some more effective follow-up with respect to their reports, perhaps in the way suggested here, than there has generally been in the past.

NOTES

[1] Canada, Royal Commission on Taxation, *Report* (Ottawa: Queen's Printer, 1966).

[2] Canada, Department of Finance, *Proposals for Tax Reform* (Ottawa: Queen's Printer, 1969).

[3] Nova Scotia, Royal Commission on Public School Finance, *Pottier Report* (Halifax: Queen's Printer, 1954).

[4] New Brunswick, Royal Commission on Finance and Municipal Taxation, *Report* (Fredericton: Queen's Printer, 1963).

Chapter Seven

Where Decision Makers Get Their Advice: How the Media Affect Citizen-Government Interaction

by
Doug Fisher

In the parliamentary press gallery at the present time there are 230 members. That is just about four times what there were in 1946 at the end of World War Two. It is just about double what there were about twelve years ago. Now of those 230 members in the press gallery, there are five or six who are listed as freelance journalists. Of the five or six that are listed only two, and I am one of them, make a good living. This is not to brag about me and Peter Ward, rather it is to emphasize to you one of the prime conditions of the media; 224 of the people who belong to the parliamentary press gallery work for organizations, most of them for large organizations. As a matter of fact, 59 of the 230 people work for Radio Canada or CBC in one of its arms or aspects. Some 31 work for Canadian Press; the *Toronto Star* has, I think, eight or nine, *The Globe and Mail* has seven, CTV seven, and so on. I use this description to make you realize that Canada is a country of very large organizations. This is mirrored in the media, and that fact is represented in the people who cover politics and government.

The second thing I want to point out is the occupational groups we have in this country. There are eleven million people in the labour force, and if you look at the labour force monthly statistics, it breaks them down into twenty-one categories and some five hundred occupations. Now with eleven million people in the labour force, let us say just ten million are working because there is usually about a million unemployed in this country. Of the ten million who are employed, I wonder if you appreciate that almost four million of them are clerks and salespersons. There are some 600,000 people who are classified as managers, some 600,000 who are working in education, 700,000 who are working in health and health occupations. Despite these statistics, we have an image in our country of being a land of great resources and our industry and work as based upon farms and mines and wood and water. And yet, of the eleven million people in the labour force, or ten million people who are working at the present time, we have only 27,000 fishermen, 55,000 lumbermen or bush workers or pulp cutters. We are now down to about 48,000 miners in all of Canada. The number of people actually working on the farm and earning a living from farms has slid down to almost 500,000.

What I am trying to suggest is that we are a very bureaucratic country. I am trying to show you that the occupational arrangements in this country are the same kind of reflection as the parliamentary press gallery. Most of its members work in large-scale organizations, and large-scale organizations are bureaucratic. This is so obvious that it probably does not need explaining. But so often I find that when we get individuals talking about the media, they do not realize that the citizenry themselves are all gathered and organized into the same kind of bureaucracies in terms of standards, modes, and dress. They push and move paper and have the same kind of facilities and machines as are found in government.

We are one of the great, white-collar bureaucratic countries in the world; we do not have to take a back seat to anybody. I can give you a classic example from my own experience. I was one of the original members that started that unbelievable long-shot enterprise, *The Toronto Sun*, back in 1971; that is only eight years ago. Last week *The Toronto Sun* broke over 350,000 copies sold in average circulation for its Sunday edition and over 290,000 for its daily edition. I can remember when the publisher took me out for a meal in Toronto about three months after we started in 1971. I paid for my lunch. As I remember, he took me to a fairly cheap restaurant and it cost me $2.50. Yesterday, I was at the Four Seasons Hotel in Ottawa and the second executive assistant to that publisher hosted a group (there were six of us around the table, five of whom will now have an Ottawa-based connection with *The Sun*) and I am sure the bill was well over $100.00. He just automatically put this on his credit card.

What is more important than the lunch was why he was there. He was there to tell us that we were going to be put on a terminal. This means that whenever we have anything ready for printing, we just have to sit down at one of those "picture things." The way they were trying to sell us this idea was by telling us there will be *nothing* between us and the printing press. Whatever you put into the terminal will go right into the paper.

Here is this young enterprise only eight years of age and what has it done. In Ottawa, there is a press building in which we all work. We work with other media groups such as Standard Broadcasting and United Press of Canada. United Press is a wire service that for a long time was not very important in Canada. Now *The Sun* has joined United Press, along with Standard Broacasting. Standard, as you know, is an arm of Argus, and Argus is controlled by Conrad Black. This begins to give you a picture of the way things operate and move in this country. In other words, it does not take very long before a small group of business people with an idea begin to get an enterprise moving. If it progresses very quickly, it becomes part of a massive bureaucratic organization.

I do not want to make predictions, but having followed the course of what Southam and FP publications have been doing in the communications area in the last ten years, I can see *The Sun* competing with them and the others in this very large context.

This is the media situation in Canada. While it is changing all the time, as technological improvements are made, it is basically made up of groups of large organizations.

How does the media affect citizen-government participation? The thrust of the conference, as I understand it, is how does the ordinary citizen or how do citizens get at the decision makers, and what role do the media play? We have to begin by asking who are the decision makers, what do they read, where do they get their ideas, and who thinks about and develops ideas for policy in this country? The answer is very simple. The people who develop ideas and influence decisions are the same ones who head up interest group organizations, many of which are corporations.

Let me take broadcasting, as an example. There are a number of different associations such as the Canadian Association of Broadcasters, the Canadian Cable Association, and organizations like CTV and CBC, each with their particular groups and lobbies. In addition, there are union groups such as ACTRA and others such as the Canadian Broadcasting League begun in the 1930s by Graham Spry. It still emerges at crucial times such as during CBC licence renewals. There are, in other words, a whole range of organizations that have a monetary interest, an occupational interest, or a promotional interest in the subject field.

This is a fairly accurate reflection of Canada and the manner in which policy making takes place. It does not leave much room for someone, as an ordinary citizen, to come along with a good idea that can get public exposure and that might be discussed and developed.

In my view, if there is anybody really in charge of decision making, it is the surrogates of elected politicians. That is, it is the upper bureaucracies in government and the upper bureaucracies of the corporations. The popular media, about which people complain so much, are largely a notice board for such men. It certainly is not a fount to which they go to get ideas.

The view I have just put forward reflects a basic prejudice of mine and I suppose it should be obvious. I suppose because I was a politician I tend to like politicians. Some people have said to me that I tend to like Conservative and New Democratic politicians. That may be, but it also reflects that while I tend to like politicians and not like bureaucrats, it is often hard to distinguish between the two in Canada because of the success of the Liberal Party. The bureaucrats and the Liberals take care of each other at either end of their careers and often they are interchangeable.

We should be concerned about this because it is a distinction that is basic regarding "party government" and "representative government." This gathering represents what is called participatory democracy; that is, the idea of groups of citizens really not having to deal with or wanting to deal with or through political parties.

In my view, representative government should be built on political parties. This view or process of government is now in eclipse. Conferences like this and the first one held in Victoria seem to be a result of the fact that our party system has broken down and failed. I do not know how to set it right and I do not know how to correct it. I do regret that it has happened, however, and I do wish we could get back to politics. I think that to get back to politics, what we have to do is change our system.

I have come here after first having read the report of the Royal Commission on Financial Management and Accountability[1] and it has left me very frustrated and unhappy. Mr. Lambert, Professor Hodgetts, and two other men had been studying this subject for a couple of years. They have come out with some marvellous prescriptions to make the federal government more efficient and more effective. There is nothing I want more than that. People have no idea how bad government in Ottawa is unless they have been there and have been a part of it. I have been calling Ottawa "fat city" for the past ten years. It has been a great delight to me that successive auditors general agree with me. Mr. Lambert and his commission agree as well. The problem is that nowhere in this very thick report does it come to grips with the fact that the party system has "gone to hell." They have these beautiful, dreamy ideas that somehow ministers are going to share their responsibility with deputy ministers. Deputy ministers are going to be open for public scrutiny. This is going to be much better. Why? Because it is deputy ministers who really know what is going on. The theory is that they should be the ones who should now be accountable rather than politicians, who come and go.

The main recommendation with regard to the political process is to make House of Commons committees efficient, and effective. I have been waiting for that for a long time. But how to do this without dealing with the issue of partisanship? The Lambert commission appears to assume that the future House of Commons will be made up of idealistic angels, not politicians, who will subdue partisanship.

What has become of political parties? Are they no longer the engine of democracy, as Dr. Corry used to say? They remain electoral machines but they are no longer the kind of engine that anybody would really want to be a part of. As a result, many people are looking for substitutes.

Having made these two general points—that is, the extent to which Canada is bureaucratized and the demise of political parties in Canada—I would like to return to the question of the media and the citizens.

I would like to deal first with the question of lobbies. At the conference held in Victoria concerning ''The Legislative Process in Canada and the Need for Reform,'' one of the papers noted that Clifford Clark, the original Canadian federal government mandarin, had the idea of organizing the farmers of this country. This organization became the Canadian Federation of Agriculture. In my view, it has become one of the most successful lobbies in Canada. It has been successful without ever having to use or to try to use the popular media.

How many people, for example, recognize the name David Kirk? I am sure very few, since he is not a major public figure. But he has been very effective as head of the federation. On the other hand, a long-time head of the Canadian Farm Union is someone I am sure many would recognize, because Roy Atkinson has been going back and forth across this country for more than a decade making headlines. I once asked David Kirk what he thought about the C.F.U., and he smiled and said they were a great help to the federation. I suggested to Mr. Kirk that the C.F.U. considered his organization and himself as ''vendus''—sell outs. He just smiled and said that somewhere between the extravagant claims made on behalf of farmers by the C.F.U. and what the government considered the farmers' due, the C.F.A. went right down the centre and did very well. The C.F.A. is almost a model, if you want, of a powerful interest group and its lack of need of the popular media.

There are a number of points I want to make about the decision makers in this country. Seeing Tom Kent here reminds me of something that happened when I was at Queen's Park in Toronto not long ago. I was with a group of high-level people, both elected and non-elected, and Tom Kent's name came up, and it is no discredit to Tom to say that he was not referred to fondly. He was given credit, all by his lonesome, for his role as an official with the Department of Manpower and Immigration in changing the whole make-up of Canada, through the immigration policy of 1967, dedicated to polyethnicism. I thought to myself when I heard them that it was another example of what I have become more and more aware of: really major significant changes and shifts in this country quite often can be the whim or the sheer desire of somebody well placed in the bureaucracy. One thing that happens repeatedly when you bring up this question of the decision makers being people highly placed in bureaucracies rather than the politicians is that so many of the bureaucrats come out and deny it. People such as Gordon Robertson make a career, a public career, of getting out and saying ''Oh, God, not me, I am just a servant.''

I want to read you a few things to show you what I am talking about. For example, Tommy Shoyama said on Patrick Watson's programme a short time ago that when governments change, you will get a set of ministers who start out by wanting to change everything. He went on to say:

I have not had a minister who has tried to change things on his own. I have had three in my four years in the Finance Department. They don't come in determined to change the whole system. After all they have been part of the government that has agreed with the decisions of the minister previously. It's certainly true that they might come in with a set of ideas of what they want to do and it is equally true, as you say, that once in and they get to know some of the complexities and the technical considerations that have to operate on the job, the permanent civil servant who is there has a great advantage. He has the information, access to the information, the technical tools for analysis, the access to skills, so it's not surprising that in very short order the minister learning his job is very likely to say, "Well I probably can't get rid of this fellow the way I thought I would, in fact he turns out to be very useful."

Now that is one quotation. I want to give you a couple of other historical ones. A very powerful civil servant who has now gone to that ideal place for a public servant is Senator Jacob Austin. I believe he was the chief of staff of the prime minister just a few years ago. Well not long ago, the Senator became stirred by some of my remarks and others writing about senior bureaucrats. Senator Austin said this of deputy ministers:

Their influence is pervasive as managers of fact gathering and of programmes, as analysts of both policy and process, of champions of this and that value judgement, advising on and influencing the decision-making process, and in acting ultimately as gatekeepers along with others in our society to ensure we maintain a balanced and effective constitutional and democratic system.

You know what he is saying there, do you not? You know that if we have a council of disciples of the Lord for Canada, these are the guys. Just listen to that: "In acting ultimately as gatekeepers along with others in our society to ensure we maintain a balanced and effective constitutional and democratic system." In talking further about the public service, he conceded that it is far from perfect. He sketched some of the evidence and some causes of trouble in which our bureaucracy is mired. Then he got to the guts of his recommendations.

Deputy heads are really not non-political and capable of serving political masters of different parties with the same intelligence, honesty, and providence. Surely, a minister is better off with a deputy minister he believes in rather than one he questions. Should not the system permit this instead of the prevailing affectation that every deputy minister is a creature that can serve whatever master comes his way equally.

When I drew attention to these remarks of Jacob Austin about this saintly class of deputy ministers, a former deputy minister waded in. Dave Golden has been in and out of the top level of the civil service and is now president of Telesat [at the time of the conference]. He sent me a speech that he made some years ago. In that speech, he said conditions of service in all large organizations are now very comparable, whether government or not. In the senior ranks of the civil service, you have managers and professionals just as in business, industry, and commerce. Golden put forward these conclusions:

It must be made easier and more acceptable, with safeguards to fire civil servants, promote them, and downgrade them. Senior civil servants should be moved more often. Incompatibility between minister and officials should be recognized grounds for movement, but of course, not for firing. The minister should have the right to have around him people with whom he likes to work. We should, frankly, admit that civil servants do make decisions for which they are and should be accountable and not waste any more time pretending otherwise. Civil servants should stop pretending that no civil servant ever had any political view. Government should quit pretending that these views have no real impact. We have the worst of two worlds in this country. In England, there is never any talk about it and no conclusion is ever drawn about it. In the United States, it is assumed that every official is a Democrat or a Republican and having made that assumption, the conclusion is drawn that it makes no difference in job execution. In Canada, we say that no civil servant has the slightest interest in or commitment to politics, and we go from there to infer that most disasters occur because secret Liberals are frustrating Conservative policies and secret Conservatives are frustrating Liberal policies.

That is my case from three top mandarins. It shows that the people who are really important in decision making tend to be the top people in the bureaucracies. It is not those whom I would call the superficial or temporary custodians, who are political and who are elected. I also want to suggest, as these examples of nobility from both Austin and Golden show, that we should follow the Lambert commission's recommendation to hold top and important people responsible. I am sure some of you are sitting there thinking this may be very interesting but what has it got to do with the media. Primarily, it shows that the decision makers in Ottawa really do not pay much attention to the popular media except when a reader begins to squeeze in on them in a direct and critical, personal way.

How did this system develop? I think there are a number of explanations. It begins with the British parliamentary system with its mystery and its secrecy, with the umbrella of ministerial responsibility, with the symbol of the Crown. This would not be bad if Canada were a unitary country. But when you have that system repeated at one level and then another and have the federal-provincial apparatus of a federal system superimposed on this, it becomes terribly complex and hard to understand.

Nothing will illustrate this better than the development that I have watched from the West Block of Parliament Hill. It is the growth and the proliferation of the federal-provincial apparatus. How are the media to cover it? Most of it is carried on in secret. How do you bring it to the public? How do you describe it? We get those odd moments when a federal-provincial conference is seen on television. But in the main, those are gatherings of people with an immense preparation behind them, based upon paper. So much of the diplomacy and exchanges is done in secret. In some ways, that is where the real governing, and many of the real decisions in this country, takes place. The media are excluded.

One of the points I want to make to you about the media in this country is that we have a really excellent distribution system. It is fast, it is very good. I am very conscious of this when I leave the country and go off, let us say, on a trip with the prime minister such as last summer to Germany. You feel when you are there that it is all very intense. Mr. Trudeau is sailing or running around with the chancellor in a very familiar way. We are planted with all kinds of stories about relationships with the United States and what is developing. Everybody is hot to send that stuff back. We do each day. Then it takes you only seven hours to fly back home where you find that already the whole trip is dead. News is every hour on the hour, and news is based and set in very, very short and staggered clips. In other words, because of the very speed and the effectiveness of our distribution system, radio and television determine topicality. As I explained at the beginning of the meeting, you know an awful lot of little things and not much in a great deal of depth and detail. This is a good description of the very effective distribution system in the media.

We should reflect upon this distribution system because it is a system or process that very soon leaves issues behind. Difficult issues get circumscribed and put off to one side to be left to be sorted out by the expert. Television and radio have widened the gap between the expert and the ordinary citizen. One of the paradoxes that I find remarkable is that as we are moving towards a "cabled or wired world" in Canada—that is, instant communication—government itself is getting more and more complex in the kind of papers and briefs that are handed out and shifted back and forth. In other words, print is flowering within the bureaucracy and in the exchange of materials. Yet in the popular media, print is, in a sense, fading away and the time span of news is shorter and more verbal and pictorial. There is also a trend in coverage toward the personal in order, I think, to somehow try and make sense through people of the challenging and difficult world of bureaucracy.

One sees our society today less and less as a population of sturdy citizens and more and more as a disparate collection of interest groups. The memberships of these groups devolve their responsibility for participation on to their occupational or economic or social lobby. Occasionally they become aroused about something government decides to do to them.

That is another point I want to make about the media. In so many ways the media are neutral. I have been carrying on a war with another columnist in *The Toronto Sun* over firearms legislation. He has been stirred into action by the National Firearms Association and its very fiery, florid organizer, Mr. Jones. Mr. Jones has come up with the theory that the Trudeau government has a plot. It is a plot to gradually take away firearms across the country, particularly from those sturdy yeoman who hunt. In time, when the government has taken all firearms away, they will then come and take over everything. The authority for this is a document supposedly prepared by two Winnipeg policemen. I have not been able to find the policemen, nobody has, but everybody has agreed that a couple of Winnipeg cops are supposed to have got the information at a closed seminar that the Mounties gave last summer in Ottawa. Now I mention that as an example of how the National Firearms Assocation is able to use the media and find people in it to propagate these scare stories. In doing so, they call in question the registration of guns and the particular approach the government adopted.

Now before you begin to clobber the media, the fact remains that it is not that difficult in this country for any kind of organization to get its message to the media. All I suppose they have to do, as the Indians have learned, is to get funds from the government and hire a public relations consultant and you are away.

The point is that given the structure and predominance of the huge bureaucracy, there is no question that the individual, the lone citizen, is left pretty much on his own when it comes to having any influence in decision making. He really has to tie in with a group or organization. I have met very few people, particularly those with a higher education, who do not belong to such organizations. This point is essentially a class view of Canada and therefore reflects a view of how the media are influenced. The class view is that in reality, all power resides with a certain group of people. It may be a bit of an open system for the upwardly mobile but, in effect, it casts off the people down below: those who have not got anybody to fight for them.

I wonder if that view is really true any more. I would be quite willing to concede that the poor, the genuinely poor and uneducated, have a much more difficult time in getting a share of the rewards of our system. But I do not think they are any longer as defenceless as they used to be. We are, for example, going to have a representative of an anti-poverty organization speaking here.

In closing, let me give you an example of how at least some of the "disadvantaged" are able to influence the media on one of the biggest industries, if I can call it that, which the government has promoted in the past fifteen years. It is what I call Indianism. Indianism at the present time is costing us somewhere between $800 and $900 million a year. I know Indians or I think I know them, and I have been in touch with many of them. When I was an M.P., the riding I represented had the most Indians at that time of any constituency in Canada. They were at the bottom of the economic ladder and many of them still are, in terms of living conditions, income, and that kind of thing. But they are not any longer without resources or organizations to speak for them.

When I came to Ottawa in 1957, the budget of the Department of Indian Affairs and Northern Development was less than $60 million, today it is over $800 million. When I came to Ottawa, the number of people working for Indian Affairs was 3,000, today it is up to between 9,000 and 10,000. I am not saying that is good, either the money or the number of bureaucrats, but it gives you an idea of the scale of the increase. Of course, during this period, the Indian population has increased from 135,000 to almost 300,000. In addition, several hundred thousand other people have emerged, claiming the same kind of rights and treatment as the Indians—the Métis. So the situation in terms of these citizens, who have had very little and in a sense were out in the hinterland without resources, is not as bad as it used to be. This change has not come about because of the media, except I suppose in arousing years ago some kind of quiet consciousness about the native people.

In closing, I must note that there are some other main topics that should be touched on. How can one really talk about the media in this country without devoting some time to the CBC? I make reference to the CBC, not facetiously, but because it has been the CBC, particularly CBC radio, and to a lesser degree *The Globe and Mail* or the letters to the editor in *The Globe and Mail* in Toronto, that have done a lot of good for the country. In other words, I am saying that there is a high-minded kind of constituency in this country that goes back to its roots in people like Escott Reid and Graham Spry. You can move across from the churches and some of the voluntary groups and see that they have had noble or idealistic intentions, and that they have built from or used the CBC and newspapers like *The Globe and Mail* to further and develop across Canada a kind of common consciousness of doing good and doing well in this country. In that sense, the media I suppose provided something. I do not know whether it is a heritage or legacy. It certainly is not as strong as it was. As a matter of fact, its influence has probably weakened because of what television and radio are doing to serious issues.

I am personally tired of complaints about the media and bitches about the media. I do not think the media are very good. I am ashamed about the kind of political coverage that we give in terms of the expertise of the people writing it. I am often ashamed myself at my lack of knowledge. But the media are a mirror, and a true one, of the qualities that we have in this country. We are not a very anarchistic or radical or wild or free or open kind of a society. We tend to sit just as I am here, looking at each other with great seriousness. The media, therefore, are both a symbol of Canadianism and a very good mirror of it.

NOTE

[1] Royal Commission on Financial Management and Accountability, *Final Report* (Ottawa: Minister of Supply and Services Canada, 1979).

Commentary

by
Jim McNiven

In his presentation of the role of the media in our society, I think Mr. Fisher put the problem quite well. I would like, in a sense, to go over the same things, perhaps not as well but in my own words. I would like to use an analogy to an industrial process. The way an industry operates is there is one group of people who acquire a raw material, a second group of people who process it into a consumer product, and a third group of people who consume it. The media work the same way and the media in our country are really the secondary manufacturers of a raw material that is then consumed. Just like any industrial process, the manufacturers and the producers of the raw material are also consumers. Their roles are interchangeable.

Let us leave them nicely fixed for a moment. The raw material is "news" if you want to call it that. What news is when it is a raw material is just like any other raw material—it is undifferentiated, and there is no meaning to it as to what is important and what is not important. Then it must be taken by somebody else and meaning injected into it: that is, it is processed. The waste material, whatever is defined as waste, is cut or thrown away. The rest is mashed up and put into a quality control process. The product is standardized and put into a decent acceptable quality deemed suitable for the potential consumer. It is then passed along to the consumer who uses it for his or her own purposes.

With this background, let me give you my perspective of the media. I come to you speaking as a primary producer. I make news. I use that word literally since I do it with malice and forethought. I give it to the *Chronicle-Herald* or the CBC or whoever else wants to process it into nice handy packages for you, the consumer, to purchase. As a source of news, I need to be aware of what the users or "secondary manufacturers" require. The first thing that the manufacturer needs is a dependable source of material. When it comes to news, this means a source or sources that can be counted on to produce enough to meet the consumer demand. As Mr. Fisher pointed out, the consumer demand is very great for news. There is a very short shelf-life to the product.

To be a dependable source of material in terms of quality, news must be something that meets what the consumer wants, and it needs to be couched at a level that the consumer is happy with. One of the ways of determining that quality is to be a personality. *People* magazine is a very good example of news that is not really news. It depends on personalities such as Margaret

Trudeau or Reggie Jackson or somebody else to provide them with a level of news that they judge the public will accept as decent quality.

You have to have quantity, too. You have to be able, as a manufacturer, to go to the primary producer and get a quantity of the material when you need it. If you cannot get it when you need it, then you do not go back to that producer. That is one of the problems with our inshore fishing industry for example. You cannot depend upon them to produce the fish at the time the airline needs it, for example, to airlift it to Los Angeles restaurants.

The same thing happens in the manufacturing of news. The media need producers who provide them with a decent quality and quantity of news on a regular basis. The news industry is a large industry and it is a large organization. It conforms to the same principles that manufacturing tomato soup does.

The next thing is that this processing must be efficient and quick. You see, it is even worse than fish. You cannot let news sit around too long before it starts to stink and nobody wants it. It has got to be in and out very, very quickly, and it has got to be to the consumer while it is still fresh. There is no way of refrigerating news. It must be processed well and efficiently. The computer interface between the columnist and the newspaper is more efficient than having him write it, send it along, and then have somebody typeset it. It will become an increasingly important news processing technique.

The next step or a quicker approach is a direct interface between the secondary manufacturer and the writer, and the consumer via electronic media. You simply turn on the television, plug in Channel 92 or 93, and out comes your news direct from him to you—bypassing editors, newspaper, everything else. Also, the process must conform to Alinsky's Law. I am sure none of you have ever heard of Alinsky's Law because I am the one who made it up. Saul Alinsky, the great citizen activist and organizer, once said that in order to get people to collaborate with you, to agree with you, to understand you, you must work within their frame of reference. If you want to confuse them, screw them up, then you work outside their frame of reference.

News must work within the frame of reference that people see as being relevant, otherwise it screws them up and they do not ''buy'' that product anymore. The media have to deal within the ''mind set'' of people that they are trying to influence or are trying to reach as consumers. If they do not, they get too far out of it. If the public do not understand the story, they turn it off. The challenge of producing news is a matter of sticking to the edge of the frame of reference and trying to push it a little bit further.

Thirdly, there is a very short shelf-life to the product, which means that new material must constantly be found. The greater part of a reporter's life is in the search for what is new and where he can find something that fits the frame of reference criterion. The pursuit is for the daily fifteen minutes worth of television news, or the two columns worth of newspaper. Sometimes, on slow news days, reporters get awfully desperate, and those are great days if you want to get in the news.

In this sense, the short shelf-life reminds me of Andy Warhol's comment that someday we will all be famous—for fifteen minutes. Last night I stayed up late and I turned on the television. There was "The $1.98 Beauty Contest" on; it is a kind of spin-off from "The Gong Show" and it amounts to a half-hour of ridicule of the Miss America kind of thing. Six contestants came on. They danced around, said a few dumb things, ran out in a bathing suit; and then a panel picked the one nobody would ever pick, and that is the $1.98 beauty. They gave her $1.98, some fake flowers, and she walked up and down in this idiot thing. Well, okay, famous until next week, when we have a new $1.98 beauty queen.

What happens is that everything is done so fast, so chopped up, and almost so irrelevant to what really is going on because the problems of today are complex. There are greys instead of blacks or whites, and as we get farther and farther into these problems, the expert or the bureaucrat gets farther and farther away from the citizen. This is what is critical to citizen participation because citizen groups today are both producers of media raw material and they are the consumers. They use it partly as a notice board and communications network. They also use it to some degree to find out what is going on elsewhere so they can find out what is relevant in terms of tactics, in terms of approach, and in terms of what is important and what is not important in our society. They are both the manipulators and the manipulated of the media.

The result is that citizen participation has to become partly theatre if it is to be relevant. You cannot avoid that. You have to play a part whether it is comedy or tragedy or something like that. You cannot just come on in a nice old-fashioned way because again you get turned off.

Now, what about the relationship between these media and the rule by bureaucrats that Mr. Fisher noted. The real problem in terms of citizen groups relating to bureaucrats with the mediation of the media is one of a difference of opinion over what is to be done. Bureaucrats generally tend to look for agreement. I am not saying that they are against change, but their interest is "how can we get these people to agree with what it is I want to do for them, to them or with them?"

People who are in a citizens' group, on the other hand, tend to look for a change from what it is that is being planned to be done for them, to them, or otherwise. It is a fundamental difference and conflict, which makes grand theatre. It is great because, for example, there are people on one side who are proposing to help society, and on the other side there are people screaming and hollering because they are being "helped" by having an airport put next door.

It makes for grand theatre and it makes for great media operations. I am not sure if it makes for an awful lot of relevance in terms of the social and economic processes of our society. In the end, bureaucratic effectiveness is hindered by bureaucratic citizens' groups, if you want to call them that, and the media manage to be the guy in the middle who is helping to trip up both sides. It is a very curious kind of situation. I am not sure how anyone gets out of it, but I have a feeling that it is going to continue as long as we have media that are processing news, people who know how to take advantage of the news, and bureaucrats who are, in a sense, entrepreneurs in terms of starting new programmes with government money.

Now, I will go quickly through a few predictions. The movement has been away from active citizens' groups, like the ones in the 1960s and early 1970s. It is a far more docile community today. Not really docile, it is a different kind of thing. Actually what has happened is that citizen activists and people who were involved in causes have tended to withdraw from the arena a bit. Now this is convenient and it may perhaps be a help to those who find that it is a nuisance to have people constantly hanging on them in terms of the policies they want to implement. This change will, I think, produce interesting forces and facets that are going to pop up in the 1980s.

First of all, there has been a tendency, especially with the latest budget cuts, to start by cutting out those people who fundamentally disagree with the way things are going. The next areas to be cut are research, then regional bureaucrats, and finally they will get to the centre, the core agencies. This seems to be the process. The first guys to go are the characters that you really cannot trust. I am being very cynical, but I think it is the essence of what is going on. The result has been that a lot of citizens' groups have gone under. Quite simply, they were on the public dole and as soon as the grants were cut off or cut back, down they went. A lot of others have transformed themselves into smaller organizations. They have changed their membership basis, gone out and tried to collect money either from corporations or from individuals, or have actually gone into sort of a fee-for-service in contract operations.

This trend is, I think, dangerous for the future of bureaucratic government in Canada and I think that should be noted. In the long run, what happens is that when groups develop that operate on their own, are used to a small budget, and are fumbling along on that, they become difficult to control very well. They are too small to control through regulations. They do not have any money, so it cannot be taken away from them, and they may get back into the theatre game again in the 1980s. When they do, it is going to be with a vengeance because, I think, like the Quebec licence plate ''Je me souviens,'' they will remember the last time they were cut off and it will not be allowed to happen again. I think that is going to be very dangerous for the kind of government that we have today. I do not mean the party, but the style.

Second, citizens' groups are moving more and more to self-help. They are tending, I think, to drop out of public debates. They are tending to look toward developing their own expertise and to understand some of the longer-term issues. I think this is perhaps why they have dropped out of public view and why they are no longer relevant to the media processing industry. I think there will be an explosion about the mid-1980s, if not earlier, and it is going to be due to the aging of our population. We are going to get more people who are going to want to be in these groups. Most of those people are going to be college educated and already are in some kind of bureaucracy. They know how the bureaucracies work, the large corporations and/or other kinds, and they simply are not going to take ''well, we know what is good for you'' for an answer. They are going to have the requisite technical skills that, say, student activists did not have in the 1960s, who perhaps just simply were engaged in one issue and then dropped out. We are going to have professional citizen participation people.

The fight will basically be over information. The struggle about freedom of information laws right now is quite simple, the tip of the iceberg, compared to what is going to happen. The essential problem of a professionalized citizen participation group is one of finding out what is going on. If there are people who want to know what is going on, it is going to be pretty hard to use that good Canadian bureaucratic motto: ''What is not released is secret.''

Third, government cut-backs are driving the entrepreneurs out of the bureaucracy. This means that we are going to have a bureaucracy in the 1980s that is going to be far more staid, far more unimaginative, and far less able to cope with the kind of professional citizen participation organization that I am talking about. If you take a look at the problems power companies have right now with citizens' groups, you can see a forerunner of what agonies bureaucracies in general are going to have in the middle 1980s.

Fourth, the weak link in the chain, the legislators, and I think Mr. Fisher pointed that out quite well, will probably remain weak as long as legislative salaries and inducements to join legislatures are so low. The average person would find trying to run for the legislature and existing on legislative salaries simply impossible. They have no alternative ways of getting money and so they stay out. If that changes and we start seeing legislative salaries looking like what they should be relative to the job to be done, then we will start seeing a change in our legislators and, I think, a change in our party system too. The quality of people that we are attracting into government right now, into the elected side, is unduly low simply because an awful lot of people cannot afford to go into government.

With regard to the media in the 1980s, there will be more theatre, more immediacy, more *People* magazine kind of stuff. I think there are going to be two slight changes that may come about but I think they are a long way away. One is this interactive mode that should derive out of the combination of the print media and electronic journalism. The idea that the television can be used to respond and to get information and to connect people up will have a great effect. I think that is going to have a lot of interesting developments in terms of the citizen-bureaucratic interaction. As well, there will be a greater concentration on specialist programming; this is programming for particular types of interest groups. Instead of trying to attract a Canadian Neilson rating equal to one third of all the population in Canada watching some show, parts of the media will start going after fairly narrow groups. You can see the splurge of magazines that have come about in the last five years in specialty areas and I think we are going to see that phenomenon as well in television and radio and other places. That is going to produce a nice new forum for citizens' participation groups.

What I see anyway is a lot of fun in the middle 1980s and I am looking forward to it. I think we may see some changes in the way in which the citizen and the bureaucrat interact because the citizen will be a bureaucrat or the bureaucrat will be playing another role. The big difference from today is that he will know how to cope with the guy on the other side of the table. I think it is going to be a rather interesting ten years.

Commentary

by
Marjorie Hartling

I am probably the person least capable of answering the question in the topic "Where decision makers get their advice" because I know they do not take it from me. Regarding how the media affect citizen-government interaction, I could not presume to answer that question either, because I am not government and the group I represent are really not citizens—they are second-class or non-citizens. I can only agree with much of what Mr. Fisher said, that while the mandarins in Ottawa wield a great power, they are influenced greatly by the press.

Unfortunately, it is virtually the only contact they have with real people; that is, picking up their paper in the morning. Outside of their government friends, and corporate friends who are tyring to make their special interests heard, they have few ties with the average person who has to live with the results of their efforts. Ottawans, I find, breakfast on *The Globe and Mail*, and they go to bed after the eleven o'clock news on television. But just this exposure is sufficient to influence everyone in Ottawa.

The media, I find, can create issues. They can create heroes or scallywags and they can ruin or make a group or person overnight.

The mandarins avoid publicity but they do not ignore it. Likewise the public is influenced by the media. The information on what the government is or is not doing is channelled through the media to the people. What we read or hear, however, is their collective version of what really happened. The media can mould public opinion; such public opinion can influence politicians, who then leave it up to the isolated mandarins to come up with a cure to the problem using their expertise and after they have consulted with their friends. It is a vicious circle and certain people are not "in." I guess the people that I am concerned with are those who are not "in." The poor of Canada are out; they are out of everything.

What is involvement, first of all? Involvement means to be able to participate or to have some kind of say. I think the most important involvement for poor people is that they would like to have some say over the regulations and the legislation that govern their lives and that essentially reach very deeply into their lives, probably more so than any others in the country. The greatest experts on government policy, I think, are probably poor people who have to live with those government policies—the ones that govern welfare, unemployment insurance, and old age pensions. You may feel that your own lives are heavily governed, but you have to be poor to understand how totally governed you can be.

For the poor to have any impact on the inner-most core of Canada's system—the government—requires a superhuman effort most people would be incapable of, even if they had the resources at hand to help them. They have to start their involvement by finding a way to become involved in society. Canadians generally have refused to accept the fact that poverty exists in Canada, let alone understand what it is. All they know is that it is a bad thing to be poor.

The media have done little to help matters—primarily, I believe, because they do not understand it either. Our office is plagued by calls from poeple in the media asking to find them a poor family they can put on television or put their pictures in the paper so that everybody can relate to them and feel sorry for them.

The only thing is that poor people, too, know that the public believes that to be poor is bad. It is not what you aim for in this life, and they are not going to expose themselves to the criticisms of the public as being one of those bad people or as one of Canada's failures. I guess the only trouble is that society itself has failed to recognize that it excludes a lot of people.

Mr. Fisher referred to the poor having a voice or beginning to have a voice and that my coming here was an indication of this. He noted that this was the way the problems of the Indians had become more strongly publicly identified. I have talked to a lot of token Indians who wound up attending a lot of conferences, so while the idea of Mr. Fisher's may be true, the problem is that 25 per cent of the people in this country live in poverty and are totally ignored by government. I do not want to deal just with Ottawa because we have ten provincial governments that have equally great bureaucracies and equally difficult structures with which to deal. And, in fact, when you get down to the city level, you have more problems. The people in our organization have problems in dealing with all of them. They have trouble getting governments to understand poverty and to understand some of the needs of poor people, to try to convince government to stop creating dependencies.

When we started looking at the dependencies and looking at poverty itself, we realized that Canada is committed to maintaining poverty in this country because a great number of people would be put out of work if we did not have poverty. When you talk about the amount of money that is spent on, say, Indian people and the Department of Indian Affairs and Northern Development, has anyone ever calculated what poverty costs us in this country? It costs us not only in terms of money given directly to poor people to cure their problem, but also in terms of creating all sorts of services and jobs for other people to maintain poverty. It is this kind of frustration that we try to take to government, that we try to take to the public. It is this kind of frustration that we talk about to try to make people realize how completely powerless we are to influence government. We are facing a federal election, and it is not even possible to get political parties to say that poverty is a problem and we should deal with it, we should try to eliminate it.

I have learned to be a person of infinite patience: to measure success in, well I do not know the metric conversions, but lillimeters or whatever. I have learned to measure success in very, very small pieces but I am still totally frustrated with wondering why it is that an organization such as ours cannot make people understand that poverty is a problem that we do not need and that we could get rid of.

Part of our problem is that the poor have very little influence of any kind with anybody. A large number of poor people do not vote and they are never invited to. A large number of poor people do not belong to a political party and they are never invited to join. A large number of people are not members of strongly organized groups in society, which might provide the kind of information and resources they could use to become involved, but they are never invited. Poor people cannot afford to volunteer, to join, or even to meet with each other. They cannot afford conferences. We had one, and only one, national poor people's conference in this country and it was such a horrifying experience for Canada that it has never been repeated.

In spite of all this, poor people are expected to participate in society, to use its rules, but not to be a part of that society because they do not fit and are not wanted. How, in such circumstances, can they accomplish anything? Maybe it is not worth being involved. Some of the things that we are saying to some of our members is that the best thing you can do is to find a way of standing on your own two legs because there is nobody who is concerned about helping you to become a member of society. You can forget your dreams. The only way you are going to do it is to do it on your own, or just give up.

Governments and political parties, and people employed by governments, the media, and universities are so busy seeking their own power and seeking to increase that power that they are not about to give some of it away in order for the poor in this country to be involved. Someone would have to give some power away. There is only one pie, one size. It is the same thing with money: power and money seem to go hand in hand. A group of prominent people such as yourselves who are concerned about improving citizen control and involvement at least have the privilege of meeting with each other and collectively pooling your thoughts and resources to tackle the problem. What hope is there for a true involvement by a group of social outcasts?

Nevertheless, we will keep trying. I and the members of our organization will continue to try to get a message through that there are some people who are being totally left behind. I think perhaps it would be useful if you, the government, the media, and all of the other groups that have been mentioned here today, first examine what power you already have before you seek more. I am a firm believer in social justice and there never will be social justice until we start working toward equality of opportunity in all things including citizen involvement for the poor. A good place to start would be to give that equality to our children, a truly significant way to celebrate The International Year of the Child.

Chapter Eight

The Limits of Direct Democracy: The Experience of Switzerland

by
Peter Studer*

Citizen involvement in government policy making, the theme of this conference, is a problem that probably confronts a Swiss more directly and regularly than any other nationality. As every travel guide will tell you, Switzerland's most famous label is that of the "world's oldest democracy." A romantic picture is presented of four fiercely democratic Germanic clans swearing in 1291 an oath of allegiance against the tyrannical Habsburgs, thus laying the roots of the present republic. Constitutional law experts are less interested in this colourful past, and more in another Swiss tag. Their emphasis is on Switzerland as the world's only "direct democracy." By this they mean the direct realization of a classical definition of democracy—rule of the people by means of maximum participation of all the people[1]—through institutions such as town meetings, "Landsgemeinde," referenda, and initiatives.

My purpose here is to give you a glimpse behind the nostalgia and labels at what Swiss democracy *really* is and how it works without fogetting the many grey zones.

First, a fundamental term should be corrected. As is customary amongst leading Swiss constitutional lawyers, it is better to refer to a "semi-direct democracy" because the Swiss system is "bound by a unique combination of representative and direct components."[2] Whichever way we label it, the Swiss political system keeps us—or, better said, the ever-diminishing number of active citizens—rather busy. When my wife and I, after a six-week break, went to vote on the wintry Sunday of 18 February, we had no less than eight sheets to fill in with a yes or no. The topics included the following:

Federal Level:
- *Do you approve a people's initiative asking for a stricter clause in the constitution for the protection of people's rights and safety in nuclear power plant construction?* (If passed, the building of a plant could have been prevented by those living within a 20-mile radius.) Some

51 per cent of those who voted rejected this proposal of the anti-nuclear lobby.

- *Do you wish to accept a parliamentary proposal for a clause in the constitution making the federal government responsible for the ground rules in establishing a network of hiking paths throughout Switzerland?* (A people's initiative, with the same goal but demanding even more powers for the federal government, had been withdrawn in favour of the parliamentary proposal.) Some 78 per cent of participating voters said yes to this popular measure.
- *Do you approve an addition to the constitution banning all advertising for tobacco and alcohol?* As expected, the initiative brought by a youthful temperance league was rejected, this time by 60 per cent.
- *Do you wish to give 18-year-olds the right to vote?* This proposal, which was supported by both Parliament and the governing Cabinet, was knocked back by 50.8 per cent of citizens voting.

Canton of Zurich:
- *Do you agree to pay 50 million francs for the improvement of a regionally important railway line?* The result: yes.
- *Do you agree to replace the 1848 law on peddling with a more liberal law?* The answer: yes.
- *Do you favour the payment of 14 million francs for the restauration of a 19th century museum?* Once again the people supported the government by voting positively.

City of Zurich:
- *Do you want to spend 15 million francs on a middle-class apartment block with 80 units?* The administration proposal won easily.

On this full and important voting day of 18 February, only every second eligible citizen went to the polls!

After giving you these few examples of what Swiss vote on, I would like to outline briefly the direct democratic elements that characterize the Swiss system.

FRAMEWORK

It must be said that this richly complex system has been built up since the early Middle Ages and continues to grow today. Most important to remember is that the structure developed from within—the communities—outwards.

- The small territory of Switzerland, not much larger than the Province of New Brunswick, has a population of only 6 million and over three thousand communities. Half of them have fewer than 500 inhabitants. Only a few communities have been swallowed up by the big cities so that the number of communities has remained almost unchanged for one hundred and fifty years.

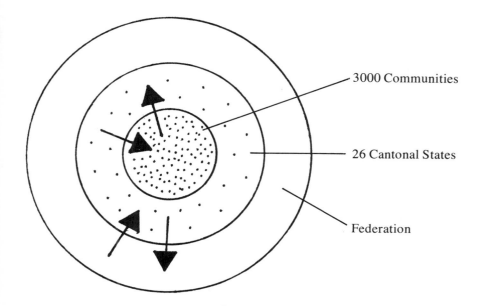

- In the middle ring are the country's twenty-six cantonal states with their often very varying cultures and degrees of wealth. Each is a miniature state with a complete administrative and legislative system. Each has a regional centre. All five French-speaking cantons have their own university.
- On the outside, we find the Swiss Confederacy, which first became a legal entity in 1848. Since then, federal power and its budget have grown continually. However, certain areas view this development with suspicion—especially the French-speaking and the small alpine cantons, which guard their 'sovereignty' with jealousy. Interestingly enough, it is these cantons that receive over half their financial needs from the federal coffer.

TOWN MEETING[3] AND "LANDSGEMEINDE"[4]

The most traditional form of direct democracy is the participation of an affected person at a decision-making meeting. Prototypes are the Athenian polis, the town meeting of Swiss and New England communities, and the Swiss "Landsgemeinde," which is a cantonal assembly.

A "regular" town meeting in the Swiss sense is when all major decisions relating to law and administration are decided at the meeting. For example, this form is valid for 138 from 171 communities in the Canton of Zurich. Larger municipalities, with a population of more than 2000, can add "extraordinary" features such as an elected legislative body or make certain decisions subject to a ballot-box vote.

In five, small, rural cantonal states, those eligible to vote (only men in two out of the five) gather once a year at the "Landsgemeinde," which is a direct descendant of the old German tribal "things" (assemblies). In a "ring," into which men from the Canton of Appenzell are allowed only if they carry a sword, the cantonal authorities and federal senators are elected. Some "Landsgemeinden" also decide their cantonal statutes in the "ring."

REFERENDA AND INITIATIVES[5]

Of course, a community can become too big and a canton too complex. Complexity and largeness make the functioning of this ancient model form of direct democracy difficult. Therefore, Switzerland has developed the referendum and initiative. These two forms of semi-direct democracy, working with representative institutions, still allow the people a decisive influence.

The referendum functions on all levels—federal, cantonal, and communal—in two forms.

• *Mandatory* referendum: certain parliamentary decisions are by constitution subject to a popular vote.
• *Non-mandatory* referendum: though a positive decision of the legislative body is sufficient for validity, if, within a specified time, a specified number of citizens ask for a vote on it, the proposal must go to the people.

On the federal level, only constitutional changes are subjected to the mandatory referendum. Both a majority of voters and of cantons have to approve. Statutory decisions come under the non-mandatory referendum regulation, meaning that 50,000 voters must ask for one within ninety days.

In cantons and communities, basically all legislative decisions, whether constitutional or statutory, are determined by mandatory referendum. In addition, various financial decisions are ruled by one form or the other.

While the referendum provides the citizen with the means to block the actions of his representatives, the initiative gives him a tool to initiate change. A specified number of voters can propose an addition to or change of the constitution or law.

On the federal level, 100,000 signatures collected within eighteen months are required to force a vote on a constitutional change. The proposal is first debated in Parliament before being submitted to the people.

On the cantonal—Zurich, 10,000 signatures—and municipal—Zurich city, 4,000 signatures—levels, constitutional, statutory, and financial changes can be initiated. They, too, are put to the popular vote.

ADVANTAGES AND DISADVANTAGES

Town Meetings and "Landsgemeinden"

How has the Swiss system of direct democracy stood the test of time? Very well, it must be concluded, from the undisputed way in which it has survived through centuries. But, on the following point, every Swiss citizen would agree with me: the town meetings'[6] smallness and cosiness embody both efficiencies and deficiencies.

The advantages are obvious:

- Because the participating citizens know each other, less formality is necessary; officials and citizens talk to one another; often the practical is more important than the ideological.
- During—or, informally, already before—the town meeting, citizens can directly influence the content of resolutions and the way in which they will be carried out. During the give and take between executive and citizen, often oral assurances will be given. Even if an administration proposal fails, the discussion has served a purpose.
- Community executives feel obliged to keep a tight budget control. If they want to buy a four-wheel-drive for the fire brigade, the gas station owner is likely to get up at the meeting and ask why they cannot get along with a two-wheel. All citizens are aware that expensive outlays affect taxes.

Now, to the disadvantages:

- In the large, rapidly growing communities, citizen participation leaves a lot to be desired. It is rare that more than 2 to 10 per cent bother to turn up at the town meeting.
- Bureaucracy may be limited, but often there is a lack of far-sighted planning and too little attention given to individual rights.
- Citizens and officials know each other. ''But in informal and intimate relationships, the agent, who is the economically and politically strongest, has certain advantages. Especially when there is pressure to conform as during open debates and votes!''[7]
- Small communities may keep an eye on the budget, but the maintenance of numerous, tiny infrastructures side by side also has a price. Political introversion dominates in many small communities; neighbourhoods take precedence over the interests of the larger community; the established over the experiment.

Even the noble ''Langdsgemeinde,''[8] one of the finest symbols of true democracy handed down to us, has its problems:

- Appenzell still refuses to give women the vote for fear, apparently, that the intimate gathering of several thousand men armed with swords might be endangered.
- ''Montesquieu (and the separation of powers) never came to Appenzell,'' complains one observer. For the cantonal administration also sits in the legislative council, which meets between ''Landsgemeinden.''

But despite these drawbacks, the ''Landsgemeinde'' is deeply anchored in its five cantons. And, it must be said, that under favourable conditions—such as in the half-industrialized Canton of Glarus—it has been responsible for pioneer social reforms, such as Europe's first factory act.

Federal Referenda and Initiatives

Years	Non-Mandatory (Statutory) Referenda		Constitutional Initiatives
1946-60	15		27
1961-79 (Feb.)	25		46
Total *voted* since 1874	**90**	Total *submitted* since 1891	**128**
1977: voter's peak year	8*		8**

   * Mandatory *and* non-mandatory referenda.
  ** Voted—two of them were coupled with parliamentary counter-proposals.

NON-MANDATORY REFERENDA[9]

First, let us turn to the non-mandatory referendum. It was thought up by the fathers of the present Swiss Confederation, the majority Radical Centralist Party, in 1874. The referendum was seen as the motor of a "peaceful, social revolution."

However, it turned out very differently to what the referendum's creators had expected. The Conservatives quickly mastered the art of this democratic tool and used it to block the legislative process. Their goal was equal representation in government. The Conservatives continued until they won: in 1891, they joined the government and they still sit there today. The up-till-then mono-coloured government became the multi-coloured compromise, which has characterized Switzerland ever since. The referendum integrated the opposition.

The battles, which marked this first phase, established the referendum as "the institution capable of regulating political conflicts irrevocably." It became accepted that a referendum set-back had no repercussions for the "defeated" government members, the government as a whole, or for Parliament. Finally, the referendum stabilized the system.

During the second phase, a further and double process of integration was played out through the referendum:

• Trade and industry, later small business and farming, followed the example of the Conservatives. Through threatening the government with "mobilizing" the referendum, they forced political concessions. They received the right to send their lobbyists as "experts" into commissions that prepared law proposals for the government. They managed to institutionalize the sending of these proposals to their associations for "appraisal." Eventually, the representatives of these associations sat on the benches of the big parties in Parliament.

• This phase ended after the social unrest of 1918-39, when Social Democrats and labour unions also tested their capacity to use the referendum's powers. Since 1943, they also sit in the federal government.

Today, the government, Parliament, and established organizations do all they can to avoid a referendum campaign. They attempt to work out a bullet-proof compromise. Switzerland's parliamentary and referendum democracy has transformed itself into an integrated "bargaining democracy."

In the long years after the war, it was mainly economic outsiders who attacked "bargains" through referenda, for example, two low-price supermarket chains. They used the referendum to fight the regulating of milk, sugar, and tobacco prices. In recent times, an active referendum scene has forced the people to make important value judgements. The right opposed laws on university reform and strict planning of zoning; the people supported them (1976, 1977). Socialists and unions, although a part of the bargaining process, were pressured by their militant wings into successfully attacking the setting up of a federal anti-riot police force and the passing of a restrictive compromise abortion law. In the first, they were joined by French-Swiss conservatives; in the second, by Catholics.

Since 1874, over ninety non-mandatory referenda have been brought before the people. On an annual average, this measures a little less than one a year. However, some years tend to be top heavy; for example, 1978, when more than nine referenda were voted on. In the last one hundred and five years, around 60 per cent of referenda have been successful, which means that the people rejected laws that had been debated and accepted by Parliament.

INITIATIVES[10]

When, at last in 1891, Parliament started to discuss the initiative, conservatives and democratic left wingers were its major proponents. The radical-centrist establishment was far from keen. Initiative supporters pointed to its success in the cantons. But on the federal level, it was to remain controversial; and is so, even today. A radical federal minister complained back in 1894: "First came Parliament, then the referendum democracy; and now we are sinking ourselves into the epic of initiative demagogy!" And recently, the dean of Swiss constitutional experts, Hans Huber, exploded: "The people's initiative has become a playground where the people's rights are misused and the constitution twisted. The authorities are diverted from important work, the voting calendar is overflowing, and voter abstinence is growing."

However, the initiative has made history. As soon as it was introduced, the initiative's influence was rapidly felt. In the beginning, it was used by Conservatives and Socialists to break the majority hold of the Radicals in

Parliament by establishing a proportional election system (1918). Since then, the established Conservatives and Radicals have rarely used the initiative.

Later, it was the Socialists who used the initiative, primarily to accelerate slowly moving or retrogressive social legislation (since 1918). In the thirties, the extreme bourgeois-right, under the shadow of Fascism, attempted through it "to tighten the people's rights."

Since the Second World War, small opposition groups from the fringes of the right and left have been emerging. Whereas such groups in other countries must form a "grass-roots movement" and struggle to contact their parliamentary representatives, in Switzerland, they gather signatures for an initiative. The Swiss rightists have used it in the service of the environment, hiking paths, and three times to reduce the number of foreign workers. The left have also pressed for clean air as well as arms control, abortion liberalization, a fair-go for conscientious objectors against nuclear power and bank power.

The referendum has served to integrate first the large opposition groups and then lobbies into the process of bargaining. On the other hand, the initiative has created a vehicle through which the neglected views of groups with little organization and power can be articulated.

Since 1891, a total of 128 constitutional initiatives have been submitted. This represents an annual average of less than one and a half initiatives. However, in the last decade, this average rose to over four; a similar development is also true for the cantons. The non-success figure is quite astounding: a total of only 6 per cent have been accepted by the people and the cantons; in the last thirty years, no federal initiative has been adopted.

But one cannot talk of failure here because those who bring the initiative are using the artful dialectic of the system to achieve their aims: "There is hardly an initiative which has left no traces."[11]

- Government and Parliament often prepare a counter-proposal, which is voted on at the same time as the initiative or even leads to a withdrawal of it (as in the case of the previously mentioned hiking proposal).

- Sometimes, it is enough when Parliament co-operates by making an unrelated statutory change. On 18 February, the anti-nuclear initiative failed because Parliament tightened the control clauses in existing statutes a few months before the people voted on the initiative. Earlier, the government had doomed three anti-foreign worker initiatives by getting in first with an ordinance restricting immigration.

- At the very least, an officially neglected subject of an initiative is put on the public agenda and discussed for a while. The opposition group has a chance to flex its muscles and a certain measure of understanding is achieved: "Alone through this safety-valve effect, it is apparent that a large amount of social and political tension is reduced."[12]

OBSTACLES AND CONCLUSION

Both the non-mandatory referendum and the constitutional initiative are faced with obstacles that reduce their problem-solving and democratic value.

• *Legal blocks:* recently the number of required signatures was raised for the referendum to 50,000 from 30,000, for the initiative to 100,000 from 50,000. Will this limit the "flood" of people's proposals? Only the future will tell.

A serious block for the initiative has always been a requirement that a majority of voters and cantons have to approve the constitutional change. This gives too much weight to the small, conservative, alpine cantons.

Under certain conditions, Parliament can declare that an initiative is "unacceptable." However, so far this has only been done in two cases. Brought by the ultra-left, one was rejected as "physically impossible" and the other as "exceeding the designated one topic." This lack of material and legal bounderies on the initiative explains why Switzerland's constitution is such a patchwork.

• *Influence blocks:* there are weakly organized interest groups, such as tenants, consumers, children, prisoners, and so forth, who find it difficult to tune into the closed bargaining of the law-making process. The gathering of signatures and the initiative campaign are dependent on voluntary manpower and cost from $1 million up. Sums can get way out of proportion. For instance, the pro-nuclear lobby is said to have spent $6 million before the 18 February vote and even the antis coughed up around $2.5 million. The predominantly bourgeois *press* does not always give initiative supporters an appropriate degree of attention.

• *Perception and participation blocks:* the more complex and technical a political topic, the more difficult it is to raise emotions, money, signatures, and votes. Unfortunately, many contemporary topics fall into this category. What does it mean that the average national voter participation has sunk to around 40 per cent in the seventies when it was always above 50 per cent till the mid-fifties and close to 70 per cent in the thirties?

Robot pictures show that the most active voter is the university-trained professional, in his mid-fifties, and living in a rural area; the typical abstainer is the young woman with elementary-school-level education, working in a factory, and living in a large French-Swiss town. She does not realize that there is a connection between politics and her daily life. She often does not understand the topic. She is disappointed because earlier fits of participation—for example, her signature for "12 car-free Sundays"—did not succeed. However, the high participation rate in the crisis-ridden thirties indicates that a basic satisfaction with the *status quo* is often an underlying motive for abstention.

My conclusion is therefore clear:

- Town meetings, "Landsgemeinden," referenda, and initiatives give the people a genuine opportunity to participate and help in the process of problem solving. They are an attempt to approach the democratic ideal of identifying the decision maker with the affected.
- Some political mechanisms are so organized that speedy innovation, competition between parties, weak groups, and open decision making are disadvantaged.
- Citizens are overtaxed by the frequency of votes. Whereas the West Germans were called to the polls 7 times within the last thirty years, the Swiss have gone 97 to 213 times depending on domicile. It is quite obvious that the frequency and complication of many modern issues strain the voter and thus do damage to the ideal of democracy.

NOTES

* I am indebted to Professor Leonhard Neidhart of Zurich, whose suggestions were of great help; fellow journalist Richard Aschinger of Zurich; and Margaret Studer-Walsh, who translated and edited the text.

[1] Pateman, 1970, quoted in R. Aschinger, *Industrial Urbanization: The Road to Serfdom?* (York University, 1975).

[2] Eichenberger, "Repräsentative und plebiszitäre Komponenten im schweizerischen Regierungssystem," [Representative and Direct-Democratic Elements] in *Zeitschrift für Parlamentsfragen* (Opladen: 1977).

[3] Leonhard Neidhart, "Erfahrungen mit den Instrumenten direkter Demokratie in Schweizer Gemeinden," [Direct Democracy in Swiss Commmunities] in *Züge unmittelbarer Demokratie in der Gemeindenerfassung*, Schriftenreihe des Deutschen Städte- und Gemeindebundes (Göttingen: Schwartz, 1977).

[4] Fritz René Allemann, *25 mal die Schweiz* (Munich: Piper, 1977), chapters on "Landsgemeinde"—Cantons, Appenzell, Glarus, Unterwalden.

[5] Codding, 1965, quoted in R. Aschinger, *Industrial Urbanization: The Road to Serfdom?* (York University, 1975).

[6] Neidhart, *op. cit.*

[7] *Ibid.*

[8] Alleman, *op. cit.*

[9] Leonhard Neidhart, *Reform des Bundesstaates* [Federal Reform] (Bern: Francke, 1970).

[10] Jean-Daniel Delley, *L'Initiative populaire en Suisse* (Lausanne: Age d'Homme, 1978); Hans Werder, *die Bedeutung der Volksinitiative in der Nachkriegszeit* [People's Initiatives in Post-War Switzerland] (Bern: Francke, 1978).

[11] Delley, *op. cit.*

[12] Werder, *op. cit.*

Commentary

by
M. André Larocque

In early 1977, Premier Lévesque asked for the establishment of a referendum act in Quebec. There was no such thing as a referendum act in Quebec. One bill had been prepared under Premier Jean-Jacque Bertrand. It was a very hasty thing, really just a reshuffling of the old *Electoral Act*. But there was no such thing as an enabling referendum act in Quebec, so I had the pleasure of being among some people who had the task of building the thing up from scratch. Now, what do you do when you do not have anything at all to start off with in writing a referendum act? What do you think of? And what country comes to your mind? Naturally, it is Switzerland. So, you start reading books on Switzerland, articles on Switzerland. You unfortunately come very quickly to the conclusion that it would be difficult to transfer the entire Swiss system into the Quebec context overnight. As we have seen, it is a complex thing, it is a multiple-level thing. The government of Quebec believes in introducing more progressively the referendum process. This imitating or closely following the Swiss experience was quickly ruled out as one approach.

The second source of inspiration was California. We had been working with people from the Fair Political Practices Commission in California for our Bill 2 on financing political parties. We thought perhaps we could enjoy their co-operation again for working on the referendum act. But that did not work out either. One thing that does come out clearly as one major obstacle when you are working on a referendum act is the parliamentary system itself. The parliamentary system is very different from the traditional presidential system where most referenda are used. In the presidental system, you have elections on fixed dates; all you do is stick a referendum question into the electoral process and all is ready. You cannot easily do that in a parliamentary system. And it was not necessarily seen as very good to call a referendum at the same time as an election in Quebec.

So in view of the obstacles of the parliamentary system, inspiration came from where you would imagine, the Parliament of the United Kingdom. The Quebec act was largely built with the co-operation of the people who had made or run the 1975 British referendum on staying in or leaving the Common Market. And there is one very major difference that I would like to mention, which is the control of finances—that is, expenditures and contributions of each national committee. Financial control has been part of Quebec's electoral tradition for years now. So, in that sense, it was more British with a Quebec touch to it than Swiss.

I welcome the occasion to get back to the Swiss experience, not for the way it would function in Quebec and I do not think it would, but for what it means ideologically, and I think Mr. Studer's paper does bring out quite a few problems that are most interesting to look at, particularly in the three conclusions. First, if I understand it correctly, participation through referendum is a good thing, especially when it grows out of a people's history. Second, the organization of those presumed less powerful. And the third conclusion is that the use of the referendum itself should be circumscribed at least in terms of the number of times you use it. Evidently, there can be excess in that field. I am no expert on Switzerland at all and I shall not try to pass any kind of judgement on the Swiss referendum, but I would like to attempt to draw some kind of a relationship between the Swiss experience and what is going on in Quebec, basically around the referendum and perhaps beyond the referendum.

Before doing that, I would like to get all this linked in with the themes of this conference generally, if it is possible to do so. So, I thought I would take a few minutes to mention a couple of assumptions. To start, I will tell you a short and true story. On 5 July 1966, I was, like a lot of people in Quebec, sitting at home watching television. The occasion was Quebec's general election. I never look at elections with a lot of people. I prefer to listen to every word, follow all the ridings, and what not. So, I managed to look at this with just one friend who was a student of mine, a student in political science at the college level. I was teaching in those days at the University of Montreal.

The 5 July 1966 election is the one, if you remember, where Mr. Lesage's government was defeated by Daniel Johnson's Union Nationale Party and that was a terrible shock for a lot of people. It looked like Quebec was headed back twenty years, back to the Dark Ages, back to the Middle Ages. The fellow I was with even went so far as to cry, very generously. He cried all evening. He intended to go into political science and kept asking himself: ''what am I going to do in political science—there is nothing to do in political science with a Union Nationale government. You can sell apples, learn to play the violin, but don't go into political science—there is nothing to do as a political scientist in Quebec with the old style of Union Nationale government.'' Now, this fellow did stick to political science, his name is Michel Carpentier. Just ten years and three months later, November 1976, and that is not very long, Michel Carpentier was the chief organizer of the Parti Québécois when it won the 1976 election. I am not trying to get a positive judgement on what he did. I would just like to get across the message that here was a twenty-year-old student who felt politically helpless, and ten years later the party he helped to build was in office. Now, I could talk about this for hours, but I would just like you to keep in the back of your minds that throughout those ten, there had to be a strong attachment to a certain number of basic values.

I think there has to be a very strong faith in people generally. You have to believe that people would do something if you got out there and worked with them. And faith in people is the basis of faith in democracy. There is a certain belief in the impossible. I think naïvety or idealism is too easily discredited in politics. They have, on the contrary, a very important part to play in politics. I do not think it is very good if you rely on naïvety alone: the point is that you really have to say, "I am going to put up with this whatever the cost." In addition, of course, you must have also a rather tremendous will and capacity to organize and to work against all kinds of opposition. This was the experience during the years the Parti Québécois was growing. Money was always on the other side and political authority was all on the other side. Statistics were all on the other side too; you had to fight those too and not to speak of ideology.

In those ten years, we were generally being called Communists. You are a Communist one day and something else the next. When flying to Halifax the other day, I was reading an article by Walter P. Stewart in the *Atlantic Advocate*. I do not know how but it turned out I was a National Socialist; I was just one step away from being a Nazi in Quebec. This kind of thing is really hard on your nerves as you go along, not to mention October 1970.

In this conference, what I would like to do is to get across the message—I am not asking you to be for or against it—and this is that what was done in Quebec during those years testifies to an attachment to, in the words of this conference, citizen involvement, popular control. There was a lot of faith in both, or nothing like this would have happened. I think citizen involvement was not a slogan, not even just an idea. It was what made, according to a lot of people, 15 November 1976 possible.* I believe that the ideals of the sixties are still with us but that they are stronger, contrary to what has been said; I believe that there is no such thing as citizens' non-interest in government, and in that sense, I do not know how you could not be interested in people who spend your money. It is very difficult not to be interested. There is, however, I believe, such a thing as governments who are not interested in citizens. Marjorie Hartling yesterday expressed that for a very important group of citizens. If there is a problem of lack of interest, it is one that the government has, I believe, much more than the people. I believe that if citizens do not show an interest in the existing political system, then changes should be made to the existing political system. I am not sure this conference is examining, as closely as it could, the errors of the system as much as it worries about the apparent lack of attention given to it by the electorate. I believe that those changes, when they are made, should be made in favour of citizens who need government most, not necessarily those who enjoy government most. And I think there can be and I think there are political parties who do not just like elections. There are political parties—and there are more than one—which are effective community channels for ideas, which are effective instruments of social consciousness, and which are mechanisms for implementing popular authority and popular control. I think there can be and I think there are governments that do believe in people very strongly.

I also believe that democracy is more than an idea; it is a relatively slow, progressive, trial and error, success and failure process. It cannot be judged too quickly. We have a tendency to do that. Governments ask for at least four years before they are judged. Why not give at least as much time before judging citizen operations? I believe the basic question for a civil servant to ask himself is not do the people understand what we are doing, but do we understand what people want. They certainly do not want to be left alone, or if they do, I am sure that they prefer not to have to pay for it! Those are just basic assumptions made rapidly without argument.

I would like to get back to Mr. Studer's paper, which I read over and over again. It was my first contact with this type of paper and it is a very balanced interpretation. When discussing the Swiss process of government, we generally get a kind of dream paper, you could call it a romantic interpretation of Switzerland—it is wonderful, it is beautiful, and it has no problems.

Well actually it is the other way around. Switzerland is where people are always voting every morning and Mr. Studer's paper tended to balance this out with a strong accent on the problems. Still, his conclusions do come down to the fact that participation through referendum is a good idea. It is an important idea but it should be reworked. In that sense, I have attempted to make some links between the Swiss experience and Quebec's experience based on his three conclusions.

The first conclusion is concerned with the individual's opportunity to participate. The referendum, he says, is an opportunity to participate and help in the process of problem solving, especially when it stems from the historic evolution of the society. That I believe is important, and it is being overlooked in the Canada-Quebec debate. Too many people see this as a break with evolution. I believe there is more to it than that. I really think in Quebec there is more attachment to evolution.

The history of Quebec in one way can very easily be seen as the evolution of a society without power, without any kind of community power. It is a society evolving from a normal situation where people discover themselves to one where they discover some kind of confidence in themselves and give themselves the political authority that goes with that confidence. In that sense, Quebec's history represents an evolution from a French commercial colony to a French Crown colony, then a period of British military conquest and rule, followed by the status of British Crown colony, and then Confederation.

There is not much popular authority through Confederation, however. I believe there is quite a bit of truth in the theory that Confederation, to a large extent, is a pretty proper deal between the Church in Quebec and the English merchants of Montreal, resulting in a pact through which the Church gave the merchants a rather passive labour force prepared for its reward in eternity and, in the meantime, enjoying low wages and hard conditions as proof that they are getting there anyway. It is ideal for a labour force and the other way around. What the Church got back from the merchants, I believe, is no government or the least government possible. No need for government or political authority, the Church will do it for you.

There have recently been two very important events in Quebec's history evolving towards normal, collective, political authority. One is the 1960 election. Mr. Lesage's election represents the first major, social reconciliation of an urban society with itself. Everything in Quebec until 1960 was rurally oriented. Political authority was based upon rural parties, rural ideas, and rural theories, in line with the way Quebec had been organized years before. What was important about 1960 is that for the first time in Quebec's history, an urban party with urban ideas, an urban administration took over. And that reconciliation was, I think, very basic. To do that, Mr. Lesage had to push back the church: not the church on a religious basis, but on a political basis. One of the two partners of Confederation, if that theory is the correct one, had to be pushed out of the way. The repeal of the Church's political authorities was the necessary foundation for the quiet revolution of the 1960s.

In the same sense, the 1976 election is a second, profound occasion of spiritual reconciliation. This was the first time in the history of Quebec that a party came right out of the French majority without its hands linked to any financial powers, without belonging to anybody else but to that majority. That party came not from an established organization but through popular support. That I call a spiritual reconciliation of a society with itself. The role of that party had to be the second step in pulling apart the deal of 1867. Mr Lesage had to push the church back to build a democratic modern urban society. Necessarily the Parti Québécois' role was to push back to a certain extent the other port; the contract of the English merchants of Montreal. The private aspect of the Quebec economy had to be opened to a French-speaking society in Quebec. That is simply normal political evolution.

Concerning Mr. Studer's second basic conclusion, I would like to say just a few words on the size of things. Switzerland always comes across as being small. The smallness is perhaps important for democracy. Bigness breeds bureaucracy and bureaucracy breeds citizen apathy by cutting off the citizen from government. Yesterday, some people spoke of the party system, the importance of the party system. I believe that, fundamentally, there is no popular democratic government on any kind of a long-term basis without the presence of political parties that are not just election war machines. I am very pleased in that sense to pay a short tribute to Mr. Claude Ryan, who in one year has transformed the Liberal Party into something more of a democratic institution in Quebec. I am very proud that Quebec does espouse two, not only one, political parties. Both are much more than war machines. The referendum will be extraordinarily interesting in that sense—you have two—much more than just organizations facing each other—but two sets of networks, social and internal networks, where people meet. There will be a lot of interest throughout the referendum on that basis.

The third conclusion that Mr. Studer draws is about political mechanisms that disadvantage certain groups. In that sense, I have found this conference a little timid, a little shy on hitting at institutions. I am afraid we are protecting our institutions a bit too much. I do not think, for example, that streamlining the rules of the House constitutes electoral reform or parliamentary reform or getting to the things that people need. Much more basic reform is needed, for instance, concerning the electoral law and the electoral system. I think many things have to be looked at straight in the eye in our institutions. A lot of things we have taken for granted for centuries should be looked at again and acted upon more closely, and it will take courage to change them.

By way of conclusion, just a word on the frequency of referendum votes. Take note that I do not think the frequency of votes in Switzerland would be a very strong temptation any place else. We have to thank Switzerland for that. Nobody would get into any kind of a situation where we would have daily or weekly votes and referenda. I would like to stress, though, that the Quebec legislation is not a referendum act for one referendum only, contrary to what has been said. I believe it is an enabling act. The government is committed to holding more than one referendum. It is committed to the use of the referendum as a tool of political participation, of popular consultation. It is also committed to introducing progressively the popular initiative and I think that is very important, but we want to do it progressively. Once we have been through a few referenda—government-initiated referenda—the government is prepared to set up referenda through popular initiative. In fact, over a very short time, we in Quebec have been trying to do a lot of things. I am not saying we are doing them correctly, but we are trying to do a lot of things, particularly in terms of electoral reform. That is my department especially. We had lots of help from California on our Bill 2, a lot of help from the United Kingdom on our referendum act, a lot of help from the Federal Republic of Germany on a proposition that will come out very shortly [24 April 1980] on a new electoral system for Quebec. I should hope that this conference has given us a close look at the constitution of Switzerland. Mr. Studer told me that there is a report on revamping the entire Swiss system, so maybe we could have the advantage of starting off anew from there.

NOTE

* The date of election of the Parti Québécois as the government of Quebec.

Chapter Nine

The Limits of the Law in Advancing
Public Participation

by
Gérard V. LaForest

Democracy and public participation are concepts that go together naturally. Our democratic ideals flow back to the Greek city state where each citizen could participate in government decisions. This approach, however, can only function fully in a small, closely knit society. In the larger, more complex, Western democracies, direct democracy has been replaced by representative democracy, and political theorists have until recent years been far more concerned with the notion of representation than public participation.[1]

The law, of course, reflected political theory. The powers of legislatures, how our representatives are elected, and so on, have long been carefully defined by law. Participation by the individual in formal political decisions, however, was left to what political or other influences individuals could bring to bear on their representatives. Few formal legal mechanisms existed to promote public participation. The law was content to accord to those who wished to participate wide freedom and protection in expressing and advancing political views.

In assessing the limits of the law in advancing public participation, it is well for us to remember how little of social activity was regulated by laws made by political authorities until this century. Organized municipalities were few, suffrage was not universal, and there were few laws governing economic activity. In fact, because there was little legislative interference with the legal rights flowing from concepts like property and contract, many of the most important decisions affecting society were taken by private individuals or corporations, leaving little room for public participation.

What I have thus far said has to do with the making of laws. Until this century, the application of law was left largely to the courts, and here there was even less room for public participation. So far as actual decisions, we have long learned the value of independent judges applying predetermined principles.[2] It is true, of course, that for many years, juries determined the facts in both civil and criminal cases. Civil juries have now largely been abolished for reasons of efficiency, except for cases closely related to community values such as those for defamation. Criminal juries, however, still afford members of the public an opportunity to soften the rigours of the law in individual cases and to make it conform to community values.

Members of the public may also initiate action in the criminal justice process. Private prosecutions may potentially be a useful technique for public participation by means of the courts. Summary conviction offences in federal and provincial environmental and consumer protection statutes may be initiated by a private citizen. Major advantages of such actions are that they attract media attention and are not too costly, particularly if the services of a public interest lawyer are obtained. One of the great disadvantages to this technique is that the information necessary to a successful prosecution may not be available to the citizen. This, indeed, applies to most forms of public participation.

Civil actions may at times also be used as a technique for advancing public participation, but the potential public interest advocate has many hurdles to overcome. This is hardly surprising. Civil actions were really never framed to advance public participation. They were intended to enforce rights, largely private rights, arising out of property, contract or, occasionally, a right to redress a tort, or civil wrong. There are no legal rights respecting many of the claims where demands for public participation are increasingly made. The stuff of a legal right is a specific claim, susceptible of satisfaction by specific action. The decisions where public participation is sought usually involve broad claims—largely respecting the environment, consumer protection, or basic social values—that require a wide variety of ongoing decisions for their resolution.

Take, for example, claims respecting the environment.[3] An individual may sue if he suffers injury to his property from some development, but he is not, of course, the public and, in any event, property rights do not include many claims that are now forcefully advanced. The individual, let alone the public, has no right to a view or generally to light and air. That property rights can afford a powerful instrument for public participation in the environmental field can be seen from the incidental protection to the environment flowing from the quasi-proprietary land claims of the Indians and Inuit. But it is evident that a judicially enforceable public right in the environment would pose awesome definitional problems and, in consequence, a heavy and unpredictable burden on entrepreneurs. A legal right must either be so defined as to make court action reasonably predictable, or it must be left to administrative authorities to define on the basis of ongoing policy development and assessment of changing factual situations. As will be seen later, the latter approach can allow for significant opportunities for public participation.

Tort actions (claims for civil wrongs) have more potential to advance public participation. But, again, these are generally available only to the individual. There is, it is true, an action for a public nuisance but it is extremely restricted. Moreover, a person has no standing to bring the action unless he has suffered "special damages" in addition to that suffered by the public generally, unless the attorney-general joins the action.

Similar problems of standing apply when members of the public seek judicial review of administrative action. Indeed, in the case of mandamus—the traditional prerogative writ against inaction by administrative authorities—there is a more fundamental impediment to judicial review. Few statutes impose a positive duty on government officials; they ordinarily only give them a discretion to act. In any event, judicial review of administrative action is largely confined to jurisdictional and procedural questions; it does not go to the merits of decisions.

Apart from the criminal process, the technique that probably offers the greatest potential for public participation by means of the judicial process is the class action.[4] This is particularly true in the consumer field. A class action is one in which the plaintiff claims not only for himself but also on behalf of others in the same situation. From a procedural standpoint, it is obviously a sensible device. By permitting a single determination of similar claims, it effects significant economies in time, effort, and expense. From the standpoint of public participation, it has the advantage of mass determination of numerous claims that might not be determined at all. For example, if a utility company charges a rate slightly higher than it is authorized to do, it would hardly be worth the time and expense for a single individual to sue. The aggregate claims are another thing. Class actions, therefore, can be effective in compensating consumers and forcing dishonest businessmen to account for improper profits. Above all, they can serve as a deterrent to improper practices and thereby constitute an additional technique of law enforcement.

Class actions are not without disadvantages of a social and technical nature. Some argue that they are slow and cumbersome, would unduly add to the work of the courts, and are a potential source of considerable expense and harassment to legitimate business out of all proportion to the violations they are intended to remedy. Such criticisms must be given due weight. And consideration must also be given to whether other measures of enforcement may not be more effective.[5]

Still there is much to be said for the view of Justice Douglas of the Supreme Court of the United States, that "[t]he class action is one of the few legal remedies the small claimant has against those who command the status quo" and that we must aim towards "creating a system of law that dispenses justice to the lowly as well as to those liberally endowed with power and wealth."[6] No business is more legitimate than the Ford Motor Company, for example, but few consumers would feel the "rusty Ford" class action constituted harassment out of proportion to the violation. For that reason, the legislatures should consider removing some of the technical defects to class actions, notably by reforming the law regarding costs. The fact that the initiator of a class action must bear the costs if he loses, and that even if he wins, he is only entitled to a portion of his costs, powerfully inhibits the use of this remedy. There are, as well, other problems such as those concerning notice to class members, the requirement of a "common interest," and so on, that also merit legislative action.

Much attention has been given to improving not only class actions but other aspects of legal procedure to advance the public participation of citizens in the courts—for example, by broadening standing to sue and by giving more substantive rights to the public. Something can and ought certainly to be done in this direction, but too much should not be expected. The structured procedure of courts, the nature of the evidence they require, the costs of judicial proceedings, and above all the fact that courts generally act *ex post facto* seriously limit their potential for advancing public participation.

The simple truth is that in focusing on courts and legislatures, we are dealing with institutions and with legal rules developed before the creation of the modern administrative state. Too many view law and judicial action as synonymous. Though judicial action may be a useful tool in the armory of those seeking public participation, it represents a relatively small, if at times crucial, part of the role of law in our society. Today, as I mentioned before, law impinges in many areas of social life not formerly subjected to public decision. That being so, we would do well to devote most of our attention to the new instruments of the administrative state if we wish to extend the role of law in advancing public participation. If we are to promote public participation, we must act before private rights are created and while they are still being determined. The courts are not the appropriate agencies for this. And neither in many cases are legislatures. Particular matters may require specific and ongoing attention. Issues may not be sufficiently focused to allow for effective public participation at the legislative stage.

That is why we have administrative agencies of all kinds and at all levels of government. It was largely through these agencies that the law moved to transfer ultimate responsibility for decisions having broad social impact from the private to the public sector. Where a developer before might have been free to decide where and how he should build, he now must obtain permission from a community planning authority acting in accordance with zoning, subdivision, and other by-laws. And the authority may have had considerable influence in the development of these by-laws. Many administrative authorities are, in fact, given broad powers to develop policy. There are agencies, it is true, where participation must often be largely limited to those who have a direct interest in the subject matter. This may be because an agency is in effect a specialized court—for example, the Immigration Appeal Board—or because of the personalized nature of the decision—for example the National Parole Board. But when the National Energy Board is authorized to license pipelines on the basis of "public convenience and necessity," it is authorized to devise policy, to make laws. The same is true of many other federal and provincial administrative bodies. In short, many are subordinate law-making bodies, and it is legitimate that the governed participate in their processes.

It is, therefore, at the level of administrative discretion and decision that we must concentrate most of our energies if we wish to use the law to expand public participation. Though created to advance the public interest, administrative authorities can become largely divorced from the concerns of the public unless they develop techniques for opening their processes to the public at every level. Public participation is required not only to respond to the democratic needs and desires of citizens to influence public decision. It is required as well to sensitize those who make decisions to the multi-dimensional aspects of the public interest and to the general and specific impacts of their decisions. In short, public participation before administrative authorities can not only foster more legitimate and acceptable decisions; it can promote more informed and effective decisions.

The precise techniques to achieve public participation must vary from one administrative authority to another. No general rule can be made. The Law Reform Commission of Canada has been engaged, for the last several years, in an extensive study of the broad problems associated with procedures before administrative tribunals.[7] If there is anything we have learned, it is that specific techniques must be devised for each separate administrative body. There are no panaceas. But there are overarching principles, and we can identify the areas where action is required. I will now speak briefly of some of the areas requiring attention in advancing public participation before administrative agencies.

Membership: As in the case of legislatures, there is room for representative democracy on some administrative boards by naming as members persons who represent particular interests. Provincial labour relations boards, for example, have representatives from labour and management. This is no substitute for participation by individual members of the public, however, since we have found that members of administrative authorities over time tend to share a common approach. But representative membership does tend to broaden that approach and give greater legitimacy and credibility to their activities. Legitimacy and credibility are enhanced, as well, when professional governing bodies have lay members. Closely related to this are situations where an administrative authority makes use of either *ad hoc* or permanent advisory committees representing a variety of interests. Such techniques can be required by law in appropriate cases.

Access: If we favour public participation, we must give as much access as possible to the individual to make representations to administrative tribunals. At the federal level, at least, administrative agencies exercising functions having considerable policy, as opposed to primarily judicial, content have been responsive to the need to grant standing to individuals and groups who wish to participate in hearings. But far more is needed if we are to advance public participation. More innovative notice techniques have to be developed to inform the public about hearings and other agency activities. A formal notice of hearing in the *Canada Gazette* is unlikely to attract a crowd. Apart from notification in the regular media, an agency could inform people or organizations it knows or suspects have an interest in the subject matter. More effort could also be taken to inform the public of an agency's activities on an ongoing basis.

I am aware that too much public intervention can interfere with the efficiency of an agency and add materially to its costs of operation. It should not, however, be forgotten that there are considerable benefits served by public participation, not only in terms of democratic theory but to the efficiency and effectiveness of agencies. There are, in any event, useful techniques for reducing excessive and unproductive intervention. Examples are screening of participants at pre-hearing conferences, an insistence that an intervener's position be stated in writing beforehand, and consolidation of interventions representing substantially the same point of view.

At times, public intervention may be supplemented by other techniques. For example, a component of an agency could be set up to represent the public interest, or again a governmental body outside the agency might be set up to defend the public interest. On the whole, these have not proved as satisfactory as intervention by the public at large, but under certain circumstances such techniques may be useful. Even more effective are "public interest" lawyers and organizations.

Information:[8] What public interest interveners need most for meaningful participation in the administrative process is information. Without it, public participation becomes a mere public relations exercise. Most administrative authorities are niggardly about the information they supply the public. Many administrative agencies do not even have written rules and, in some cases, the rules of those that do are not easy to obtain. On the substantive side, it is simply not possible to participate intelligently in proceedings involving a proposed project without being privy to the information on which the proposal is based.

The courts will compel the revelation of information to participants at formal hearings when that information may affect a decision. But information generated before a hearing, such as staff studies, is essential to the proper preparation of a submission before an agency. Ultimately, the solution to problems of this kind is freedom of information legislation. I am aware, of course, that there are limits to the information that can be supplied to participants. Individual privacy, confidential business information, and security must be protected. But properly framed exceptions and adequate procedures for weighing the competing claims of freedom of information and confidentiality are obviously what are required here.

Time: Interveners also need time to respond. Cases abound where planners have worked on a scheme for months and years, and the public is given a matter of weeks to respond. This occurred, for example, in relation to the impact assessment procedures respecting the proposal to build a nuclear energy plant at Lepreau, New Brunswick.[9] Interested parties were given three weeks to comment on complex technical reports that had taken a year and a half to prepare. Obviously, enough time must be allowed to absorb the information and test the assumptions of those proposing a project. Provisions for notice could take this into account.

Procedures: Much can be done to foster public participation by properly framed procedures. Formal court-like hearings to determine particular applications make public participation difficult and expensive. Some agencies—notably the CRTC—have helped to promote public participation by informal hearings. In any case, what participants are usually more interested in, and where their contribution is usually most valuable, is in relation to the broad policy grounds on which specific applications are determined. Different kinds of hearings may be called for to determine policy. These can be less formal than hearings to determine specific applications, and so less expensive. They can also settle a general course of action once and for all (or at least for some time). They can, therefore, prove more efficient for an agency. And it is also far more convenient for interveners. Despite this, most agencies develop policy on a case-by-case basis.

It may be necessary at the inception of a regulatory scheme to develop policy on an incremental basis at specific hearings, but as time goes on, the broad underlying policies are more or less set. Why should people be constrained to determine an agency's policy by reference to previous decisions, sometimes not adequately published, if at all? Why not establish rules? Why not consult the public when these general rules or principles are established? Laws could be so framed as to encourage this type of development.

Costs:[10] Meaningful participation can be expensive. Often legal representation and scientific and other research are required. If we are to look at participation as not just a public relations exercise but as a useful way for agencies to obtain information about all relevant interests so that their decisions may be acceptable and sound, then some means must be found to finance it. Otherwise, only those who have the financial means are represented, an undemocratic situation that is the antithesis of the underlying rationale for public participation. Those who are being regulated are given a say, but often not those for whom a regulatory process is established.

One of the means of financing public participation is by awarding costs to participants—as the CRTC does—when they make a useful contribution to an agency's deliberations. But who is to pay these costs? An obvious way in some instances is to award them to the applicant for a government licence or privilege. This is then passed on to those who use the services of the applicant and thus directly benefit from the intervention. Another way is to establish a public fund out of which such costs are paid. Government can also assist, as it has, in fostering public interest groups, such as the Consumers' Association of Canada.

What I have thus far said, though hardly new to those who have thought about the subject, is far from being realized in practice except in specific instances. Yet it is far removed from the structural legal changes that have to be effected if we are to move closer to the ideal of participation by the public in decisions that affect them. Generally, a member of the public can only participate at the later stages of the planning process. The issues have already been formulated—not only that an airport must be built, but where. Indeed, often the public's first opportunity for participation is in a process that was never intended for the purpose. Thus pre-expropriation hearings under the federal *Expropriation Act* are frequently the occasion for members of the public, not only to make objections to the expropriation of particular land, for which the hearing is intended, but to question whether the project for which the expropriation will take place is necessary and whether some alternative site might not be better.[11]

Many other structural difficulties to effective participation in the planning process could be mentioned. Sometimes a decision is pre-empted because a series of low visibility minor approvals from separate departments or agencies have been obtained and financial commitments undertaken on the strength of these. Again, there are few statutes permitting a citizen to take the initiative—to ensure, for example, that certain lands are retained for recreation. Usually, he must wait until someone proposes some development in the area before he has an opportunity to do something.

I have not, as you will surmise, begun to describe the limits of the law in advancing public participation. Those limits have yet to be explored. That is hardly surprising. For as Léon Dion has noted, until the last few years, "Western liberal political philosophers [had] made little effort to develop a theory of political participation."[12] Under these circumstances, can it be expected that the law should yet have moved beyond mere groping? What movement there has been, however, seems to have been in the most appropriate areas. Dion noted that there is more potentiality for real participation in the new and less formal modes of participation than in the more traditional forms. As he puts it, "Nothing less is needed than . . . the creation of an elaborate network of mechanisms of participation throughout the planning apparatus."[13]

The law can be a major tool in this endeavour. Where in the past it concentrated on rights, it must now concentrate on structures and on goals. It must provide for and insist that those who wield economic or political power listen to and accommodate public concerns. Statutes can be so written as to encourage public participation, and procedures can be modified accordingly. Legislative or administrative guide-lines can be developed to assist agencies in developing adequate procedures in this and other fields. And an administrative body can be set up to supervise and promote the adoption of such procedures.

These are but a few of the avenues that can be explored in extending the frontiers of the law in this area. Much, much more remains to be done. It is far too early yet to begin to define the limits of law in advancing public participation.

NOTES

[1] See Léon Dion, "Participating in the Political Process," *Queen's Quarterly* 75 (Autumn 1968): 432-47.

[2] For the dangers of public participation in decisions in the judicial process, see Reginald Allen, "The Trial of Socrates," in *Courts and Trials: A Multidisciplinary Approach*, edited by M.L. Friedland (Toronto: University of Toronto Press, 1975), p. 31.

[3] See Alastair R. Lucas, "Legal Foundations for Public Participation in Environmental Decisionmaking," *Natural Resources Journal* 16 (January 1976): 73-102; R.T. Franson and P.T. Burns, "Environmental Rights for the Canadian Citizen: A Prescription for Reform," *Alberta Law Review* 12 (1974): 153-71.

[4] See Neil J. Williams, "Consumer Class Actions in Canada—Some Proposals for Reform," *Osgoode Hall Law Journal* 13 (1975): 1-88.

[5] See J. Robert S. Prichard and Michael J. Trebilcock, "Class Actions and Private Law Enforcement," *University of New Brunswick Law Journal* 27 (1978): 5-17.

[6] *Elsen v. Carlisle & Jacquelin* (1974), 94 U.S.S. Ct. 2140.

[7] Many of the ideas for this paper flow from the Law Reform Commission of Canada's studies of various federal tribunals, including the following:
— Ian Hunter and Ian Kelly, *The Immigration Appeal Board* (Ottawa: 1976).
— G. Bruce Doern, *The Atomic Energy Control Board* (Ottawa: 1976).
— Pierre Carrière and Sam Silverstone, *The Parole Process* (Ottawa: 1976).
— Pierre Issalys and Gaylord Watkins, *Unemployment Insurance Benefits* (Ottawa: 1977).
— Alastair R. Lucas and Trevor Bell, *The National Energy Board* (Ottawa: 1977).
— H.N. Janisch, A.J. Pirie, and W. Charland, *The Regulatory Process of the Canadian Transport Commission* (Ottawa: 1978).
— Philip Slayton, *The Anti-Dumping Tribunal* (Ottawa: 1979).
— Pierre Issalys, *The Pension Appeals Board* (Ottawa: 1979).
— David Fox, *Public Participation in the Administrative Process* (Ottawa: 1979).
— Stephen Kelleher, *The Canada Labour Relations Board* (Ottawa: 1980).
— Chris Johnston, *Canadian Radio-Television and Communications Commission* (in preparation).
There are also unpublished studies prepared for the commission, including Sandra K. McCallum, "Citizen Participation."

[8] See R.T. Franson, *Access to Information: Independent Administrative Agencies*, a study prepared for the Law Reform Commission of Canada (Ottawa: 1979).

[9] Doern, *op. cit.*

[10] See Sandra K. McCallum and Gaylord Watkins, "Citizens' Costs Before Administrative Tribunals," *Chitty's Law Journal* 23 (1975): 181-90; the article is based on a submission of the Law Reform Commission's Administrative Law Project to the CTC. The commission has proposed that commissions of inquiry be empowered to pay expenses of interveners: *Administrative Law; Commissions of Inquiry*, Working Paper No. 17 (Ottawa: 1977), pp. 28, 54.

[11] See *Expropriation*, Working Paper No. 9 (Ottawa: 1975), pp. 24-28; *Report on Expropriation* (Ottawa: 1976), pp. 10-12.

[12] Dion, *op. cit.*, p. 432.

[13] *Ibid.*, p. 445.

Chapter Ten

Regulation and Public Participation: Recent Versus Desirable Trends

by
William A.W. Neilson

INTRODUCTION

In this paper, I propose to analyse the relationship between the regulatory process and citizen involvement in Canada. I will probably trespass on some of the points raised by Dr. LaForest, but I hope that these unintended incursions will be viewed in a complementary light. I will explore the objectives and the operations of our regulatory agencies, both provincial and federal, and assess the opportunities for public participation before these agencies.

In particular, I will argue that the time is ripe for a clarification of regulatory goals, procedures, and public accountability. As part of this appraisal, it is to be hoped that fresh attention will be paid to the question of public access to the decision-making process of our regulatory bodies. Among other matters, this should profitably involve some new thinking on the difference between adjudicative-type duties and policy-making responsibilities of regulatory agencies. Although the dividing line between these two tasks is not always clear, the more the agency in question gets into a rule-making capacity, then the more we should be thinking about the "participation points" for the representatives of public interest groups.

Finally, I will make a few comments on the question of cabinet or ministerial involvement in the regulatory system and its implications for public access to the system. My conclusion may be shortly stated: while there is growing evidence that provincial and federal cabinets are exercising more direct political control and influence over regulatory agencies—breaking the mystique of the "technical experts" and recognizing that "the regulatory process is in very large part a political process"—this assumption of executive direction is not necessarily synonymous with the development of an accessible, reasoned, and fair system of decision making. The system may well be more politically responsive, but more in the direction of permanent, well-funded, professionally staffed pressure groups than of public interest groupings and coalitions and individual citizens.

Regulation is the newest buzz-word in political, legal, and economic circles—its ascendancy marks a fever-level interest in the growth and importance of statutory regulation in Canada. The interest is evidenced, perhaps most significantly, in the establishment of a national inquiry called the Regulation Reference established by the federal and provincial governments under the aegis of the Economic Council of Canada,[1] and by separate studies such as the Regulation and Government Intervention Program of this conference's co-sponsor, The Institute for Research on Public Policy. Interest in the general subject area is further borne out by the ambitious series of studies of federal agencies sponsored by the Law Reform Commission of Canada,[2] the 1978 report on government regulation of the Ontario Economic Council, and the influential writings of commentators like Messrs. Doern, Stanbury, Janisch, Hartle, and Trebilcock, to name but a few.

In my own province of British Columbia, however, we have achieved the unique situation of having a minister for deregulation appointed at the time of the last Cabinet shuffle in December 1978. At that time, the gentleman in question variously described his task as "cutting red tape," "reducing the paper burden" in dealing with government, "getting rid of useless statutes and regulations," and "cutting back" on unnecessary or inefficient government regulation.[3] Such is the apparent determination of the government to accomplish these many tasks that the ministry has been given but two years to perform its surgery because after two years, Canada's first "sunset" ministry is to self-destruct, a victim of its own success. Students of institutional survival will be watching with interest as the second anniversary date approaches.

So it is not surprising that the topic of regulation is on our agenda—it is certainly on the lips of politicians of every stripe and analysts of every persuasion and discipline.

At this point, allow me to define more precisely the type of regulatory activity that I want to discuss today. In basic terms, my "model of regulatory intervention . . . is the semi-autonomous regulatory agency created with a broad legislative mandate to act in the public interest," a definition gratefully borrowed from the 1978 study on government regulation by the Ontario Economic Council. As pointed out in that report's summary:

> Governments, in addition to administering a vast network of regulations through traditional departments, also delegate general regulatory powers to a host of independent or quasi-independent agencies that they create for the purpose. These may be designated as boards, commissions, councils or have other titles. Whatever the nomenclature, the numerous regulatory agencies can and do impose a multitude of rules and regulations that have, in aggregate, a great influence on many activities, both economic and non-economic, throughout the country.[4]

Until recently, there was very little public understanding about the economic and political significance of these diverse activities. Although important work has been done by Professor Brown-John[5] and initiatives have been taken under the auspices of the Regulation Reference, we do not even have a firm fix on the number of such agencies in Canada today. I might also acknowledge here the helpful work of the Canadian Consumer Council[6] and the Law Reform Commission of Canada. Suffice to say that there appear to be more than 1,000 regulatory agencies of the type described presently operating in Canada in such diverse areas as energy planning, public utilities' rate setting, broadcasting, all forms of transportation, agricultural products marketing, environmental protection, securities, the arts, industrial relations and, of course, liquor and lotteries.

Because the regulatory presence operating by way of delegated power has heretofore been studied in an *ad hoc*, piecemeal fashion in most jurisdictions, it comes as a surprise to first-time researchers when they collect data on regulation. In British Columbia, for example, the first systematic search was not conducted until 1978,[7] and based along the general lines of the semi-autonomous agency described above, over fifty statutorily created agencies were quickly identified. The more prominent included the B.C. Energy Commission, the Agricultural Land Commission, the Pollution Control Board, the Motor Carrier Commission, and a total of twelve marketing boards.

By indicating these numbers, my only intention is to underline the significance in everyday terms of regulatory activity in Canada. This is not the place, nor am I qualified, to debate whether Canada has too much or too little regulation. Happily, that task is for the Regulation Reference to resolve, and it will be a minor miracle if they accomplish that part of their mandate. In the preliminary report issued in November 1978, the chairman of the Economic Council adroitly noted:

> [w]hile those who are alarmed at the growth (and costs) of government regulation have been most vocal, the demands for new and/or higher regulatory standards in various areas have been far from insignificant. It is, moreover, a mark of the complexity of the general subject that, in some cases, the strongest proponents of continued and increased regulation are not consumer groups but business and producer interests. . . . At this early point . . . the Economic Council cannot even begin to appraise the conflicting demands for less regulation by some Canadians and the demands for more regulation by others.[8]

SOME ASPECTS OF THE REGULATORY PROCESS RELEVANT TO CITIZEN INVOLVEMENT

A. Delegation of Powers

The focus of our discussion is the semi-autonomous agency established by statute to deal with a particular problem of public policy. Their *functions* are normally clear from their founding legislation, and there is a basic assumption that they are to be conducted ''in the public interest.'' How—that is, the *objectives* of their functions—the agency is to accomplish its statutory purpose generally is left by the legislators to the members of the agency to work out on their own—sometimes on a case-by-case basis, sometimes by way of policy rules evolved and identified as such, and sometimes by a combination of both processes in which the statements of basic policy and principle are given a more detailed meaning and interpretation in the individual cases decided by the tribunal. Thus, the B.C. Motor Carrier Commission is told by Section 37 of the *Motor Carrier Act*:

> It is the duty of the Commission to regulate motor carriers with the objects of promoting adequate and efficient service and reasonable and just charges therefore, and of promoting safety on the public highways, and of fostering sound economic conditions in the transportation business in the Province, and the Commission may make such investigations and inquiries and such regulations and orders as it deems to be necessary for the carrying-out of such objects.[9]

Similarly, the object of B.C.'s Agricultural Land Commission is to ''preserve agricultural land,'' and ''encourage the . . . preservation of farms,''[10] and the Pollution Control Board of British Columbia has the power and duty, *inter alia*, ''to prescribe standards regarding the quality and character of the effluent or contaminant which may be discharged into any waters, land or air.''[11]

In each case, and these are only examples for present purposes, it is either clearly stated or assumed in the statutes establishing the agencies that their objectives will be pursued *in the public interest*. As Professor Brown-John has argued, it follows that the

> activities of statutory agencies charged with regulative responsibilities are an intrical component of public policy evolution in the context of a particular field.[12]

While it is to be admitted that ''a fairly high proportion'' of regulatory statutes either ''do not contain any statement regarding the objectives of the legislation'' or ''often'' contain conflicting objectives in the same statute,[13] the fact remains that, in most cases, the most important policy-making responsibilities are initially left to the agencies. This has not happened by accident. Various explanations have been given for the creation of these largely autonomous agencies. As one American commentator recently observed:

> In theory, Congress created regulatory agencies and gave them power because it had neither the time nor the expertise to do the regulating itself.[14]

Others trace the establishment of the agencies in the 1930s and 1940s

> to the view that most major policy issues were susceptible of ''right answers'', if only enough *experts* were given enough time and enough resources to analyse them. Policy issues were thus conceived of as susceptible of objective resolution against a discoverable talisman of technical virtuosity.[15]

In recent years, however, the realization has struck home that a good amount of the regulatory process "is not merely a technocratic search for scientifically 'right answers',"[16] but rather, in K. Kernaghan's words, that "the regulatory process is in very large part a political process." He goes on:

> Regulatory agencies are involved in politics in the sense of the authoritative allocation of society's resources. The agencies contribute significantly to the development and implementation of public policy through their discretionary powers to make decisions in particular cases and to interpret the very general policy guidelines contained in their constituent acts. Some agencies contribute directly to policy formation by providing advice to the government in the policy field for which they have regulatory responsibilities.[17]

As Professor Jaffe noted in 1956,

> ... the autonomy of 'expertness' as an objective determinant of policy is, I am afraid, an illusion. Policy-making *is* politics.[18]

We have thus begun to recognize, at least in the case of those regulatory agencies that formulate their own policies or exercise their own form of legislative authority, that their jurisdictions are very wide ranging and more self-defined than delegated. To some observers, they are a separate executive. These perceptions of their powers and operations are interesting in several respects. First, their pivotal political role has long been appreciated and acted upon by the business and professional interests directly regulated or otherwise affected by their deliberations. The broadcasting licensee, the trucking firm, and the telephone utility have known the score since Day One. But, and this is the second point, the "public interest" connotations of their decision-making process were not firmly identified until the 1960s and 1970s as consumer groups, community organizations, and *ad hoc* pressure groups sought access to agency hearings and conferences. The door opener is the duty of the agency to act "in the public interest." As one observer has put it:

> ... a statutory agency charged with acting in the public interest must be seen to be acting in the public interest. "Being seen" involves the pluralist requirement of access and provision of access to the policy process by parties or persons principally concerned with the specific area of policy. Public interest, while often considered vague in meaning, is interpreted in this context as "policies government would pursue if it gave equal weight to the welfare of every member of society." Access is interpreted to mean the implicit or explicit rules of procedure which permit reasonable participation by interested parties in proceedings before statutory agencies.[19]

B. Access to the Regulatory Process

Once the pivotal significance of regulation in Canada and the weighing of choices that goes on in that process have been appreciated, the *merit* of public access to these agencies attracts little debate. Speaking of the U.S. experience—and his remarks are quite applicable to the Canadian situation—Robert Reich recently observed that regulatory agencies are or should be in the business of reconciling the diverse and often conflicting demands of competing interest groups. Accordingly, administrative law and procedure should have as their aim the adequate representation of all interests affected by the agency, and agency policy-making should reflect adequate consideration of all of these interests.

The intellectual foundations of this premise [of political responsiveness] lie deep in democratic theory. Not only is it assumed that regulatory decisions will better match the "public interest" if those whose interests are affected participate in them, but the very process of public involvement and scrutiny is deemed to be a public good, encouraging confidence in regulatory fairness and reducing the sense of alienation and helplessness that bureaucracies inspire. Moreover, fundamental principles of fairness dictate that individuals should be represented in decisions that seriously affect their own welfare.[20]

The legal means by which citizen involvement has been recognized and advanced have been discussed in a more general context by Dr. LaForest. In terms of specific experience, we may point to the proposed procedures of the Canadian Radio-television and Telecommunications Commission[21] governing its conduct of telecommunications hearings, and at the provincial level, the programme of the Alberta Public Utilities Board[22] whereby the advocacy costs of non-industrial user groups are recovered through cost awards of the board against the utility companies. These are but two examples of what is happening, at least in some cases, in turning a perceived *need*, if not *right*, of public access into an economically viable *practice* of consumer-citizen participation in regulatory policy making.

Public or citizen participation comes at two levels. The first is the *individual* level; the second might be described as the *representational* level. In the first situation, the citizen participant is in a position analogous to that of a litigant or a person directly affected or aggrieved by a decision made or to be made by a regulatory body. In the second situation, the citizen intervener participates as a representative or advocate of a more broadly based constituency, often described as a public interest lobby group, community organization, or consumer group.

Keeping in mind that we are dealing here with agencies operating outside departmental structures on the basis of delegated authority (and that we are also excluding *ad hoc* bodies and tribunals such as public inquiries and royal commissions), let us turn to the relationship between these two levels of citizen involvement and the regulators' discharge of their statutory responsibilities. The more that an agency is engaged in the adjudication of specific, competing claims, the higher the incidence of *individual* citizen involvement.

The individuals, for instance, may be two truckers arguing over the granting of a carrier licence where one already has a licence for the route in question and the second seeks a licence, perhaps on slightly different grounds, for the same route. The normal situation in those provinces maintaining this system of trucking regulation is for these two immediate interests to argue their case and then for the commission, with or without written reasons, to make its decision. In the great majority of such cases, they are the only citizens, corporate or otherwise, to appear and to involve themselves. Administrative law, including the potential for judicial review in certain circumstances, has focused in the last two decades (excessively in the view of some observers) on the protection of procedural fairness in the handling of these adjudicatory functions.

Let me return to my example of trucking regulation to illustrate the next point. In making its decision, which is *prima facie* between two competing carrier interests, the Motor Carrier Commission, to use the B.C. example, is invited by its legislation to

> take into consideration, amongst other matters, . . . the general effect on other transport services and *any public interest* which may be affected by the issue of such licence.[23]

Their adjudicatory function immediately takes on an external horizon and this is hardly surprising, for apart perhaps from the particular functions of licensing appeal bodies and compensation-oriented tribunals, regulatory agencies exercise a policy-making function in many proceedings which, to the inexperienced observer, appear only to involve a choice between A and B. The incremental development of regulatory policy where the initial capacity for policy-making responsibilities has been delegated to an agency is very much a fact of life in Canada. Particularly where policy guide-lines and rules are either not given to the agency by legislative statement or by executive direction provided for in the empowering statute, the situation can lead to significant uncertainty and an unfortunate potential for abuse, both of which do little to encourage public confidence in the process. Too often the development of the actual policy goals and guide-lines has been left to be developed on a case-by-case basis almost in the tradition of the common law, which is ill-suited to the structured, accessible resolution of significant policy matters in the larger public interest. This is not to undermine the view that policy statements and guide-lines quite properly are the subject of interpretation and refinement in the individual cases coming before the statutory agency. But the point is that they fall into an announced policy framework for their resolution and that there is an element of predictability at the outset as to whether or not parties, in addition to the immediate claimants or participants, should become involved in the proceedings.

My concern is not to suggest that adjudicatory and policy-making functions in a given regulatory area should be meticulously differentiated and perhaps even given to separate bodies. Others have commented critically on ''the manifest imprecision in statutory role definition,''[24] and while there is admittedly room for improvement in that respect, the mingling of roles is understandable and, in many cases, eminently sensible.

The jurisdiction of the CRTC, for example, to develop a broadcasting policy for Canada within the context of a very broadly defined authority and to adjudicate competing claims for broadcast licences is an appropriate statement of tasks, whatever one's views about the performance of those tasks.

Too frequently, however, in the name of delegation, our regulatory bodies have been allowed to drift into an individualized pattern of decisions from which only seasoned, regular participants are capable of privately constructing the actual policy parameters of their legislative purpose. Little wonder that we hear complaints about the close relationship between the regulators and the regulated, for apart from a handful of high visibility federal agencies, the involvement of other interests on any systematic basis is close to non-existent.

C. Policy Statements and Rule Making

The failure to provide policy direction through parliamentary or executive direction to regulatory agencies is not uncommon in Canada. Nor is it unusual, as I have noted, for such bodies simply to slip into their skeleton statutes and go about their business on a day-to-day basis. The result of this type of exercise for a regime of delegated intervention *in the public interest* may assume ludicrous proportions in some cases. In 1973, for example, the new chairman of the B.C. Motor Carrier Commission issued this plaintive cry:

> It is a curious aspect of the regulatory system with which we are concerned that the principles on which it is to be operated are neither apparent from the two statutes concerned . . . nor have they been laid down in recorded decisions rendered by the Courts, the Lieutenant-Governor in Council, or our predecessor Commission during the 43 years which have elapsed since motor carrier regulation was introduced in this Province by the Highway Act of 1930.[25]

These remarks were made in the course of extensive reasons on a licence application matter, the first statement of any consequence by the commission in over forty years on the policy goals declared to be significant in the discharge of its supervisory responsibilities. Except for the brief tenure of that chairman, the B.C. commission has never developed a readiness to articulate the reasons for its decisions. Its process of decision making and the policy rationale therefore remain unknown to all but a handful of industry people who have developed their own "feel for" the workings of the commission. It is not that the agency is not doing anything—far from it. The commission exercises a crucial influence on surface transportation policy in a very large province closely tied to scattered population centres, resource industries, and a rugged terrain. What we are unclear about is *why* the commissioners are making their decisions, which touch upon questions of market entry, rates, and alternative forms of transport.

The statement of delegated objectives in the *Motor Carrier Act*[26] is purposively vague and singularly unhelpful in attaching any precision to the commission's policy goals. Those goals, we must conclude, are to be developed by the commission. How? Either by a process of case decisions, for example, on carrier licence applications, which over time would speak to the commission's policy priorities on market entry and service to the public; or by a combination of "policy statements" on the subjects of entry and service and ensuing case decisions, which would interpret and flesh out the guide-lines. The latter approach, in contrast, is regularly practised by provincial authorities engaged in securities regulation. Although it has not been used often, the power is also expressly given to the B.C. Labour Relations Board, which is authorized "from time to time [to] formulate general guidelines in furtherance of the operation" of the Labour Code.[27]

Unfortunately, the end result in too many other cases in Canada is that the exercise of discretionary powers by regulatory agencies has been akin to private law making in the name of the public interest. Citizen participation at the *representational* level may look in vain, or at least with great uncertainty, for those moments of potentially profitable involvement where their scarce energies might be usefully co-ordinated to influence the basic policy goals of the agency in question. There is a dilemma here that saps the strength and the longer-run vitality of public interest groups—*collective representation*—and serves to undermine the participation of directly aggrieved or affected individual citizens.

Where, for any of the reasons cited, adjudicatory-type proceedings are the principal policy rudder of the agency vessel, then the odds are stacked against significant public involvement. The process tends to look inward and becomes unduly private. As Professor K.C. Davis has noted in a related context:

> In most circumstances, the more the private party can know about the agency's law and policy the fairer the system; the less the private party can know the lower the quality of justice.[28]

An obvious response to this problem is for regulatory agencies to proceed more often by way of promulgated policy guide-lines or statements. Rather than simply concentrating on incremental policy making by the process of adjudication, there would be a new emphasis on forward planning and policy priorization. If this rule-making approach were more widely exercised, the agencies would be forced to think through the objectives of their delegated authority in an open forum more appropriate to maximum citizen input and involvement. This is not to minimize "the difficulty and importance of drawing a workable distinction between rule making and adjudication,"[29] but this is not a sufficient obstacle to stop the exercise.

In Canada, as Professor Janisch has noted:

> ... rule making procedure remains singularly underdeveloped. Neither the McRuer Commission nor the MacGuigan Committee felt that there was any need for formal pre-regulation making procedures, being satisfied that widespread informal consulta-

tion took place in any event. Neither undertook any empirical research to determine whether informal consultation is truly representative of all interests. My concern is, of course, that less organized and influential interests such as consumer, safety and environmental will not be consulted unless a formal forum for participation is created.[30]

It is clear, however, where the use of policy statements is authorized by the agency's statute, that the practice will be upheld by the courts.[31] The judiciary is not the problem. The barrier to rule making is regulatory inertia.

D. Public Access and Political Control

Recent Canadian reactions to these trends have been most interesting and carry important implications for public participation in the regulatory process. In general terms, and frequently regardless of the distinctions between choosing rule making or adjudication in developing regulatory policy, the emphasis has been on the assertion of *executive or ministerial control* over the discretionary authority of the agencies. This is not to deny the several recent federal initiatives whereby it is proposed at the agency level to establish pre-promulgation procedures for the dissemination and discussion of policy statements and regulations—procedures in which ''a reasonable opportunity shall be afforded to interested persons to make representations.'' But the brunt of the change in thinking has been on the question of *political* control.

One of the most interesting examples at the national level may be found in Bill C-14, the Nuclear Control and Administration Act,[32] introduced by Mr. Gillespie in late November 1977. By Part II, Section 61 of the bill, the minister is made solely responsible for regulating ''commercial and promotional activities in relation to nuclear energy . . . .'' Under Part I, Section 20, the objects of the Nuclear Control Board are ''to regulate, control and supervise the development, production, possession and use of nuclear energy . . . '' in the interests of health, safety, security, and environmental considerations. In the discharge of these duties, the board is directed to follow a carefully prescribed series of steps involving public hearings (for proposed nuclear installations), public notices, and the disclosure of information in its possession.

By Section 19 in the same part, the Cabinet is empowered, ''on the recommendation of the Minister,'' to ''issue *policy directives* to the Board and the Board shall comply therewith'' (emphasis added). The same provision requires any such executive directives to be ''forthwith tabled in Parliament and published in the Canada Gazette.''

It will be noted that the instructions do not pertain to a particular matter before the agency but rather to questions of larger import. The approach may also be found in recent provincial legislation. It signifies a new assumption of *political control* over the previously delegated responsibility for policy making. The right of *ex ante* Cabinet intervention has been met with favour in principle by most observers, basically because the process will increase the

> accountability by agencies to the political process to ensure [the] proper weighting of competing interests and values.

Moreover,

> [c]orrelative with this prerogative of intervention [will] be [the] assignment of more political responsibility for failure to intervene, in the event that circumstances are seen to call for it.[33]

I will be interested in the observations of our commentators on such expressions of faith in the responsiveness of executive government. For myself, I would not quarrel with the need to replace political abdication of responsibility with appropriate lines of political direction and accountability. However, it is most unfortunate, as noted by the Ontario Economic Council report last year, that the increasingly favoured path of *ex ante* direction by Cabinet appears devoid of the simplest procedural safeguards. Binding directions may be issued without any provision for public discussion, a process increasingly denied to the agencies when they are engaged in the same task of policy making. The Ontario study minces few words on the point:

> The process of directive-formulation is *unilateral* and *invisible*, in sharp contrast to direct legislation or delegated policy-making by an agency. Attempts to ensure publicly accountable decision-making at these levels are liable to be subverted by the substitution of a bureaucratic process which severely attenuates accountability. Some form of public notice of a proposed directive and a procedure for written comment on the public record seem minimum requirements before a directive becomes binding. Moreover, the credibility of an agency's decision-making process is likely to be undermined if interests are induced to believe that they can be short-circuited, whenever inconvenient, by secret and perhaps well-couched entreaties to a minister.[34]

The concern here, then, is that the *directive process* up front must be accessible and must be seen to be weighing the affected interests properly represented in the regulatory process. In the name of political responsiveness, executive policy orders may dictate the parameters of action to the agency but they are not to become dictatorial in the wider sense. Perhaps this is an area for increased oversight or review by legislative committees although, in most cases, the dominance of executive government would render them paper tigers.[35]

The rationale, in the words of Professor Janisch, "would seem to be that accountability and not participation is what counts," and, as he would argue,

> ultimate accountability, important as it is, is no substitute for openness in policy making which allows for the interplay of competing ideas *before* any final position is adopted.[36]

In addition to this right of *ex ante* intervention by directive, *ex post* review is also provided for in section 57(1) of Bill C-14, the Nuclear Control and Administrative Act:

> On the petition of any person who is directly affected by an order or decision of the Board received by the Clerk of the Privy Council within one month of the making of the order or decision, the Governor in Council may confirm, vary or rescind in whole or in part the order or decision.

"Political appeals" to the Cabinet are fairly commonplace in Canadian regulatory statutes. Examples may be readily found in both federal and provincial jurisdictions. In terms of the visibility of this final stage of political control, however, considerations similar to those applying to *ex ante* directives tend to arise. They speak directly to the issue of *representational due process*. In a nutshell, the same procedural safeguards are called for—public notice of any decision to review, request for submissions from affected interests for the public record, and published reasons for the government's ultimate decision. The recent Inuit decision of the Federal Court of Appeal[37] reveals the judiciary's interest in the formulation of a basic procedural fairness in a Cabinet review system. In that most interesting case, it was decided, absent statutory language to the contrary, that the Cabinet, or a committee thereof, is the master of its own procedure *provided* that every private intervener is allowed to respond to the evidence given by any other intervener. The result has been appealed by the federal government to the Supreme Court of Canada.

The lack of procedural regularity in regulatory appeals to the federal Cabinet has also come under sharp attack by lawyers representing the Consumers' Association of Canada in the Cabinet's handling of the Telesat review in 1977. Attempts to require a minimum basic standard of natural justice in the process were rebuffed by the prime minister and later in the trial and appeal divisions of the Federal Court of Canada.[38]

In the past two years in Ottawa, public interest groups have tested the Cabinet appeal route at least four times on decisions in the broadcasting or telecommunications field. The questions included cable licence transfer policy, domestic rate-setting criteria, and telephone service for low-income people and for natives. Their experience has basically confirmed the concerns expressed earlier in the report of the Ontario Economic Council and by other observers like Professor Janisch. The growing trend towards *ex post* review by Cabinet testifies to and confirms the importance that Parliament has attached to a political review of regulatory decisions.

The problem, however, is that Parliament has not set out the procedures that the Cabinet should follow in handling the appeals. The ministers are worried, perhaps with some cause, that formal procedures will regiment and constrict unduly an essentially political process. Yet, as Geoffrey Stevens has observed, it does not make sense to require openness, fairness and impartiality from regulatory tribunals and not require the same from ministers when they review the rulings of tribunals;[39]

and

[t]here should be procedures to ensure fair consideration. Natural justice is more than a narrow legal principle. It's an important political principle, too.[40]

The need to reconsider the framework for political appeals has taken on a new urgency with the Inuit appeal and continuing evidence that the policy of *ex post* review is putting down firm roots, namely, the Northern Pipeline Agency, the latest proposals for the new Competition Board, the new *National Transportation Act* and the *Telecommunications Act*. The pendulum of political responsiveness has swung too far. In the name of political accountability, we may end up with government control and departmental interference. The "squeeze play" of policy directives at the front end and Cabinet appeals at the other end will lead to regulatory eunuchs. The trends, ironically enough, come at a time of increasing readiness by many agencies and tribunals to encourage public participation, and a strong approval by the Supreme Court of Canada to the development of policy guide-lines by such bodies employing full and fair opportunities for public comment by all interested parties.[41]

CONCLUDING OBSERVATIONS

What is to be done? Here are some suggestions:

1. Reconsider the wisdom of unilateral policy edicts and devise a front-end approach that will give the first opportunity to the regulatory agency. Under this proposal, the agency is requested, within a time limit, by the department, to establish a new policy or amend an existing one through its rule-making procedure. The department takes part in the proceedings and only after the agency has completed its task does the minister consider the question of requesting his Cabinet colleagues to vary or replace the agency's product. This stage would not involve a hearing. As one respected observer has commented:

In view of the ample opportunity which will be provided to the department to call its policy concerns to the attention of the regulatory agency, it is likely that resort will only have to be made to the failsafe political power in the most exceptional situations. On the other hand, the regulatory agency need not feel intimidated by the department's having the last say because the department will have to be prepared to speak out at the hearing as to its policy and the agency's decision will have a sufficient degree of legitimacy as a product of the open decision-making process to discourage casual reversal by Cabinet.[42]

2. With respect to those *ex ante* policy directives that are retained, basic procedural requirements for prior notice, public comment, and appropriate consultation ought to be guaranteed by legislation.

3. Every encouragement by legislative and other means should be given to the development of policy guide-lines and related rule-making activities by regulatory agencies in a manner supportive of open and substantial citizen involvement.

4. The reasons for allowing Cabinet or ministerial review of individual regulatory decisions should be critically examined.[43] Particularly if policy directives are employed or if my first suggestion is accepted, then the agency should be left to do its job in such cases. Otherwise, we run the risk of political interference operating in the guise of accountability. If political appeals are viewed as necessary, if only for a very small minority of cases, then a basic standard of procedural fairness should attach to the system of political review.

Canada is now in the midst of its first national inquiry into regulation. The mandate of the Regulation Reference is very broad and includes close consultation between the three levels of government, the private sector, and public organizations. The Reference's major objective is to come to terms with the amount of government regulation judged to be compatible with private initiative and public responsibility.

In respect of those questions touching upon public access and participation in the regulatory process, recent legislative and political developments call for immediate study and comment by the Reference and other interested commentators. Otherwise, the potential for political meddling in the shaping of regulatory policy and the review of individual decisions will crystallize and threaten the carefully defined areas of independence best reserved to the statutory agencies.

Political oversight of the regulatory process is necessary and the vigorous employment of parliamentary committees to that end makes eminent sense, as well as the use of open and accessible forums for the development of policy directives by Cabinet and a corresponding diminution of Cabinet reviews of individual regulatory decisions.

However, in the search for better standards of political accountability, the standard bearers have been too heavy-handed and created a potential for unnecessarily secretive decisions that will ultimately undermine the public credibility of the regulatory system. That system will not wither away—for a great number of reasons—however vocal the cries for deregulation. At a time that more and more windows are opening on the actual process and rationale of regulation, it is ironic that *ex ante* and *ex post* measures taken in the name of political accountability threaten to lower the blinds at opposite ends of the exercise.

In the absence of substantial rethinking, we may simply end up with the worst of both worlds—unelected departmental ''experts'' and ministerial ''advisers'' managing the important facets of the regulatory process from both ends of the spectrum with the consumer, environmental, and community-based groups watching from the sidelines, mounting an occasional rally here and there as their resources will permit. The very model of unaccountability ascribed for so long to many of Canada's tribunals and commissions will now be replaced by an equally faulty design that will only aggravate our fundamental concerns about openness and responsiveness. The public will be the loser in this battle between departmental and regulatory power centres.

NOTES:

[1] See *Regulation Reference: A Preliminary Report to First Ministers*, by Chairman, Economic Council of Canada (Ottawa: November 1978).

[2] Including studies on the Canadian Transport Commission (1978), National Energy Board (1977), and Atomic Energy Control Board (1977). An overview study paper on the federal administrative law process is due to be published shortly. For shortened versions of the studies published to date plus useful original research papers, see G. Bruce Doern, ed., *The Regulatory Process in Canada* (Toronto: Macmillan, 1978).

[3] Newspaper advertisements in late March 1979 were placed by the minister, proclaiming: "Fed Up with Red Tape? My job is to cut through red tape and make government simpler, less costly and more efficient for everyone. Your examples of unnecessary bureaucracy at all levels of government will help me in this task." Letters, not phone calls, were invited from the public. The government, but not the minister (Sam Bawlf), was returned with a reduced majority in the provincial election on 10 May 1979. "Deregulation," according to the Throne Speech read on 6 June, remains a high priority of the government.

[4] Ontario Economic Council, *Government Regulation: Issues and Alternatives 1978* (Toronto: The Council, 1978), p. 1.

[5] C. Lloyd Brown-John, "Defining Regulatory Agencies for Analytical Purposes," *Canadian Public Administration* 19 (Spring 1976): 140-57.

[6] The Canadian Consumer Council (an advisory group to the Minister of Consumer and Corporate Affairs and disbanded several years ago) commissioned a number of studies in 1972 that broke new ground in regulatory analysis in Canada. Titles included G.B. Reschenthaler, *The Performance of Selected Regulatory Commissions in Alberta, Saskatchewan and Manitoba;* D.A. Dawson, *The Canadian Radio-Television Commission and the Consumer Interest;* E. Richardson, *Consumer Interest Representation: Three Case Studies;* J. Erkkila and J. Palmer, *The Role of the Consumer in Affecting the Decisions of the Hydro-Electric Power Commission of Ontario;* W.T. Stanbury, *B.C. Public Utilities Commission and the Consumer Interest;* P.L. Arcus, *The Consumer Interest and Marketing Boards;* and the Council's *Report on the Consumer Interest in Regulatory Boards and Agencies* (1973).

[7] Richard Brown, *Inventory of B.C. Regulatory Agencies* (Victoria: University of Victoria, Centre for Public Sector Studies, 1978). It is understood that a second and more comprehensive study has been started by the B.C. Ministry of Deregulation.

[8] *Regulation Reference, op. cit.*, pp. 5-6. For details of the Reference's significant programme of research and inquiry, see its occasional publication, *Update*.

[9] *Motor Carrier Act*, R.S.B.C. 1960, c. 252, as amended.

136 / *Sovereign People or Sovereign Governments*

[10] *Agricultural Land Commission Act*, S.B.C. 1973, c. 46, as amended, s. 7.

[11] *Pollution Control Act 1967*, S.B.C. 1967, c. 34, as amended, s. 4 (b).

[12] Brown-John, *op. cit.*, p. 141.

[13] *Regulation Reference, op. cit.*, p. 22.

[14] James C. Miller III, "Regulators and Experts: A Modest Proposal," *Regulation* (November-December 1977), p. 36.

[15] Ontario Economic Council, *Government Regulation, op. cit.*, p. 46.

[16] *Ibid.*, p. 47.

[17] K. Kernaghan, "Political Control of Administrative Action: Accountability or Window Dressing?" *Cahiers de Droit* 17 (1976), pp. 931-32.

[18] L. Jaffe, "The Independent Regulatory Agency—A New Scapegoat," *Yale Law Journal* 65 (1956), quoted in Ontario Economic Council, *Government Regulation, op. cit.*, p. 46.

[19] Brown-John, *op. cit.*, p. 141.

[20] Robert B. Reich, "Warring Critiques of Regulation," *Regulation* (January-February 1979), p. 37.

[21] C.R.T.C. Draft Rules of Procedure (1978), ss. 49-52.

[22] Described by W. Horton, Alberta Public Utilities Board chairman in "The Role of the Alberta Public Utilities Board," *Transcript of a Seminar on Effective Participation in Alberta's Energy Planning, Decision Making and Regulatory Process (Vol. 1)* (Edmonton: Dept. of Consumer & Corporate Affairs, 1978), pp. 24-43.

[23] *Motor Carrier Act, op. cit.*, s. 7 (2) (b) (emphasis added).

[24] Brown-John, *op. cit.*, p. 142.

[25] *Per* M.R. Taylor, Chairman, Motor Carrier Commission, *In Re P. Dickson Trucking Ltd.*, Reasons for Decision, Nov. 26, 1973, p. 20, Annual Report of M.C.C. (1973).

[26] *Motor Carrier Act, op. cit.*, s. 37 (1), discussed above.

[27] *Labour Code of British Columbia*, S.B.C. 1973, c. 122, as amended, s. 27. For the first (and apparently only) *Statement of Policy*, see *Canada Labour Relations Board Reports* 2 (1976) 17, "Statements of Policy: Section 96 of the Labour Code."

[28] K.C. Davis, *Discretionary Justice: A Preliminary Inquiry* (Baton Rouge: Louisiana State University Press, 1969), p. 24.

[29] D.L. Shapiro, "The Choice of Rulemaking or Adjudication in the Development of Administrative Policy," *Harvard Law Review* 78 (1965), p. 924.

[30] H.N. Janisch, "Review of K.C. Davis, *Administrative Law of the Seventies*, and Bernard Schwartz, *Administrative Law*," *Dalhousie Law Journal* 4 (1977-78), p. 834.

[31] *Capital Cities Communications Inc. v. C.R.T.C.* [1978] 2 S.C.R. 141, 81 D.L.R. (3d) 609.

[32] Bill C-14, *An Act to provide for the regulation, control and supervision of the development, production, use and application of nuclear energy and matters related thereto*, 3rd Sess., 30th Parl., given First Reading, 24 November 1977.

[33] Ontario Economic Council, *Government Regulation, op. cit.*, pp. 48-49.

[34] *Ibid.*, p. 49 (emphasis added).

[35] For a general discussion of legislative committees and their members, see John M. Reid *et al.*, "The Backbencher and the Discharge of Legislative Responsibilities," in *The Legislative Process in Canada: The Need for Reform*, edited by W.A.W. Neilson and J.C. MacPherson (Montreal: The Institute for Research on Public Policy, 1978), pp. 139-63; see also H.N. Janisch, "Policy Making in Regulation: Towards a New Definition at the Status of Independent Agencies in Canada," *Osgoode Law Journal* 17 (1979), pp. 103-4.

[36] H.N. Janisch, paper to University of Ottawa Conference on Administrative Justice, 27 January 1978, mimeo, pp. 24-25.

[37] *Inuit Tapirasat of Canada v. Léger*, Federal Court of Appeal, Nov. 17, 1978, *per* LeDain, J., speaking for the Court reversing the Trial Division reported in (1978), 87 D.L.R. (3d) 26.

[38] Discussed in H.N. Janisch, "Policy Making . . . ," *op. cit.*, pp. 81-84.

[39] Geoffrey Stevens, *Globe & Mail*, 2 February 1979, p. 6.

[40] Geoffrey Stevens, *Globe & Mail*, 28 September 1978, p. 6.

[41] In *Capital Cities Communications Inc. v. C.R.T.C., op. cit.*

[42] H.N. Janisch, "Policy Making . . . ," *op. cit.*, p. 106.

[43] For the latest discussion of this whole subject, see Douglas G. Hartle, *Public Policy Decision Making and Regulation* (Montreal: The Institute for Research on Public Policy, 1979), particularly Chapter 6, "Regulatory Agencies: The Independence-Accountability Issue," pp. 121-34.

Commentary

by
Kitson Vincent

The role of the Member of Parliament and his relation to his electors is worthy of more serious consideration than has been given at this conference. Dr. Rabinovitch touched on this point yesterday when he said that all of us got a smattering of the problem in first-year political science. Indeed we did, but it is time we swam back into the historical mainstream.

The country tradition of English politics stressed the importance of a short Parliament on the grounds that the elected representatives were exposed to the temptations of power and the corruption of the court. This gave rise to a series of debates and polemics on the relation of the electors to the elected. And what you and I got in first-year political science was Edmund Burke propounding to the electors of Bristol the view that their representative had been chosen to act for the good of the whole realm, and thus to play a part that they could not play themselves. This representative exercised his judgement concerning the common good even when it conflicted with theirs, and similarly they, the electorate, exercised their judgement if they decided not to re-elect him at the close of his term. The elector, according to Burke, should not seek to impede his representative's judgement by instructing or recalling him. Now in some sense that is the kind of debate we have overlooked.

Dr. Corry's anecdote about the students at Queen's trying to find out what was going on in the governing councils, finding out, and then going on to better things, is rather appropriate. I also agree with Stefan Dupré that many people aggressively seek to be left alone. One thing, however, that fuels the cry for participation today is the suspicion that the people we send to elected assemblies no longer make decisions for us and, even worse, no longer hold accountable those who do. It is fine for Messrs. Pitfield-Smith to insist that the system is shaped by the delegation of power. According to their version, however, it starts at the top. Cabinet decides what to do and it is ultimately left to Parliament to give or withhold its seal of approval, and on down the line. With all due respect, it is actually the other way around. It starts at the bottom, with the first and most important delegation of power made between the citizen and his representative. To me, that is the linchpin of parliamentary government, and to say, as Messrs. Pitfield-Smith suggest, that public interest groups are partly responsible for Parliament's demise is nonsense. I do not want to minimize the burdens that participation causes, but the cry for participation came not as a precursor of parliamentary decline but in response to its demise—as an attempt to re-establish a connection.

In answer to Doug Fisher's question, "How do we get back to politics," I say, "Start there." In common with Fisher, I too like politicians; I like them a lot better than bureaucrats, regulators, advisory boards, and I like them much better than the disgruntled academic who sat on the Carter commission. Yesterday we were presented with the view of Parliament as syndrome. Poor Professor Graham—once his great work was finished, the interests of private people were thrown to the dogs and our elected representatives fought over the scraps. Special interest groups, he says, know they can bend the ears of politicians better than regulators or academics. What we have here is a view of Parliament that needs the experts to protect it from the citizens. Follow the unspoken premises of the professor's argument a little further and you will come up with some ominous conclusions. I do not like politicians because they are nicer or morally better; it is just that they are more exposed, accountable, they get there through competition. I know how to get to them and I know how to speak to them.

The arrogance of the expert and technician, concurrent with their ridicule of elected assemblies, has infected a number of papers at this conference. It is no wonder that the main topic—namely, the gifted amateur—has yet to surface. Professor Graham, however, should be happier these days because Parliament is certainly deferring more and more to professional and academic opinion. If they chewed over the Carter report,[1] they barely gave lip service to the Berger report.[2]

I spoke with Mr. Justice Berger shortly after he published his report. I questioned the popular assumption of the time that Berger killed the pipeline. To me that view was equivalent to saying that Parliament no longer played a role. But role or no role, one had to ask about the status of inquiries appointed by executive order and why Parliament should not be at the forefront. Berger answered that we would never have parliamentarians of the stature, power, and public acceptance of such figures as Kennedy, Johnson, and Fulbright. We must have other means, he said, and inquiries are one of the main vehicles.

I was stymied then, and still am. What about the representative functions? Is it not obvious that the executive makes all the appointments? On asking these questions, I felt the same frustration that I did on my first fund-raising campaign across Canada for the Canadian Arctic Resources Committee. In those days, to get acceptance, you had to have a tripartite composition of the board, something like The Institute for Research on Public Policy. We ended up with the chairman of Imperial Oil who told us, "Fellows, when there are two elephants around, there is no room for a mouse." That summed up a lot about what participation meant in those days.

There we were, running between the federal government and the oil companies. In doing all that running we raised no money, but we learned a lot about Canada. And one of the things we learned was that every time we came into a boardroom or government agency, we had to start with a political talk on accountability and the rights of citizens. I did a lot of fund raising in the United States subsequently and found out that nobody ever asked me that question. We may have been thrown out of a number of offices; they may have said we were crazy, but nobody ever said, ''You don't have a right to be here, why doesn't the government do it, or why doesn't somebody else do it?''

We have talked a lot here about participation, and yesterday Doug Fisher put holes in another fallacy about Canadians as entrepreneurs. According to Fisher, we are mostly working for large corporations, and we are really bureaucrats. The same thing applies to participation; we do not have vital participation in this country's political life; we never have. There are very few groups that are privately funded. The abject experience that the Consumers' Association has to undergo each year, cap in hand, over to the Department of Consumer and Corporate Affairs, is something I wish on nobody. Before we act smart about it, we should understand more about what kind of qualities are needed; perhaps we will find that self-reliance and risk taking have long been bred out of it.

If this sounds familiar, it should. In one of the more politically turbulent times, the end of the fifteenth century, the Florentines often debated this topic: how can a people who once possessed certain qualities, and lost them, ever hope to regain them? They came to a very pessimistic conclusion. Machiavelli, in particular, thought long and hard about it. Although this is a nebulous kind of item for a conference like this, I suggest somebody deal with the problem because it is a very important one.

Yesterday, when Professor Dupré reached for his Bible, it happened to be the *Federalist Papers*, number 51—famous 51. Whatever we say about the U.S. system, if what you are looking for is accountability, then they are far ahead of us. They have an identifiable birth, the advantages of an easier referral, and a necessity of celebrating that point in history. That particular period deals with the problem of how we keep government in check and how we treat men in power.

Professor LaForest talked about accountability and participation and seems to favour participation. May I suggest that they are rather closely related, and the link is power. I am not speaking solely in the Actonian sense of that word—''power tends to corrupt, and absolute power corrupts absolutely.'' That is an obvious use, and for that we have devised systems of checks and balances. But corruption in the classical tradition also occurs when men are denied the possibility of partnership and self-rule. In other words, power, when it excludes people from sharing in it, prevents the development of the qualities needed for self-rule. Accountability and participation are very close.

Now, let us move on to some of my old friends. Yesterday, Mr. Bryce referred to the Porter commission as a glowing example of public participation, but he obviously did not like the evangelical overtones of the

Berger inquiry. I can tell this group that without the pioneering efforts of Mr. Justice Berger, the Porter commission would not have been able to go very far. Unlike Mr. Bryce, he dealt with the complexities of participation and he made some extraordinary innovations. He was truly the gifted amateur.

Now a gifted amateur never accepts terms of reference without at least subjecting them to scrutiny. Power and concentration are not just corporate phenomena, they equally infect government and unions. I would have expected some discussion on this matter, yet found nothing but a slavish adherence to order-in-council. Berger, by contrast, took seriously the idea that is found in the Institute's third objective on organizational purpose, which reads, "find practical solutions to important public policy problems." In other words, how do we implement the results of our research? First we must realize that policy research is usually conducted at arm's length from events. If a study or session like this contains recommendations, follow-up is usually not addressed or, if it is, it takes the form of another recommendation. We not only ignore the practical aspects of implementing results, we fail to realize that follow-up contains a moral dimension. Sydney Hook referred to this dilemma when he said, "All of us assumed too easily that the achievements of intellectual conviction carried with it the moral courage to act upon it. Unfortunately, this has not been the case, especially in recent years."

Let us put the challenge to the Institue. A year ago, a finance minister from one of the western provinces asked my advice on whether his government should give money to the Institute. I said, "Definitely no," and gave him my reasons. Now, if it happened again, I would say the same thing, only this time I would add one more reason. My additional reason would be, "There is no room for the gifted amateur." I use the phrase metaphorically to suggest that there is something dynamic lacking here. The business of government has indeed preferred the professional and the expert. It has also favoured the Institute. In fund raising all over this country, I have run into business and provincial governments that said, "Sorry, we've done our thing for public policy, we gave to the Institute." For what?

What I suggest is that the Institute hold another conference, one that deals solely with the gifted amateur. And when we know a little bit more about what we are looking for, let us strike up a small group and allow it to give a third of the Institute's budget to gifted amateurs—no strings attached. I can assure you, ladies and gentlemen, this will do a lot more for Canada than conferences like this.

The gifted amateur is not an inspector, a bureaucrat, a regulator, or a technician. He is a creative person. Like all creative people, he has a vision of the whole. We could transpose here Nietzsche's concept of greatness, which should be determined, he says, "by the amount and variety that an individual could carry within himself by the distance his responsibility could span." This is no mere aspiration. The amount of diversity that individuals can carry may determine whether we remain a self-governing people or whether we continue to turn over the direction of our lives to professionals and experts. The M.P. as gifted amateur is an exciting theme and one we should be looking at. We may have to delegate, but let us delegate to people we trust and admire. I suspect that what we are looking for is a gifted amateur.

NOTES

[1] Canada, Royal Commission on Taxation, *Report* (Ottawa: Queen's Printer, 1966).

[2] Canada, Mackenzie Valley Pipeline Inquiry, *Report—Vol. I: Northern Frontier, Northern Homeland; Vol. II: Terms and Conditions* (Ottawa: Minister of Supply and Services Canada, 1977).

Commentary

by
Jalynn H. Bennett

Dr. LaForest and Professor Neilson, it seems to me, clearly focused their attention on areas critical to citizen involvement and control, within the context of law making and policy formulation. This has been a subject that has received too little public attention.

The first part of Dr. LaForest's paper was most interesting—interesting because he described not the limits of the law, but the *limitations* of the judicial process in the application of the law to broad social claims.

In our society, there is a broadly held common assumption that it is the right of citizens to participate in law making and in policy making. Historically, the public have exercised this right through the election of representatives to the legislature. Whether citizens choose to vote or not, the right to vote is irrefutable.

With the rapid growth in administrative government over the last several decades, with the delegation of adjudicatory and policy-making functions to regulatory agencies, incorporation of effective public participation into the regulatory process has become crucial. It is crucial in terms of protecting the right of the citizen to have a voice in how he is governed. The "why" is not in question in a Western democratic country. Consequently, we must focus on the "how." Fortunately, both these papers have offered some constructive suggestions about what such methods and procedures might look like.

It is important to note Dr. LaForest's reminder that "Judicial review of administrative action is largely confined to jurisdictional and procedural questions. It does not go to the *merits* of decisions."

Consequently, the fact that both papers address the question of how to modify the operations of the administrative arms of government so that public participation can be better affected is very helpful. Again, I suggest that it is fundamentally a matter of adequate access during the process of decision making, and the design of mechanisms to ensure that such access is not only widely available but also broadly perceived to be so available.

Professor Neilson has observed that interest in regulation is very evident; such interest is long overdue. The lives of all of us are substantially affected by the pervasiveness of the decisions of regulatory bodies. Many people carry strong feelings of being excluded from these processes whereby governments shape their lives. Where these feelings exist, they increasingly manifest themselves in citizen frustration and apathy and alienation from the whole political process. As Professor Neilson says, when "the exercise of discretionary powers by regulatory agencies has been akin to private law making in the name of public interest,'' and where manifestly there has been no public involvement, the public has every right to be sceptical, and ultimately cynical, about the equity not only of the outcome but also of the process. And where there is scepticism and cynicism, inevitably comes a sense of alienation.

Let me pick up Professor Neilson's point about the impact of regulatory activity in Canada. Among those who are focusing their attention on what constitutes appropriate activities for government are various different collectives: business, labour, consumer groups, public policy advisory organizations, the academic community, environmental groups, and others.

I have had some direct experience with four types of collectives. Specifically, business, an environmental interest group, a public policy research body, and also from the perspective of being a member of the board of directors of a Toronto-based adolescent treatment centre, whose budget is provided for by the Ontario Ministry of Community and Social Services. Let me talk, very quickly, about my experience from these four various points of view, in the context of Professor Neilson's articulated goal of the regulatory process as ''an accessible, reasonable, and fair system of decision making.''

First, business. Recently, I completed for my organization, a large insurance company headquartered in Toronto, a survey of our involvement with government. I knew intuitively that we dealt extensively with government. As a federally chartered company, operating in both Canada and the United States, clearly many people in head office, and we employ some 1200 people, have dealings with various governments on an ongoing basis. I did not know how many people were involved in this or how many man-hours were spent on complying with various governments' regulation of the various aspects of our business when I started. After many weeks of extensive interviews, I came to the conclusion that fully one third of head office staff spent at least part of their time on the job in analysing, assessing, or complying with government legislation and regulatory initiatives.

Second, my experience with the public interest group, an environmental organization, actively involved, among other things, with issues related to energy conservation. One of our frustrations in this group was the nature of the regulatory process and how to mobilize sufficient volunteer time to offset our exceedingly modest financial resources. We had to be very selective because we could not afford to fund appearances before each and every regulatory agency or commission. If we were to put forward an articulate and well-researched position and to file appropriately documented briefs on each and every hearing held by each and every agency involved with monitoring the activities of Ontario Hydro, we would have had to have access to resources substantially greater than those we possessed.

Third, the work of the Ontario Economic Council on Regulation. When the OEC began research in this area, over two years ago, it proved very difficult to pick specific research topics. Difficult because as the research management team began to look at regulation in the Ontario context, it discovered that there were some thirty-six regulatory bodies, thirty-four licensing and appeal bodies, nine compensation bodies, and nine arbitral bodies, among other regulatory agencies. The question arose: where did one begin to look at the design and impact of the regulatory process?

Fourth, the family treatment service in Toronto. This is a small agency. Senior management includes the executive director, the clinical director, and the director of the seven-bed residence for adolescents. These people spend a lot of time dealing with municipal and provincial governments on licensing requirements and in responding to proposed standards of treatment, which the ministry is anxious to put in place: too much time, in my estimation—time that could be better spent treating adolescents and their families. However, if the management of this agency does not negotiate with the fire marshal on whether an extra door is needed in the residence, the house could be closed. And if the management does not respond to ministry green papers and white papers around various matters, the end result could be regulation that does not incorporate appropriate measures—from this agency's professional perspective, measures that should be designed to permit adequate treatment for disturbed adolescents and dysfunctional families.

The basic conclusion I can draw from my own experience is that the regulatory process is accessible, but you have to learn how to get in. You need a lot of time to learn, to gather information. You need a lot of volunteer talent and considerable financial resources. Kitsen Vincent, commenting on his experiences, referred to the frustrations in trying to collect money for public interest groups in Canada. There have been very real constraints to achieving public participation in the regulatory process in this country.

Professor Neilson's point about accountability through the political process is well taken. He clearly suggests an alternative in terms of mandatory rule making and policy framework statements by a regulatory agency. His concerns around *ex ante* and *ex post* political control, exercised through the executive, constitute an appropriate warning. This does not mean that political accountability should not be strengthened, I believe, but that due consideration must be given to the design of the process by which accountability is built in.

I would take issue with Professor Neilson's statement that ''the pendulum of political responsiveness has swung too far.'' Where we run ''the risk of political interference operating in the guise of accountability,'' I believe that his points are well made. A clarification of procedures is most important, particularly the development of policy directives to the regulatory agencies, which are open and accessible and are perceived to be such. However, there is a concomitant risk around substantive strengthening of the regulatory process, so that its executive function around policy making begins to rival that of the elected executive.

I would be interested in hearing more about his suggestions around reinforcing open and substantial citizen involvement in the regulatory process. After all, accountability is in many respects a means of ensuring that equity prevails, that the public interest is truly the overriding criterion of the regulatory function. Surely this area must be strengthened. We need more openness and visibility in the whole process. I think that there is a very important role for the legislature to play here, such as the function outlined by Trebilcock *et al.*[1] in their study for the OEC. The vesting of *ex post* review powers in a standing committee of the legislature may help to provide stronger assurances of accountability and openness, as would periodic and regular reporting on the part of the agencies to the legislature.

Fundamentally, the problem is one of design to achieve balance—a regulatory process that is open and accessible and an accountability process that is seen to ensure that the competing societal interests are appropriately weighed in a consistent fashion.

NOTE

[1] Michael J. Trebilcock, Leonard Waverman, and J. Robert S. Prichard, "Markets for Regulation: Implications for Performance Standards and Institutional Design," in *Government Regulation: Issues and Alternatives 1978* (Toronto: Ontario Economic Council, 1978), pp. 11-66.

Chapter Eleven

The Limits of Political Parties in Citizen Involvement and Control of Government

by
Dalton Camp

My subject is "The Limits of Political Parties in Citizen Involvement and Control," and let me say at the outset that I agree that there are limits. The problem for me at this conference in speaking about political parties at all is that it is plainly a subject about which everyone here can claim to have as much and as good an opinion as I do. It is like tourism or the weather or the advantage of fossil fuel, windmills, or solar heat over nuclear energy upon which everyone knows as much as anybody else. The question is not really of knowledge but of values. I know we are all experienced in politics and we practice it every day of our lives. Without a knowledge of politics we could not survive. I have been saying for some time now that I am not a member of any organized political party but I am a Conservative. Audiences usually enjoy this remark, especially Liberal ones. This is not intended to suggest partisanship but rather it is a confession. It is meant to say that as a Conservative I do not have a party, and for that matter as Liberals neither do Liberals nor Socialists, unless they subscribe to the tenants of the Social Democrats, whatever these may be or whomever they might be.

But let me say respectfully, what do I believe the political parties do today, and what is their function or their mandates? Their supreme function is to decide who will lead. For example, in the present excitement we are now enjoying, we are allowed a choice between Messrs. Trudeau, Clark, Broadbent, and I suppose someone called Fabien Roy. These are our choices, or the illusion of it, as to whom shall lead. But if you were to walk down Barrington Street tomorrow, you would walk a long way before you found a living soul who had anything to do with the fact that these gentlemen represent the choice that we are to make.

This is a remarkable condition, and it struck me forcibly in Miami Beach in 1968 when fewer than 3,000 Americans, out of a population of hundreds of millions, literally chose Richard Nixon as President of the United States. It is a comment upon democracy that so frail a thing as a political party should

147

determine who shall lead. Parties and nations, that is how it works. Anyone is free to tax their minds as to how it could be done otherwise or better. The reality remains, however, that political parties have this unique authority and power invested in them by no one other than tradition, and the selection of leaders is easily the most significant visible function that they have. Today our national parties have the further power of disposing of their leaders even if their leaders should be prime minister. So they determine not only who should lead but for how long. This relatively new procedure of so-called ''leadership review'' in the Canadian party system was adopted by the Liberals under Mr. Pearson when he was Prime Minister and by the Conservatives under Mr. Diefenbaker while he was not. It is only an irony of history that the Liberals who were in power found it easy to institute such a review and the Conservatives who were not found it almost impossible.

The right to dispose of a party leader, or more precisely the right to decide whether or not to do so, is not really new to the democratic process. The most potent and prolific democratic model, the American party system, requires even more of their presidents. An incumbent must contest the leadership of his party every four years. In Britain, dumping party leaders and prime ministers has been historically the blood sport of caucus cabals usually led by newspaper publishers. One remembers Stanley Baldwin's exhortation to the parties that they either back or sack their leader. It was not until 1966 that Canadian parties enjoyed the luxury of both these options.

If we did not have political parties, as the cliché goes, we would have to invent them. Someone has to narrow down the choices that we have to make as to who shall lead and similarly the choice as to who shall represent us in the parliamentary system we have. The parties provide for the electoral war and the voters provide the survivors. This latter function cannot be discharged by an infinite number of parties of one, but only by parties of many. Because of that, of course, independence in the parliamentary system is unique. The pre-selection of representatives is accomplished by identifiable partisan political organizations that give sanction to candidates and simplify the process of choice. That right of choice, of course, is not merely basic to the democratic process but also to the capitalistic system itself, or free enterprise if you like a softer phrase.

I would argue that the less free enterprise or capitalistic the economic system is, the more illusory is the concept of choice in the political system. I would also argue that the total experience with the party system both here and in the United States has been considerably strengthened with respect to the role of providing leaders for the system. With regard to all other real or imaginary responsibilities, the influence and power of political parties has been subject to a prolonged paternal influence. That is, the influence of the parties continues to wain as does their relevance. Apart from providing a minimal life support and survival system for candidates for public office, you have to take refuge in symbolism or mythology.

It would be hard to make a substantial case for the proposition that political parties influence public policy and government priorities, or even interaction between parties to influence policies or priorities. If you watch this campaign or any other, you will be quick to see the other true function of political parties (in addition to picking leaders), which is to serve as handmaiden to the communications technology that now exists. The parties essentially provide visible crowds for television, the sound of applause to radio, and the tangible evidence of support for newspapers. This role, of course, had its primitive beginnings in politics in the day of the torchlight parades, but today, because of the vast pervasiveness of the media, the roles become enormously significant.

I can remember campaigning, before the media became so pervasive, with Mr. Diefenbaker in 1962. We took him or he went on the campaign trails through the hinterlands of Quebec, which immediately suggests there had to be some tactical circumstance. We put the press in the front of this train and we had a car in the back in which we put a crowd. Whenever the train stopped the crowd got off and demonstrated. It took about five stops before the press became wise to the idea and were so impressed by the "chutspah" of the organization that they never reported it.

Plainly, over time, the role of political parties has changed and is changing. If I were asked what the future might hold for the parties, I would answer that the future of the parties is probably behind them. What they do now is not only what they can do best but all they can do best.

Someone then should ask, would ask, "what of policy?" It has been my experience, and one applicable to both major parties, that while policy formation was once an illusory function of parties, it is now no longer even an illusion.

The last time the Conservative Party attempted such a thing as a party manifesto was at the 1956 convention that chose John Diefenbaker as its leader. The first act of the new leader was to order that the manifesto be put to the torch and expunged from the records of the convention, which it did, and Gordon Churchill supplied the fuel. The last time a policy issue surfaced within the Conservative Party was in 1962 at an annual meeting where there was a concern with the issue of nuclear arms. While the policy committee of the party produced a policy statement on the issue of nuclear arms and incorporated it in a printed eight-page blue and white pamphlet dealing with overall policy, the same party leader ordered that it be destroyed before the delegates could see it. The leader, who was also prime minister at that time, gave the delegates his own policy on nuclear weapons, which they overwhelmingly endorsed. That policy was "don't tie my hands." At the most recent leadership convention of the Tory party in 1976, policy was never discussed other than by the candidates who gave only their vaguest notions about it. At the most recent annual meeting of the party in 1977, policy was never discussed there, either, because the delegates were giving all their time and interest to the vote on leadership review. Policy was not discussed and there was no discussion at all as to why it was not being discussed.

Now Liberals who might be enjoying all this have no right to. They, of course, have the ongoing responsibility of governing the country. Serious consideration of policy by the party at large has generally been abandoned as an exercise ever since the Kingston conference. This was an event that proved to the satisfaction of most that when you compel party members to write policy, you drive them mad. Instead, the Liberals have computerized the ritual of policy involvement among their rank and file. They recently adopted the practice of distributing questionnaires among delegates attending party conventions, asking them skill-testing questions such as do you favor national unity, world peace, motherhood? Answer yes or no.

Finally, I recall the pitiable vision of Ontario's NDP leader, Stephen Lewis, in 1977. He struggled through the election campaign, bearing upon his slim shoulders the impossible burden of a policy drafted by his party and imposed upon him in a solemn convention and which called for a $4 an hour minimum wage. The policy pleased the majority of convention delegates, obviously, who voted for it, but no one else in the electorate at large. The party fell from second to third place in standings in the legislature. It is my opinion, better still an opinion shared by Mr. Lewis, that the minimum wage commitment sunk him in that campaign.

There remains, admittedly, some primordial ambition that lurks in the heart of a few citizens to participate in the formulation of policy through the party apparatus. I would advise them that if they insist on doing so, not to join a political party. The very least they should do is join a parapolitical pressure group. The very best thing they could do is join the civil service.

In today's practice of forming policy, participation is not necessary. It would be naïve of anyone, I think, to believe that the resolution to privatize Petro-Canada was passed in the Tory convention, and I am sure none of us can remember such a thing as a "Decade of Development" being mooted about at the last Liberal rally. It was not even mentioned as a matter of fact in the gathering of its caucus. Mr. Broadbent's divinations of policy yesterday, today, and tomorrow will come as much of a surprise to his party as it does to me.

Policy formation, like political partronage, has been bureaucratized. John White, the chairman of the National Committee of the Democratic Party, summed it up pretty well when he said recently, speaking in the context of American politics, "I don't see either national party being the great spiritual leaders of political thought in the country. So what role should they play? It would be silly of me," he said, "to try and do what Jim Farley did and what Bos Promote did in Tennessee or is now being done by the Department of Health, Education and Welfare."

The analogy to the Canadian circumstance is precise. Party involvement does not any longer presume policy involvement. In the *New Yorker* magazine a few months ago, Elizabeth Drew put it even more succinctly. "Politics" she writes, "has in effect been removed from politics." And she goes on to say, "one gets the sense from talking to people in Washington that they feel that the nature of politics is changing very fast and they don't know where it is going. One man told me that the political system is changing much more rapidly than our ability to see it." I agree, and I agree that it is changing very rapidly in Canada where very few people really want to see it, even if they could see it.

Of course, if you look closely at it, you have to see it. For example, the relationship between the elected representative and his party has changed, and changed not to the party's advantage but to his advantage. While the elected member may be eternally grateful to his local party organization for the gift of their nomination, he will know immediately he is elected that they did not elect him and they will not re-elect him. He also comes to know the powerful advantage in our present system of the incumbent. In our system, it is far easier to get him re-elected than it is to get him out once elected.

Let me illustrate the power of incumbency by example. In the thirtieth Parliament, recently dissolved, almost a third of the membership of the House of Commons were also members of the House in 1965, fourteen years ago. If you look at the names of those who are still there they are not, with few exceptions, the stars of Parliament. They are merely among the membership of Parliament. What has been happening in the system is that the Members of Parliament themselves have been steadily and, in a way, stealthily increasing that power of incumbency in every Parliament. This is not happening, I would add, in the British experience, not yet anyway, although it is happening in the United States.

How has that incumbency power been strengthened? Of course, the franking privilege has always been a modest help to Members of Parliament, since it allowed for postal communication between members and constituents. Today, the free telephone is a considerable extension of that franking privilege. In addition, unlike their British counterparts, our parliamentarians have long enjoyed their own office space on Parliament Hill. I can remember when M.P.'s shared offices, shared secretaries. Today, they all have private offices, they all have executive assistants, and some have research assistants, and tomorrow they will have more. We can remember when a member's office, if he had an office in the constituency, belonged to his party organization who rented it and staffed it at party expense in his and their interests. Today, every member has his own contituency office, financed by the taxpayer with clerical and administrative support salaried by the taxpayers. We can remember, of course, when the members occasionally travelled home by train and now they travel by warrant, by air, and by compulsion.

One of the most difficult things that I have on my own conscience is with respect to the Camp Commission in Ontario, which was called upon to inquire into members' services and purposes, and salaries and pensions, and to make recommendations to the legislature. Those of us working on the commission knew that whatever we were doing was almost certain of legislature acceptance. I was, very frankly, a long hold-out against the provision of constituency offices financed from the public treasury: not because I am a reactionary, not because I am mean, but because I resisted somehow this continual tranformation of the role of the legislator as a "case worker" in his riding.

It is argued that the substantial increase in support services enables the member to share the needs of his constituency better as a case worker. This is undoubtedly true, but it also emancipates him from his party. It liberates him from many of the restraints of caucus and it frees him from many of the more wearisome duties of a member of the House of Commons. These were once endured by Members of Parliament because they had no other thing to do and had no excuse for not doing it.

The member's role has changed and with it his traditional relationships have changed. The Members of Parliament have an occupational responsibility to disagree with one another in many matters. But on one matter they do stand united. It is their common feeling, I suspect, that whatever else might happen, they will continue to act in concert in any effort and on any matter to ensure that they remain where they are. If, as a matter of fact, Parliament were a place for our superiors and not our peers, one would put a greater value in the eternity of tenure that they are coming to enjoy. But what we have done and what they have done either out of our ignorance or our consent is to develop a system that almost guarantees or makes difficult the possibility of changing the representation of Parliament. Indeed, the result has been that whomever a parliamentarian may represent, they no longer represent the hopes and aspirations and gospel and penance and dogma of their parties. Of course, when Parliament revised the *Elections Act*, it revised it in favour of its members: that is, they revised it in favour of incumbency.

For example, when you limit the use of the media in a campaign (that is, when you just allow the party access to media through its own purchase to a statutory period of time), it is to the advantage of the incumbent who is better known rather than his challengers who are less well known. In addition, the financing arrangement now provided under the new act favours a candidate. Subventions that the member enjoys throughout his tenure in Parliament allow him to campaign continuously for re-election. And, of course, and I mean no offence, personal or otherwise, incumbency is also enhanced by the structure of members' pension plans. Now I have known voters to sublimate their political impulses in order to express their compassion so as to re-elect the member, rather than to deny him his pension.

The bureaucratization of politics leads unerringly to the continual down-grading and de-emphasis of the role and place of the party, and the people in the party. In 1953, the national director at the national headquarters of the Conservative Party had a larger staff than the leader of the Opposition had in his office on the Hill. Today, even prior to the election, the office of the leader of the Opposition in his research arm on the Hill would outnumber not only the personnel at national headquarters, where there is no longer any national director, but would outnumber the caucus of the party itself. All this apparatus is deemed essential to the function of the leader and is of course funded out of the public treasury.

Finally, and probably terminally, we have the "Goldfarb syndrome." It used to be that the ultimate source of wisdom as to the basic question in all politics, which is, "how are things going?" was the wisdom of the party's source. I can remember again Mr. Diefenbaker coming to Nova Scotia and he asked one of Mr. Stanfield's many organizers, a gentlemen named Don Haggard, "how many seats" and Haggard would say "all of them." You could not get better research than that for Mr. Diefenbaker's purposes. But as a source today, who really cares? Goldfarb knows, Peter knows, the party leader and his immediate advisers know, and they are determined that the party will never know.

It is not my intention to sound disparaging. Only we would wish to be realistic when we consider the party as an outlet for citizen involvement in the formulation of public policy. Of course, the parties have given themselves up where they can, and where they are able to, to professionalism. Professionalism need not be the enemy of politics any more than the bureaucracy. So much has changed in society that there is no reason to expect that politics and the party system could remain unchanged. While you have to search your mind for them, there are rewards for those in the party system, even though there are only a few (but I think even though there are few, those that are, are comforting). Perhaps best of all, people involved in party politics do enjoy an access to politicians that others do not. They do get a glimpse of the mechanisms of politics that others are not able to see. I suspect that access, even for the gifted amateur, may be the remaining redemptive personal benefit most partisans expect to enjoy and still enjoy. However, access is not influence; more often than not, it is merely contact, and perhaps in the judgement of history, that ought to be enough. It may therefore be that people in politics, as they come to understand the impact of modern technology, will throw off a system that has become so rooted in tradition, and as a result will begin to rescue themselves from incipient obsolescence.

Perhaps there has been some wisdom in leaving until the end of this conference questions of reform of an institution that has somehow been the most enduring and looks, in fact, to be indestructible. There are only three or four things that I could think of, which I am sure will be repellent to almost everyone, that could rescue parties and make them once again a viable instrument in the political process.

First of all, and this would occur to me if not to anyone else, the stricture with respect to accountability, which the parties now apply to leaders, is of course not applied to leaders in terms of annual conventions, it is applied to leaders outside of conventions. That is, the party meets not to elect a leader but to assess the leader. There might be some wisdom in applying that same system of accountability in making Members of Parliament responsible for that accountability in their constituencies, by a constituency convention in non-election years. This will guarantee one thing. It will improve communications between the members of the party and their man or woman in Ottawa.

Second, and this is a liberal notion, on the assumption that man is educable, we should have more emphasis in our society, not on teaching people politics but on teaching them journalism so that we all could develop a more critical capacity. With respect to the impact and influence of the media upon ourselves, upon government, and upon our political system, we really lack a fundamental understanding of all the factors involved. As a result, politics suffers from the lack of public understanding and, of course, politicians suffer, even though they scarcely understand it themselves.

The third and most important thing that has to be considered is that if we could and if we would and if we did recreate not only some greater degree of patronage in the political system, and if we could educate the public to a better understanding of it, then I think the party system would begin to revive. People talk about the bureaucracy, everybody does. The people who blame the bureaucracy, and most people do, for its failure to maintain some kind of realistic contact and, as a result, no longer feel some honest involvement in the whole process of politics in government have really done it to themselves. At the very least, in the American system, there are some ten thousand jobs in Washington that change when the administration changes. It is an assumption in the American political system that partisan identification and loyalty—which carries with it the assumption at least of some ideological conformity—is helpful to governing and is helpful to the government governing. I do not often detect any great improvement in the quality of judges appointed to the benches since the Canadian bar has been appointed as a consultant. It seems to me, with respect to appointments to the Senate, that people of certain parties are somehow rewarded. I must tell you I do not have any problems flying Air Canada because Bryce Mackasey* is there and I do not think it does any damage to Air Canada. Indeed it might even do it some good; there is that possibility. However, what we have done to a system that was based on loyalty and was based on the capacity of the party to advance its interest in association and in league with its supporters is to have cut it off at the polls.

Finally, I think the most important possible solution to all of this is the ideas of people themselves. Most people have not thought of parties, and

ministers' offices, caucus research bureaux, and the prime minister's office—these organizations essentially are fulfilling the role of a political party. I am troubled, however, when Mr. Camp seems to imply that M.P.'s should return to the austerity of earlier days. It may come as a surprise to some of you, although certainly not to him, that barely twelve years ago, M.P.'s shared offices. In fact, in the mid-1960s, it was not uncommon for two M.P.'s to share an office with two secretaries often with only one telephone line. Undoubtedly, this kind of austerity did mean that M.P.'s had to rely more upon the party, if they wanted a constituency office, for example. The party was important, but it would be a mistake to conclude that in order to re-establish a party presence, we must return to the state of affairs where M.P.'s were deprived of essential resources. On the contrary, I would argue that the role and the resources of M.P.'s ought to be vastly increased and, at the same time, that we should seek additional means of asserting an effective role for parties.

I completely agree with the so-called "Goldfarb syndrome," noted by Mr. Camp. The syndrome, the polling syndrome, is really part of modern image making and what I regard as leader-dominated politics. It does tend to leave the party out. The leader and a small coterie of advisers have a monopoly of information and they act on the basis of that information. Beyond all of this, a much more serious question concerns the implications of the Goldfarb syndrome for what we might want to call innovative or creative leadership. There is a disturbing tendency to use polls in a way that is reminiscent of Frank Underhill's description of the leadership of Mackenzie King. Underhill used to say that Mackenzie King would try to find out which way the mass public was moving and then hustle like hell to get up front. That was his concept of leadership. Whether it is an apt description or not, I am sure the politicians in the audience will agree that the King approach had an element of legitimacy that is lacking in the Goldfarb syndrome.

The final comment of Mr. Camp was on patronage. For a long time I have believed in patronage at the highest level of government, but now, from time to time, I find myself believing in patronage at the lowest level of government as well. I have always thought that patronage was conducted backwards in Canada. We need to go the American route and change policy makers and advisers at the senior level when we change governments. *Political* leadership and *political* control of government need to be stronger in Canada, and to do this we should ensure that our ministers have fellow travellers around them. Governments should be served by people who share their sense of mission—people who have come to power with them. I have always believed that this kind of system would enrich the total society by facilitating greater movement between the governmental and private sectors. Canada has suffered very much from this lack of cross-fertilization, which is a product of the permanent public service system.

With regard to patronage at the lower level, as I mentioned, I am tending increasingly to agree with this idea as well. I recall when I was in Saskatoon a couple of years ago, I went to speak to Professor Norman Ward's class at the University of Saskatchewan. As you may know, Ward is one of the foremost analysts of western politics and particularly of Jimmy Gardiner's Liberal Party machine on the Prairies. Ward had reached the position where he concluded that one of the reasons for the decline of party politics, as well as a significant contributor to alienation in western Canada, was the steady elimination of patronage at the grass-roots level. For example, the Prairie Farm Rehabilitation Agency played a vital role in involving people at the poll level in party politics. People understood that it was either a price they paid for being in politics or a benefit they reaped from being in politics.

My general position is that I agree with what Mr. Camp has said about the decline of political parties and the party process in this country. Much has been said about the decline of the party process at this conference. It was mentioned by Mr. Smith and was mentioned in an oblique way by Dr. Corry when he talked about special interest groups. The decline of parties in Canada can be attributed to a number of factors, none of which will come as much of a surprise. It can be attributed in part to the pervasiveness of government; to the rise of the bureaucratic state; to the proliferation of governmental committees, advisory boards, departments, agencies, councils, task forces, commissions, and so on. It can be explained, in part, by the massive development of special interest groups, very powerful special interest groups, which interact directly with government.

The decline of political parties and the party process has been affected by the electronic media and by journalism. To a large extent, the electronic media have reinforced the leadership orientation of political parties and have encouraged the extravaganza nature of the process that Mr. Camp has mentioned. Investigative journalism and the increasingly pervasive activities of the media have tended to erode many of the traditional communication functions of politicians and M.P.'s. In turn, this has reinforced the reliance on imagery and style as the substance of politics. Parties, therefore, have become dominated to a very large extent by style-conscious leaders who are advised by high-priced image makers.

The party system has also suffered to a very real extent from a lack of alternation between the major parties in this country and by one party having been in power for an inordinately long period of time. One-party dominance in our national politics has worked, in different ways, to the detriment of both the Liberal and Conservative parties.

I would like to turn now to what I regard as some of the solutions. We have highly disciplined parliamentary parties that are leader dominated, that do not involve the people in a meaningful way, and are organized in a sort of "tinsel-town fashion" for election purposes. There are two basic changes that would go some distance toward remedying this situation. One is that parties themselves should "pull up their socks." Canadian parties should look seriously at their constitutions and the extent to which they are living up to those constitutions. Parties need to examine their own structures, their attitudes, and the role and nature of their leadership. Dissidents in the Liberal Party, in particular, are too easily suppressed. Principles are too easily overlooked and political expediency is too readily accepted. This contributes to the general decline of political parties to the same extent that it contributes to the general sense of cynicism in this country.

I believe, for example, that there was all too little concern within the Liberal Party about its position on wage and price controls in the last election and especially in light of the actions subsequently taken. Similarly, there was too little concern within the party concerning the courtship and acceptance of Jack Horner as a Liberal. Too few were concerned about the fact that Horner was a leading opponent of the Liberal Party's position on the official languages and bilingualism, a major part of the party's national policy. This kind of sowing the seeds of confusion and failing to stand up on basic principles does not, in any sense, strengthen the party process or reinforce the position of a political party. In the long run, a political party has to pay a price for duplicity and short-term political expediency.

This brings me to the second change required in parties, and is in line with what a number of participants have said in this conference. I believe we must, as soon as possible, reform our political system in a way that will strengthen political parties. It has been mentioned that we might reform the electoral system. This is something that has been studied by a number of commissions and committees. The Pepin-Robarts commission, for example, has advocated moving in that direction. The Canada West Foundation, in its many reports, has advocated the same thing in order to allow political parties to fulfil more of a national role. Such reforms would provide a more integrative role for parties rather than encourage, as is now the case, the creation of regional bastions of party support. Changes in the electoral system could contribute significantly to strengthening the growth of national parties within a more viable party system.

The representative role of Members of Parliament could, and should, be effectively increased. I realize that a number of speakers here have pointed out that the role of M.P.'s has in fact improved. Nevertheless, it is essential that we devise means whereby M.P.'s can be freed from the constraints of party discipline so that they will be able to more readily involve the public in the political process. It is not simply, as Mr. McNiven said yesterday, a case of offering members more money. Providing higher salaries would not automatically result in better Members of Parliament, better representation, and a greater sense of citizen participation.

We need to seriously begin the search for more open and responsible methods of federal and provincial government interface. In recent years, a growing number of analysts have come forward with proposals in this area. It has often been noted that federal-provincial conferences, which employ extensive closed-door consultations at the bureaucratic and executive level, do not work to the advantage of responsible government in Canada. Nor do they work to the advantage of political parties and the party process. A means of addressing this problem has been suggested by the Pepin-Robarts Commission. They have recommended that the Senate become a public forum that would normalize and establish lines of responsibility that bear some relationship to the party and level of government to which premiers, ministers, and public officials adhere.

Generally I would endorse what has been said by many speakers about the need to provide more open government and less secrecy. We should revise our system in such a way that we do not have to rely on secret Cabinet meetings or secret caucuses as the main means by which people relate to government. In this sense, I believe the position of Cabinet itself has to be restored in this country. I have a theory, which I am presently developing for other purposes, that Cabinet is in serious decline in Canada. The decline of Cabinet, much like the decline of the legislative branch, is a result of the growth of bureaucracy, particularly central agencies, and the orientation of our politics toward electoral values and leadership images.

This is the essence of the problem. We must free our politicians and give them a role that ensures that they, rather than bureaucratic tribunals or interest groups, are the primary contact point between people and the government. This, I believe, can be done, but it will take dramatic changes in what we perceive to be the parliamentary system operating within a federal structure.

The kinds of changes I have suggested at the federal level have the added advantage of allowing the people of our far-flung regions to relate more readily to their national government. Surely, if we can increase the legitimacy and relevance of the national government, we will have gone some distance toward curing our national ills.

APPENDIX

Program of the National Conference on Citizen Involvement and Control, April 5-6, 1979

THURSDAY, APRIL 5, 1979

9:00 A.M.
Opening Remarks
H.V. Kroeker
Conference Chairman

Dr. Henry H. Hicks
President, Dalhousie University

Dr. Michael J.L. Kirby
President, The Institute for Research on
  Public Policy

9:15 A.M.
**Keynote Address: Sovereign People or
Sovereign Governments?**
Dr. J. Alex Corry
Chairman, Council of Trustees, The
  Institute for Research on Public Policy

10:00 A.M.
Coffee

10:30 A.M.
**The Citizen and Government:
Co-operative Forms of Public Policy
Making**
Mr. Michael Pitfield
Clerk to the Privy Council and Secretary to
  the Cabinet, Government of Canada

Commentators:
Dr. Victor Rabinovitch
Canadian Labour Congress

Dr. Stefan Dupré
William Lyon Mackenzie King Visiting
  Professor, Harvard University

12:00 P.M.
Luncheon

1:30 P.M.
**Where Decision Makers Get Their
Advice: The Limits of Advisory Councils,
Committees, and Commissions**
Mr. Robert Bryce
Former Deputy Minister of Finance, and
  Chairman, Royal Commission on
  Corporate Concentration

Commentator:
Professor John F. Graham
Department of Economics
Dalhousie University

2:30 P.M.
Coffee

3:00 P.M.
**Where Decision Makers Get Their
Advice: How the Media Affect
Citizen-Government Interaction**
Mr. Doug Fisher
Syndicated Columnist, *The Toronto Sun*

Commentators:
Ms. Marjorie Hartling
Executive Director
National Anti-Poverty Organization

Mr. Gerald Doucet
Atlantic Provinces Economic Council

4:30 P.M.
Discussion Sessions

**The Citizen and Government:
Co-operative Forms of Public Policy
Making**

**The Limits of Advisory Councils,
Committees, and Commissions**

**How the Media Affect
Citizen-Government Interaction**

7:30 P.M.
Reception

8:00 P.M.
**Dinner and Address:
Has Public Policy Formation Become Too
Professionalized? "Whatever Happened
to the Gifted Amateur?"**
Professor King Gordon
Senior Adviser, University Relations
International Development Research Centre

FRIDAY, APRIL 6, 1979

9:00 A.M.
**The Limits of Direct Democracy: The
Experience of Switzerland**
Mr. Peter Studer
Editor, *Tages-Anzeiger*
Zurich, Switzerland

Commentator:
Mr. André Larocque
Associate Secretary General
Executive Council, Government of Quebec

10:00 A.M.
Coffee

10:30 A.M.
**The Limits of Law in Advancing Public
Participation**
Dr. G. LaForest
Commissioner
Law Reform Commission

**The Limits of Regulation in
Citizen-Government Conflict Resolution**
Professor William Neilson
Faculty of Law
University of Victoria

Commentators:
Mr. Kitzen Vincent
Former Executive Director
Canadian Arctic Resources Committee

Ms. Jalynn Bennett
Member of the Ontario Economic Council,
   and Chairperson of the Council's
   Committee on Regulation

12:30 P.M.
**Luncheon and Address:
The Limits of Law as a Substitute for
Community Responsibility**
Mr. Bayless Manning
Paul, Weiss, Riskind, Wharton and
Garrison, New York, and
Former Dean of Law
Stanford University

2:30 P.M.
**The Limits of Political Parties in Citizen
Involvement and Control**
Mr. Dalton Camp
Former President
Progressive Conservative Party of Canada

Commentator:
Professor Blair Williams
Concordia University, and
Former Executive Director,
Liberal Party of Canada

3:00 P.M.
Coffee

3:30 P.M.
Discussion Sessions

**The Limits of Direct Democracy: The
Experience of Switzerland**

**The Limits of Law in Advancing Public
Participation, and The Limits of
Regulation in Citizen-Government
Conflict Resolution**

**The Limits of Political Parties in Citizen
Involvement and Control**

5:00 P.M.
Summation
Mr. Tom Kent
President
Sydney Steel Corporation

6:00 P.M.
Reception

Conference Oganizers
The Institute for Research on Public Policy
Government Studies Program, Dalhousie
   University
School of Public Administration, Dalhousie
   University

The Institute for Research on Public Policy
PUBLICATIONS AVAILABLE*
March 1981

BOOKS

Leroy O. Stone & Claude Marceau	*Canadian Population Trends and Public Policy Through the 1980s*. 1977 $4.00
Raymond Breton	*The Canadian Condition: A Guide to Research in Public Policy*. 1977 $2.95
Raymond Breton	*Une orientation de la recherche politique dans le contexte canadien*. 1978 $2.95
J.W. Rowley & W.T. Stanbury, eds.	*Competition Policy in Canada: Stage II, Bill C-13*. 1978 $12.95
C.F. Smart & W.T. Stanbury, eds.	*Studies on Crisis Management*. 1978 $9.95
W.T. Stanbury, ed.	*Studies on Regulation in Canada*. 1978 $9.95
Michael Hudson	*Canada in the New Monetary Order: Borrow? Devalue? Restructure!* 1978 $6.95
W.A.W. Neilson & J.C. MacPherson, eds.	*The Legislative Process in Canada: The Need for Reform*. 1978 $12.95
David K. Foot, ed.	*Public Employment and Compensation in Canada: Myths and Realities*. 1978 $10.95
W.E. Cundiff & Mado Reid, eds.	*Issues in Canada /U.S. Transborder Computer Data Flows*. 1979 $6.50
G.B. Reschenthaler & B. Roberts, eds.	*Perspectives on Canadian Airline Regulation*. 1979 $13.50
P.K. Gorecki & W.T. Stanbury, eds.	*Perspectives on the Royal Commission on Corporate Concentration*. 1979 $15.95
David K. Foot	*Public Employment in Canada: Statistical Series*. 1979 $15.00

---

* Order Address: The Institute for Research on Public Policy
P.O. Box 9300, Station "A"
TORONTO, Ontario
M5W 2C7

Meyer W. Bucovetsky, ed.	*Studies on Public Employment and Compensation in Canada*. 1979 $14.95
Richard French & André Béliveau	*The RCMP and the Management of National Security*. 1979 $6.95
Richard French & André Béliveau	*La GRC et la gestion de la sécurité nationale*. 1979 $6.95
Leroy O. Stone & Michael J. MacLean	*Future Income Prospects for Canada's Senior Citizens*. 1979 $7.95
Douglas G. Hartle	*Public Policy Decision Making and Regulation*. 1979 $12.95
Richard Bird (in collaboration with Bucovetsky & Foot)	*The Growth of Public Employment in Canada*. 1979 $12.95
G. Bruce Doern & Allan M. Maslove, eds.	*The Public Evaluation of Government Spending*. 1979 $10.95
Richard Price, ed.	*The Spirit of the Alberta Indian Treaties*. 1979 $8.95
Peter N. Nemetz, ed.	*Energy Policy: The Global Challenge*. 1979 $16.95
Richard J. Schultz	*Federalism and the Regulatory Process*. 1979 $1.50
Richard J. Schultz	*Le fédéralisme et le processus de réglementation*. 1979 $1.50
Lionel D. Feldman & Katherine A.Graham	*Bargaining for Cities. Municipalities and Intergovernmental Relations: An Assessment*. 1979 $10.95
Elliot J. Feldman & Neil Nevitte, eds.	*The Future of North America: Canada, the United States, and Quebec Nationalism*. 1979 $7.95
Maximo Halty-Carrere	*Technological Development Strategies for Developing Countries*. 1979 $12.95
G.B. Reschenthaler	*Occupational Health and Safety in Canada: The Economics and Three Case Studies*. 1979 $5.00
David R. Protheroe	*Imports and Politics: Trade Decision-Making in Canada, 1968–1979*. 1980 $8.95

G. Bruce Doern   *Government Intervention in the Canadian Nuclear Industry.* 1980 $8.95

G. Bruce Doern &   *Canadian Nuclear Policies.* 1980 $14.95
R.W. Morrison, eds.

W.T. Stanbury, ed.   *Government Regulation: Scope, Growth, Process.* 1980 $10.95

Yoshi Tsurumi with   *Sogoshosha: Engines of Export-Based Growth.*
Rebecca R. Tsurumi   1980 $8.95

Allan M. Maslove &   *Wage Controls in Canada, 1975 – 78: A Study in*
Gene Swimmer   *Public Decision Making.* 1980 $11.95

T. Gregory Kane   *Consumers and the Regulators: Intervention in the Federal Regulatory Process.* 1980 $10.95

Albert Breton &   *The Design of Federations.* 1980 $6.95
Anthony Scott

A.R. Bailey &   *The Way Out: A More Revenue-Dependent Public*
D.G. Hull   *Sector and How It Might Revitalize the Process of Governing.* 1980 $6.95

Réjean Lachapelle &   *La situation démolinguistique au Canada: évolution*
Jacques Henripin   *passée et prospective.* 1980 $24.95

Raymond Breton,   *Cultural Boundaries and the Cohesion of Canada.*
Jeffrey G. Reitz &   1980 $18.95
Victor F. Valentine

David R. Harvey   *Christmas Turkey or Prairie Vulture? An Economic Analysis of the Crow's Nest Pass Grain Rates.* 1980 $10.95

Stuart McFadyen,   *Canadian Broadcasting: Market Structure and*
Colin Hoskins &   *Economic Performance.* 1980 $15.95
David Gillen

Richard M. Bird   *Taxing Corporations.* 1980 $6.95

Albert Breton &   *Why Disunity? An Analysis of Linguistic and*
Raymond Breton   *Regional Cleavages in Canada.* 1980 $6.95

Leroy O. Stone &   *A Profile of Canada's Older Population.* 1980
Susan Fletcher $7.95

Peter N. Nemetz, ed.   *Resource Policy: International Perspectives.*
1980 $18.95

Keith A.J. Hay, ed.   *Canadian Perspectives on Economic Relations with Japan.* 1980 $18.95

Raymond Breton and   *La langue de travail au Québec: synthèse de la*
Gail Grant   *recherche sur la rencontre de deux langues.*
1981 $10.95

Diane Vanasse   *L'évolution de la population scolaire du Québec.*
1981 $12.95

Raymond Breton,   *Les frontières culturelles et la cohésion du Canada.*
Jeffrey G. Reitz and   1981 $18.95
Victor F. Valentine

David M. Cameron, ed.   *Regionalism and Supranationalism: Challenges and Alternatives to the Nation-State in Canada and Europe.* 1981 $9.95

Peter Aucoin, ed.   *The Politics and Management of Restraint in Government.* 1981 $17.95

H.V. Kroeker, ed.   *Sovereign People or Sovereign Governments.*
1981 $12.95

OCCASIONAL PAPERS
W.E. Cundiff   *Nodule Shock? Seabed Mining and the Future of the*
(No. 1)   *Canadian Nickel Industry.* 1978 $3.00

IRPP/Brookings   *Conference on Canadian-U.S. Economic Relations.*
(No. 2)   1978 $3.00

Robert A. Russel   *The Electronic Briefcase: The Office of the Future.*
(No. 3)   1978 $3.00

C.C. Gotlieb   *Computers in the Home: What They Can Do for*
(No. 4)   *Us—And to Us.* 1978 $3.00

Raymond Breton &   *Urban Institutions and People of Indian Ancestry.*
Gail Grant Akian   1978 $3.00
(No. 5)

K.A. Hay   *Friends or Acquaintances? Canada as a Resource*
(No. 6)   *Supplier to the Japanese Economy.* 1979 $3.00

T. Atkinson   *Trends in Life Satisfaction.* 1979 $3.00
(No. 7)

M. McLean
(No. 8)

The Impact of the Microelectronics Industry on the Structure of the Canadian Economy. 1979 $3.00

Fred Thompson &
W.T. Stanbury
(No. 9)

The Political Economy of Interest Groups in the Legislative Process in Canada. 1979 $3.00

Gordon B. Thompson
(No. 10)

Memo from Mercury: Information Technology **Is** *Different*. 1979 $3.00

Pierre Sormany
(No. 11)

Les micro-esclaves: vers une bio-industrie canadienne. 1979 $3.00

K. Hartley, P.N. Nemetz,
S. Schwartz, D. Uyeno,
I. Vertinsky & J. Young
(No. 12)

Energy R & D Decision Making for Canada. 1979 $3.00

David Hoffman &
Zavis P. Zeman, eds.
(No. 13)

The Dynamics of the Technological Leadership of the World. 1980 $3.00

Russell Wilkins
(No. 13*a*)

Health Status in Canada, 1926 – 1976. 1980 $3.00

Russell Wilkins
(No. 13*b*)

L'état de santé au Canada, 1926 – 1976. 1980 $3.00

P. Pergler
(No. 14)

The Automated Citizen: Social and Political Impact of Interactive Broadcasting. 1980 $4.95

Zavis P. Zeman
(No. 15)

Men with the Yen. 1980 $5.95

Donald G. Cartwright
(No. 16)

Official Language Populations in Canada: Patterns and Contacts. 1980 $4.95

REPORT
Dhiru Patel

Dealing With Interracial Conflict: Policy Alternatives. 1980 $5.95

WORKING PAPERS (No Charge)**
W.E. Cundiff
(No. 1)

Issues in Canada /U.S. Transborder Computer Data Flows. 1978 (Out of print; in IRPP book of same title.)

John Cornwall
(No. 2)

Industrial Investment and Canadian Economic Growth: Some Scenarios for the Eighties. 1978

Russell Wilkins   *L'espérance de vie par quartier à Montréal, 1976:*
(No. 3)   *un indicateur social pour la planification.* 1979

F.J. Fletcher &   *Canadian Attitude Trends, 1960 –1978.* 1979
R.J. Drummond
(No. 4)

** Order Working Papers from
The Institute for Research on Public Policy
P.O. Box 3670
Halifax South
Halifax, Nova Scotia
B3J 3K6